LOOKING
—— INTO ——
PAINTINGS

LOOKING
— INTO —
PAINTINGS

Norbert Lynton, Alistair Smith, Robert Cumming
and Diané Collinson

General Editor: Elizabeth Deighton

in association with

faber and faber
LONDON · BOSTON

and

Channel 4 Television Company Limited

First published in 1985
by The Open University
Walton Hall Milton Keynes MK7 6AA
in association with
Faber and Faber Limited
3 Queen Square London WC1N 3AU
and Channel Four Television Company Limited

Designed by Julia Alldridge
Printed by The Bath Press

The cover illustration shows the complete painting framed by details:
Georges Seurat
Sunday Afternoon on the Island of La Grande Jatte
Oil on canvas
1884–6
81 × 120⅜″
Helen Birch Bartlett Memorial Collection
© The Art Institute of Chicago
All rights reserved

A CIP record for this book is available from the British Library

ISBN 0 571 13669 9

6 8 10 9 7 5

CONTENTS

COLOUR PLATES

10

BLACK AND WHITE ILLUSTRATIONS

12

14

INTRODUCTION

This book is the major component of a kit designed and produced as a short course in the Open University's Continuing Education programme. The course is intended as an opportunity to add to or develop existing interests. There are cassettes, together with additional illustrations, to complement the material offered here. The whole, planned by an institution experienced in this kind of teaching-at-a-distance, should be seen as half the material of the course. The other half is you.

It is a course without a timetable, without required written work, without an examination, and so without the pressures that go with the Open University's degree courses. Nonetheless, it places a considerable onus on the student. We ask for your patience as you follow us through information and explanations that may at times seem too basic or even too remote. The course does not assume any special preparation on your part, but it does assume a desire to know art better, to go beyond the nodding acquaintance that seems to keep many gallery-goers on the move past marvellous things.

Appreciation of anything, certainly of art, goes with a certain kind of attention and with a slow pace. Working through this book requires both, and they are under your control. At various points we ask you to examine illustrations and consider specific questions before reading further, and we hope that in doing so you will use the methods and concepts we offer you. But the whole book is meant to encourage you to extend your looking at and thinking about art, your 'looking into paintings' especially, to art wherever you can find it—in local galleries and public buildings, in private collections open to you and at exhibitions. We do not set out to persuade you of the superiority of one kind or period of art over another, or of one artist over another. We do not tell you what to like. We are concerned, rather, to display a method and an attitude that will lead to closer intimacy with art and also to true discrimination.

We can use only words and reproductions here. Reproductions are not art. They can mislead one quite fundamentally: sometimes the better a reproduction is the more misleading it becomes, just because it is so persuasive. We all use them, and the more works we know in the original as well as in reproduction, the more we know the ways in which a reproduction helps and the ways in which it is dangerous. This again is a reason for venturing forth and using what your locality offers. It can, for instance, be a useful exercise to make a close comparison of, say, a postcard of a painting with the actual painting, perhaps noting some of your findings on the back of the card. The only essential advice is: take your time when you are looking at the real thing. Works of art reveal themselves by means of a kind of dialogue that we have to begin. Our aim in this book has been to suggest good openings. We believe that the way most people encounter art works against intimacy with it. That is why we have chosen the particular approach used in this book.

Art is news when it is stolen, sold at enormous prices, or said to be faked. It comes to us as cultural entertainment through the media, and also in 'popular' art books, in a dramatized form: the emphasis tends to be on rebellion and shock, 'the shock of the new'. The artist is presented as a rebel against society and against all art but his own, enjoying the anger of persons in authority and the misunderstanding of people in general. The art that is glorified is the art associated with this sort of disruption; the rest is labelled 'academic' and treated as though it were not art at all.

It is true that much of the best art produced during the last two hundred years in the Western world has been innovative. This has been much less so in other periods, but there have also been other times when change was rapid—in fifteenth-century Italy for instance. Yet artists have always looked to other artists, living and dead. They know they are contributing to something that is rooted in its own long history. Those artists who have claimed to be against tradition have usually rebelled against only a particular aspect of that history, or been expressing their distaste for seeing a great tradition devalued by routine repetition.

We encounter actual works of art mainly in museums and public galleries. These are excellent places, good at conserving and displaying individual works in a way that makes historical sense of them. We are able to see things that in past ages we would not have had access to or would have had to make a special effort to see. But they make it more difficult for us to understand individual works properly.

Imagine you are going into one of our major national art collections. Look around one of its rooms. Hanging in their frames on the walls, harmoniously grouped and probably well lit, are a number of paintings belonging to one period or place. The labels tell us the names of the painters or at least what school a work came out of, and what it represents. You may see a *Madonna and Child with Saints*, a religious subject most of us recognize whether or not we are believing Christians; and then by its side a portrait, a young man in fine clothes and arranged to look elegant and thoughtful; then a dramatic painting with lots going on in it, that reveals itself as the martyrdom of a saint; then another portrait, the head and shoulders of some important-looking person; and finally a cheerful-looking scene with a title like *The Rape of Europa*, appealing to our eyes yet telling us about something we cannot fully comprehend.

In a museum such paintings might well belong together in that they represent a period of art and show its dominant styles or idioms. But each of them was almost certainly done for a particular place and purpose: the *Madonna* to stand on an altar; the young man's portrait to hang beside others in one of the more public rooms in his family's mansion; the scene of martyrdom to dignify and give meaning to the meetings of the trade or craft association whose patron saint the martyr is; the important-looking person's portrait to go alongside others in a town hall or other civic headquarters; and the mythological story to hang in the private apartments of an educated man. They have been removed from these places, and so have lost their original function. In being put side by side in this way they lose much of their value as 'communicators'. Mythological stories have often been given religious interpretations and we may or may not want to see this one as a piece of worldly visual poetry, but in any case it does not make a good partner for the *Madonna* at the opposite end of the wall. In consequence, most of us tend to take little account of the subject of a painting in a gallery, or of its deeper content and its implications. Too much attention is paid to the artist and the period, and above all to the artistic flavour they present together.

Even this flavour may have been falsified by the particular arrangement of works on one gallery wall. Imagine the large canvas of the martyrdom still on the wall for which it was painted. It probably fitted the wall, needed only the slightest framing strip to hold it in position, and echoed in its lit and shadowy areas the actual fall of light in that room. That visual experience has been changed by the transposition to the gallery wall. The altarpiece was similarly planned for a particular position, possibly high up on an altar removed from us by steps as well as by horizontal distance; we should be looking up at it from some way off, not close to and at our own level. Different functions call for different ways of painting, and at times also for different media which suit the purpose and the location but which look arbitrarily different lined up on a gallery wall.

In *Looking into Paintings* we have tried to put the paintings back into their most appropriate context. Until the nineteenth century, when most museums opened, it was generally understood that different categories of art related to different functions, and also that some of these were more serious, more elevated, than others. There was in fact an agreed scale of values according to different 'genres' of painting. Those paintings which dealt with important themes, religious or secular, in a carefully considered manner that suited the subject, were thought to be more important than paintings representing particular individuals, however lifelike and elegant, because these offered less food for the mind. Other sorts of paintings were thought of primarily as decorative, as pleasing backgrounds to civilized living; that applied to still-life and landscape paintings, and to paintings of animals and ships. This hierarchy of genres gradually collapsed as painters of the 'lower' types of painting brought into them symbolism and other forms of significance borrowed from the higher, but it was not under serious attack until the nineteenth century.

The three initial sections of this book deal with four of these genres. Narrative painting belongs primarily to that most elevated of categories known as History painting (the term will be explained below); Portrait painting, discussed in the second section, is shown to serve a range of purposes and to meet needs that have changed over the centuries; and Landscape and Still Life painting, in the third section, are discussed as forms of art that were invented to convey something more than a mere description of a chosen motif.

Two general points emerge, more implied than stated, and both need emphasizing in our museum and media-dominated world. One is that different kinds of subject demand different kinds of painting. They pose different problems to the artist and offer different solutions. The other is that artists tend to be intelligent and thoughtful, often learned people. The post-Romantic notion of the artist spilling out his heart or soul through impulsive action has obscured this general truth. The first point will become clear as the four major genres are discussed in the pages that follow; the second will appear from the demonstration, again and again, that the artist is the conscious inheritor of ideas in art and practices relating to these ideas, and that exceptional status among artists—what the Romantics called, all too readily, genius—is accorded to those who add to or redirect the particular tradition they are working in.

Nowadays there is little or no reference to the genres when art is discussed outside the professional literature of art historians, as though they were thought unfit for general consumption or too obscure to be of general interest. In fact, they are basic to the way art communicates. Perhaps this is best shown by way of analogy. Music lovers know that they are engaging in different kinds of experience, requiring particular sorts of attention and answering to particular expectations, when they settle down to listen to a symphony, a song, a sarabande for a harpsichord or a mazurka for a piano, an opera, or a sonata for unaccompanied violin. Similarly, you do not need a doctorate in literature to recognize that an epic poem by Homer or Milton, a sonnet or a long autobiographical poem by Wordsworth, a lyric by Shelley or a verse drama by Shelley or Eliot, are wholly different kinds of poetry. To mistake one for the other, to bring to one of these the expectations associated with another, is to court disappointment and mis-understanding. To have an agreed system of genres means that the artist (in each department of the arts) can assume that we, the art-consumers, will be prepared to meet him halfway by recognizing the form he is using and thus also the skill and originality with which he is using it. Mixing the genres—in the later eighteenth century and after—loses much of its point if we are not aware that they are being mixed and that this itself carries meaning. What is more, the genres continue to play a role, openly and latently, in much modern production. There are unmistakable signs that, in painting especially, they are again becoming categories of acknowledged importance.

In discussing types of painting in this way we are working against the grain of art history and art criticism written for the general public. Often this focuses on an individual work and points out its virtues without reference to its historical context; sometimes it offers simplified, diluted art history which may deliver part of that context but leaves the reader at a loss how to engage with a particular work. Biographies and personalities of artists tend to dominate. These can serve to dramatize and even glamorize an individual artist's output—Van Gogh cutting off his ear, Gauguin's escape to the South Sea Islands, Picasso's restless way with women—but they hinder us from engaging with the works they left behind.

Our method is not wholly historical, although it necessarily refers to historical developments and situations, but it does not attempt what is usually meant by art appreciation. No way of writing or talking about art that draws attention to actual works can be entirely bad. However, appreciation (judgement with enjoyment) is developed through contact with art, not by being told what to appreciate. Our basic task is that of offering ways of spending time with paintings, and our hope is that the discussion in the first three sections of this book will encourage students in their approach to many other examples. At the back of the book there is a glossary of some of the terms that are needed in discussing art purposefully.

The fourth section of the book raises and discusses some of the questions that anyone interested in art will come up against. What is involved in 'enjoying art'? Why do we do it? Does art matter? This essay has been contributed by a philosopher who has also been involved from the beginning in discussing and shaping the course. She introduces very large topics in a way that reflects ordinary experience, and thus bridges the gap between the approach of the average gallery-goer and the professional development of a philosophy of art.

As we said in the first paragraph of the Introduction, this book is the major component of an Open University course, although it is in a real sense 'free-standing'. Many readers may already have bought the complete course (i.e. the book plus 'study items'), but those who have purchased only the book by itself may wish to buy the additional 'study' components as well. Details of these are given on the enclosed slip. But there is one very relevant item to which we wish to draw your attention. This is an 'introductory postcard' which you can send to the Open University. Looking into paintings is, first of all, a one-to-one business, you and it. But it can become a productive social action when people of similar interests compare their understanding of a work of art or collaborate on a systematic questioning of it. By means of the postcard, the Open University hopes to link up people following this course who are interested in meeting others. You may decide to form a group and make visits to galleries and other such places together. Given proper notice, a gallery may be willing to offer you an introductory talk about particular works in the collection, or about the collection as a whole, or to let you see things not normally on display. There are several ways in which you might be led further in your venture into what we think of as an essentially human activity, constructive and peaceable: the informed appreciation of individual works of art.

The philosopher is Diané Collinson, a staff tutor at the Open University. The three art historians are Robert Cumming, director of Christie's Fine Arts Course, who has written introductory books on art and has taught for the Open University; Norbert Lynton, a teacher of art history for many years, former art critic for the *Guardian* and director of exhibitions for the Arts Council of Great Britain, for a time visiting professor at the Open University and now professor of the History of Art at the University of Sussex; and Alistair Smith, keeper of education and exhibitions at the National Gallery in London, author of various National Gallery publications, initiator of the gallery's much-praised 'Painting in Focus' and 'Second Sight' series of exhibitions, and contributor of texts and television programmes to the Open University's course on Renaissance Art. The instigator of, and executive chairman for the course is Elizabeth Deighton, a staff tutor for the Open University since its inception.

Elizabeth Deighton
Norbert Lynton

NARRATIVE PAINTINGS

Norbert Lynton

Section One

NARRATIVE PAINTINGS

Perhaps the title of this section surprises you. Can pictures tell stories? There is the saying that 'every picture tells a story' which sounds clear enough until we try to think what exactly it means. Obviously not every picture does, nor is intended to. 'Every picture tells us *something*' is probably more generally true. Works of art are forms of communication.

Let us test this briefly on what appears a very modest painting, one of Cézanne's simpler still lifes, shown in Figure 1. Fourteen apples on top of a wooden chest and, only partly seen, a plate with two biscuits. Behind them is a background of wallpaper with leaves on it; there seem to be a few leaves also on the front of the chest. Only the apples and the metal hasp below them are at all emphatic. The colours are mostly restrained; the overall effect is very peaceful. The painting describes the still life; that is, it confronts us with touches of paint so selected and arranged as to suggest these objects to us. But of course the same things might have been arranged very differently.

If you look at the picture as a whole you will notice that it consists basically of three horizontal bands: wall, top of chest, and front of chest, all seen frontally. Experience tells us that the wall and the front of the chest confront us vertically and that the top of the chest is a horizontal surface coming between them, but we get very little sense of the top of the chest receding from us. In fact, with the apples on it and its relatively firm edges (and the projecting hasp) it appears more positive, a vertical plane closer to us than the front of the chest, and we feel the apples could tip off it. Had Cézanne shown us one end or both ends of the chest we should probably have a better sense of it as a three-dimensional box, and therefore of the space in which the apples and plate are. Instead, his frontal arrangement and close-up presentation have the effect of pressing the apples and plate towards us and giving us a sense of their precariousness.

With these last words we clearly enter the area of interpretation. Until I used the word 'precarious' I was speaking objectively, about how anyone would be likely to see the painting. But 'precarious' implies an element of peril, and since there is no reason why the painted apples and plate should fall off the painted surface the word must have emerged out of me, triggered but not called for by this work of paint and canvas. The slight sense of peril, of instability at any rate, is in me.

The apples are red or yellow-green. They were put there by the painter; whether he took time over arranging them or did it quickly, he presumably decided that the way they are arranged, their number and the way they are placed in relationship to each other, would suit his purpose—i.e. would be worth making a painting of and would perhaps serve as exactly the subject he was looking for. We find that some of the apples form groups, some stay alone. Some of them are firmly outlined, some are not, or only here and there, and some of them lose outlines that would otherwise separate them from an apple close by.

FIGURE **1** STILL LIFE (APPLES AND BISCUITS), Paul Cézanne, c.1880
Oil on canvas, 46x55 cm, 18x22 in, Musée du Louvre, Paris

Saying this I am not sure to what extent I am interpreting or describing. The fact that I am going on about the placing and relationship of the apples at all reflects an awareness created in me by Cézanne's emphasis on the apples and by my sense of their precarious placing. On the other hand, there are larger and smaller gaps between them, and there are outlines that are sometimes strong and sometimes lost so that one apple may even seem to be linking up with another. I am certainly interpreting when I go on to say that I have come to sense these apples as being like humans, and that I feel about this painting as though it was describing relationships of the human sort and their precariousness.

If I then read about Cézanne I find that he lived amid very uncomfortable human relationships, that he was both passionate about individuals and very shy in company, that he was driven by strong sexual feelings but painfully diffident about expressing them in ways that would release them constructively. He could not bear friends to touch him in the way friends will when they are talking. Obviously he was hypersensitive to the physical and the psychological spaces between people. He was also a notoriously slow painter, looking endlessly at what he was painting, hesitating between brush-strokes, doing a touch here and a touch there with long gaps in between for looking again and feeling his way into his subject: into, that is, what he is painting and the meaning it carries.

You will have gathered from this that I am convinced my reading of the painting, that is, my account of what it shows and what that implies, meets and to some extent matches the feelings and intuitions that led Cézanne to paint the picture in this particular way. In other words, I feel that he has communicated with me, and I, in a sense, with him. There was only one Cézanne and he painted this unique picture. There are many people who have looked at it, and many more will, and I cannot help thinking that many of them will see it in much the same way. And this thought produces in me the notion (it cannot be more than that) that a work of art can link people of all sorts and over time. In this particular case, I am saying that my small sensation of precariousness, emerging out of some degree of identifying with the apples on that apparently tilting board, is not only mine and that, insofar as others respond similarly, the painting serves as a kind of meeting place or exchange for human beings and their experience.

Yet Cézanne's picture is only a still life (just as a breath-taking phrase in Mozart may be only a few notes that in themselves are ordinary and without meaning; 'Tyger! Tyger! burning bright' is only $2 \times 1 + 2 = 4$ words, that do not tell us a lot and don't make very good sense). We are going to be discussing paintings that were made at various times to convey stories to us via images of people apparently involved in them. The kind of looking and intuitive responding we have used for the still life will be essential for them too, but in addition there will be an important story element, in every case the starting point of the narrative paintings we shall look at.

At once we are up against a problem. Stories are surely sequential and need time: this happens, and then that, and the consequence is as follows. We tell stories, we read them, we see and hear them in the cinema and on television, we run them through in our minds, waking and dreaming. Sequentiality seems to be an essential component. Obviously a single image cannot do that (as opposed to a comic strip, coming halfway between the single image of the painting and the successive images of cinephotography). What it can do is to suggest a story.

Before we go on to see how a painting can do this, and indeed do this in ways that make us feel it is doing much more besides, consider for a moment how stories are presented visually. Take the daily news, on television and in the newspapers. On television we see a newsreader whose voice goes on to explain inserted footage of news film. In the paper we see illustrations made from photographs, and these are accompanied by captions, verbal explanations that are usually developed further in the report alongside the picture. Words and images reinforce each other. Without the words most images would be without meaning or at least uncertain in their meaning. When the images can stand by themselves, they do so because our minds are prepared for them; the words that make the image specific and enable it to carry a particular meaning are, in a sense, already lodged in us and all we have to do is to match the image to them. In fact images very rarely come to us without words.

In the Introduction, on page 17, it was suggested that the way we normally see paintings tends to diminish their communication by taking attention away from the subject and by focussing it on the individual artist and on period and style. This matters particularly with narrative paintings when the story presented and its implications are remote from us. Unless we have some recollection of the story which the Latin poet Ovid relates in his *Metamorphoses*, we cannot know what is going on and why in the painting of *The Rape of Europa*, nor guess at the meaning behind it. At the time, however, the artist knew that the people likely to see his painting would have no difficulty with it, and might well have seen other versions. He could hope that they would give their attention to how he is presenting the story in his painting, and how that brings out particular aspects of it, for enjoyment and instruction. Today we do not, on the whole, carry with us a store of commonly known stories that a narrative painting could build on, and because of this we perhaps do not expect paintings to address themselves to that kind of knowledge. This distances us from some of the greatest paintings ever done. Moreover it silences, or comes close to silencing, an important type and function of art. My hope, in this section of the book, is both to help people to engage with narrative painting and, in the process, to breed a taste for this kind of communication. There are plenty of signs today that artists are trying to develop forms of narrative painting for our own times.

Let us look carefully at a well-known narrative painting and see how it works, what it can tell us and what it cannot.

And When Did You Last See Your Father?

(Plate 1) I imagine you did not read that heading as a direct and possibly impertinent question. It is the title of a painting that was once very famous and still ranks as one of the more popular paintings produced in this country. The caption that accompanies Plate 1 tells you the painter's name, what the painting is made of, its size, and also where it is. Ideally you should go and look at the actual painting, in this and every other case. Even good reproductions are poor substitutes, often hiding the very qualities that make a particular painting great.

We are going to look at the painting in detail, which will take a lot of words and a lot of looking, but please don't take any of it for granted. Remember that the painter started with a blank canvas. He probably made drawings before he started on the canvas with his paints, but in any case, he had to make countless decisions, all following upon his basic decision to paint this particular subject. All we have is the outcome: the more inevitable it feels the more we must conclude that the painter made good decisions. At the same time, he worked using his knowledge of art, and undoubtedly remembered works by other artists that helped him to make his own decisions. In making his painting he may well have been original, but no artist is ever wholly that.

i Size, format and general character

We see quite a large canvas, roughly four feet by eight (if you are working from the reproduction, try to visualize that size). I find I remember this picture as larger than it really is, partly because it is so firmly composed; one can imagine it on a large or a small screen, a Vista-Vision film. Its general colour is warm: bright colours here and there in small quantities, but mostly browns. The figures and other elements in it are arranged across that long rectangle. There are quite a number of figures and a definite sense of something dramatic going on, but hardly any suggestion of movement. The drama does not reside in a physical action but a verbal and perhaps mental one.

ii Composition

The arrangement of the figures seems to ask us to read from left to right; the climax comes in the right half. What hint of movement there is is from the left going towards the right. Two well-dressed young ladies in the doorway on the left seem distressed; the little girl has been led away from them by the soldier; the little boy presumably preceded them. He stands on a footstool, picked out by the lighting, by his fair hair and his silky blue suit. He confronts, profile to profile, the man who has asked him the question by which the painting is known.

iii Space

The picture is designed to give a very clear idea of a particular space and where everything is in it. About the space beyond the doorways we know nothing: our attention is not invited to wander out of the room we are shown. The wall between the doors, with its embossed leather covering that glints in the light, combines with the floor boards to give us a precise container for the people and furniture.

iv Light

Without an effect of light within the picture there would be little sense of space and no sense of the roundness and the solidity of things. Can you see how the painter has planned his lighting? There are no sharp shadows, but there are plenty of signs that the most important source of light is a window behind the viewer's left shoulder. This kind of room would have windows in the outer wall which we cannot see. The light seems to fall on the young ladies from a second window further to the left. Perhaps we are being shown part of a long gallery, quite typical of the period represented.

v Story and action

I have already had to refer to aspects of the story. A picture does not consist of discrete elements that can be treated in isolation. The little girl is probably sobbing: the rest of the picture is still, silent as well as motionless. We guess that the question of the title has been asked. It fills the room and waits. Notice the dramatic gap between the questioning man and the questioned boy. The clerk, on the other side of the table, looks down. If he were to look up, and we could see any expression on his features, the dramatic tension would evaporate. As it is, we feel part of the picture; we witness the event and hold our breath, wondering what the boy will say. This is partly a matter of sympathy: we get involved. It is also a matter of presentation: the composition is open to us, not a self-contained cluster, and the chest (front left) and the chair (front right) show us an empty space at the front of the picture and invite us into it.

The title tells what was said, and our imaginations provide the rest. Here we depend on our knowledge and experience. Anyone totally uninformed about seventeenth-century England and the civil war between the supporters of Charles I and those who wanted to limit the authority of kings—Cavaliers versus Round-heads—will be able to make only the most general interpretation. The contrast in the clothes, elegant versus functional, may not be obvious to people from very different cultures.

The painter clearly assumed a general awareness of what went on in the England of Charles I and Cromwell. He had a reason for doing so. Historical novels and histories were widely read in his day. Sir Walter Scott had written historical romances around the theme of the Civil War, *Rokeby* (1813), *Old Mortality* (1816) and *Woodstock* (1826). About 1836 Daniel Maclise painted a picture in which we see Charles I with two of his children and a dog as a group of dignity and harmoniousness, observed by a dour and silent Cromwell (Figure 2). The painter of our picture must have known Maclise's. That table, the clerk on the far side of it, the emphasis on profiles right and left, and above all the figure of the young prince (in silky red) obviously stayed in his mind.

Our picture does not especially glorify one side as against the other. The man who asked the memorable question leans forward without aggressiveness or bullying. These Roundheads are not ruffians. The feet in the painting we glimpse on the wall behind the questioner are no doubt those of the absent aristocratic father, and there could just be a hint of satire in showing them there. But all in all we are not offered a simplistic polarity of heroes and villains. This may tell us something about the painter himself. William Frederick Yeames (1835–1918), born in Russia, son of a British consul, worked in St John's Wood, London. He was elected a member of the Royal Academy in 1877, the year before he completed this painting. He is not a major figure in the history of painting in Britain and we know little about his thinking, but by the 1870s others, historians and artists, had come to take a relatively unpartisan view of the struggle.

But what is the story? The interesting fact is that there isn't one. Yeames's picture represents an anecdote rather than a story, a moment describing a situation perhaps typical of its period, not a pre-existing text. We can guess what happened before this moment, but we shall never know what ensued. The implication is that our foothold in the seventeenth-century context is firm enough for us to cope with the invitation offered by a story-less picture. And I think this goes beyond merely wondering what answer the boy might have given. If we dwell on the issue referred to in the painting—inherited power and authority

FIGURE **2** AN INTERVIEW BETWEEN CHARLES I AND OLIVER CROMWELL, Daniel Maclise, c.1836
Oil on canvas, 184×235 cm, 72½×92½ in, National Gallery of Ireland, Dublin

versus the rights of all and the power of the many when joined together—it takes us well beyond the seventeenth century and national frontiers.

vi Style

I have said nothing of Yeames's style, and would ask you think about it for a while before I make my comments. Does this picture have a style? The word 'style' refers both to a personal manner and to the idiom of a period or school. Do you think this painting has a style in either sense?

You may well feel that it has no personal manner. It has been painted carefully and solidly, and there is nothing in it that suggests a particular painter's touch or handwriting. Is there a school or period style in it? Again you may feel not: the painter is just recording the scene as he planned and envisaged it, thinking of nothing but truth and informative fullness, and of being what is called 'realistic'.

This realism is a style, a broad style within which there can be variations. It has a long tradition, going back to Greece and Rome, and also a shorter tradition born at the end of the sixteenth century and developed especially in the Holland of Rembrandt and Vermeer. This is referred to again in the section on landscape painting (page 223). It relies partly on perspective, a device developed and refined in Renaissance Italy by the sculptor and architect, Brunelleschi, by which internal and external spaces, and the place of objects in them, are convincingly represented. It also relies on conventions of light and colour that other artists have shown to be inaccurate, and on what one might call organizational decencies: for instance the way our side of the room is kept clear of people so that we get a good view and, as I have suggested, imaginative participation. In some respects Yeames avoids realism. He has gone to some trouble to find out about period clothes and interiors, but he has shunned period and functional blemishes. There should be dirt on some of those boots and on the floor. Few grown-ups at that time were free of the marks of some infection or other. And he has stretched the sitting officer's left arm more than a little to get his fist on to the corner of the table. It makes an important contribution as a link across the picture, but imagine the young boy's figure away and you are left with a very distorted limb.

There is another convention at work here. Fiction was the major growth area of Western culture in the nineteenth century, reaching most levels of society, but not only fiction in the form of books and part-publications in weeklies and monthlies. There was also the stage: plays and operas, good, bad and indifferent, but lots of them and fairly ubiquitous. (Bellini's opera *I Puritani*, based on a French play based on *Old Mortality*, was given its premier in Paris in 1835 and performed the same year in London.) A particular kind of drama was developed in the nineteenth century and is still very popular today. In this the audience is made to feel that it is observing actual life on the stage. Everything is made to seem very naturalistic or realistic; the set, the language, the action. We are persuaded to forget that the actors have learned their lines and are pretending, pretending above all that they are unaware of us. What is called 'naturalistic drama'—which many people today think of as the *normal* sort of drama—was being developed about the time when Yeames was painting his picture, primarily by companies in Germany and France.

It is often useful, in discussing narrative painting, to think of it as a form of drama. *And When Did You Last See Your Father?* could well be a 'still' representing a stage performance; that is, a photograph (usually posed by the performers for the photographer, not shot during a performance) done to record the production and to advertise it. Yeames can be said to have acted both as playwright and producer, inventing at least the outline of a story and imagining how to present the most telling moment from it on the stage of his picture. He was also, of course, his own designer and casting manager. And, like anyone else, he was helped by precedent—by, for instance, Maclise's painting.

I referred to 'the most telling moment'. You can see, I think, how for Yeames the unanswered question provided the psychological climax of whatever story he had imagined. You can also see how important it is, when planning a narrative painting that will present only one moment, to pick the moment that most fully represents the whole story. The German philosopher, Lessing, discussing the problem of how art communicates actions and feelings in an essay of 1766 (he focussed his discussion on the Greek sculpture known as the *Laocoön*, to which I shall be referring below), labelled it the 'pregnant moment' because it carried the workings of past and the promise of future in it. Yeames has, in effect, given us that moment without there ever having been a story that it refers to. His choice has been so effective that we sense the story around the moment, inventing what he has not provided any information about. But where would we be without the title?

There is another point in thinking about narrative paintings as though they were stage productions. When there is a story, and particularly a well-known story, the painter acts very much like a producer who is putting on a well-known play. When producer Z puts on *Romeo and Juliet*, he may well feel that he envisages the play in ways that bring out meanings and beauties that the productions of X or Y did not bring out. He may also feel that he can use his production to comment on the present day, making points about social behaviour or politics that the play can carry for him. So what he puts on stage is Shakespeare plus his own response to Shakespeare (and to others' productions of his plays), plus a reading of Shakespeare that he feels is relevant to the audience. He is combining many elements received from the author and from the long and rich tradition of staging Shakespeare with elements that belong to himself and elements that belong to his time.

Yeames did not have a particular story to tell, but he could rely on his public's familiarity with at least the outline of the political history that is the context of his picture. Given that familiarity, he could and still can appeal to our appetite for stories and our readiness to engage interest and sympathy in a human situation. We will now look at a much earlier painting, presenting a passage in the Bible, and use much the same method as for the Yeames painting.

The Tribute Money

(Plate 2) This is a wall painting, done in the early fifteenth century in Florence, part of the decoration of a side chapel in the church of a monastery. The family who endowed the chapel, the Brancacci, asked for its three walls to be painted with scenes from the Gospels and from the Acts of the Apostles, showing Peter's leading role among Christ's disciples and in founding the Christian Church after Christ's departure from earth. The fourth side, opposite the altar and window wall, is open to the transept of the church. *The Tribute Money* occupies almost the whole length of the left side wall in the upper register (there is another long painting below it). It dominates one's memory of the chapel partly because it is a very strong painting, but also because of its position. Its subject is of importance to the meaning of all the paintings together, and it also has a particular relevance to the commissioning family.

The painter and patron planning a representation of what we summarily call the Tribute Money have only a few verses in the Gospels to base it on: Matthew, chapters 17 and 22, Mark 12, and Luke 20. There is not much drama implied in any of these, not much action, but the problems raised are of perennial importance to a Christian. How are we to act when the demands of religion and country are in conflict? But this painting focuses on something more particular.

Its textual base is Matthew 17. I quote the relevant verses as given in the King James version:

> 24. And when they were come to Capernaum, they that received tribute money came to Peter and said, Doth not your master pay tribute?
> 25. He saith, Yes. And when he was come into the house, Jesus prevented him, saying, What thinkest thou, Simon? Of whom do the kings of the earth take custom or tribute? Of their own children, or of strangers?
> 26. Peter saith unto him, Of strangers. Jesus saith unto him, Then are the children free.
> 27. Notwithstanding, lest we should offend them, go thou to the sea, and cast an hook, and take up the fish that first cometh up; and when thou hast opened his mouth, thou shalt find a piece of money: that take, and give unto them for me and thee.

Masaccio's painting is surprisingly vivid, given this text. It looks and feels dramatic. Study Plate 2. Ask yourself how one might stage or represent those verses in St Matthew's Gospel in a succinct and memorable way. The painter cannot bring the curtain down on his production; what he presents becomes a permanence, a visual statement that must go on existing. This painting, worked into the plaster of the wall, a fresco, by a man in his early twenties, has been there for more than five-and-a-half centuries. It was greatly admired when it was done. Michelangelo, seventy-five years later, in his youth, made drawings of parts of it. It is greatly admired today, for all the flood of art and other images that sweeps past our eyes. So please pause and consider: consider the text and the pictorial possibilities inherent in it, and the reproduction.

Then let us look together.

i Size, format and general character

This is an exceptionally long painting, Vista-Vision plus; almost two-and-a-half times as long as it is high. The figures in it that are closest to us are nearly life-size. The main group of figures occupies about half the width of the whole; a crowd of figures it seems, in fact only fourteen. There is also something going on to the right and the left of this group. You probably noticed the two figures to the right: one man handing something to another. You may not have noticed, at first, the smaller squatting figure near the left edge of the painting. The whole scene is rather solemn. People make gestures but there are few actions of a larger sort. The colours of their clothes dominate the general visual impression: quite strong reds and greens. Apart from that the general effect is brownish-greyish. A building on the right, silhouetting the two men there, recedes into the distance; the rest of the figures are seen against the background of a fairly distant landscape.

LOOKING
— INTO —
PAINTINGS

The Open University

SUPPLEMENTARY PACK ORDER FORM

There's a whole new world of pleasure in visiting art galleries and museums and looking at painting with a fresh and informed eye. *Looking into Paintings* could be your key to unlocking this world of art. This book is also part of a multimedia study pack which brings painting to life with video programmes, fine art reproductions, linked audio commentaries, practical guidance on where to go and how to look at works of art. It will help you develop your taste in art at your own pace in your own home, without the pressures of exams and assessments.

Now that you have bought this book, you can order all the other items for £21.95.

Contents Boxed set including:
  Three audio cassettes containing six
  programmes, linked to
  Twenty fine art reproductions on cards
  VHS video cassette containing six video
  programmes
  Pack guide with list of galleries and museums
  and suggestions for gallery visits

Looking Into Paintings is presented by the Open University in association with Channel 4 Television, Faber and Faber and the Arts Council.

Price The price given may be subject to change. Price includes postage to UK addresses, packing, and VAT at £1.60 per pack. Available in the UK only.

14 Day Money Back Guarantee If, when you receive your order, you decide that the materials are not what you require, simply return them to us in the original packing and in mint condition within 14 days, and we will refund your payment in full. You must include the green despatch note or a note of your name and address with the returned materials.

Delivery Materials will normally be despatched within 30 days of receipt of your order.

Please return your order to: The Learning Materials Service Office, The Open University, PO Box 188, Milton Keynes, MK7 6DH

To: LMSO, The Open University, PO Box 188, Milton Keynes, MK7 6DH

Please send me .... copies of the supplementary pack 'Looking Into Paintings' at £21.95.

I enclose cheque/postal order for £ .... payable to The Open University

Or debit my credit card.

Access ☐ ☐☐☐☐☐☐☐☐☐☐☐☐☐☐☐☐
               card number

Visa ☐   expiry date ....

Signature ....

Name ....

Address ....

....

.... Postcode ....

TELEPHONE YOUR ORDER. If you are a credit card holder, you can save time and trouble by phoning 0908 655955 giving your name and address, credit card no. and ref. PA786SUP.

ii Composition

This is in three parts, unified by the single setting; three actions on one stage. Notice that the two figures on the right stand close to the bottom and front edge of the painting; the big group stands a little way further upstage except for the man who has his back to us. The squatting figure on the left is in the middle distance (he has taken off his red robe and is seen in his green undergarment, which makes him less noticeable). I find I take in the main group first, the group of two on the right second, the single figure on the left third.

Notice that the heads of the figures are pretty well on one horizontal line. Where their feet come tells us how far back on the picture stage they stand. The line of heads comes a little above half-way up; the area of painting above that is without significant events.

iii Space

The relative emptiness yields a strong sense of space and air. This painting is one of the first to make calculated use of the new perspective system, though Masaccio makes only sparing use of it here. The house on the right, with its porch and especially the steps on the extreme right, is a clear demonstration of the effectiveness of perspective as a means of suggesting space. Situated to the right of the main group, the building tells us about the space in which the men stand, and prepares us for the larger and less defined space of the landscape.

iv Light

There is no very strong sense of light and shadow, but what light there is serves to give the figures a three-dimensional and weighty presence. It falls from the right, from above our right shoulders, and that is where, in the actual chapel, there is a window over the altar. It is not dramatic lighting, but it makes good factual sense. There is no light in the sky, and the darkness there feels a little like a ceiling over the scene; a blue sky would suggest more space beyond the mountains, and this deepening of the effect of space would interfere with the unit of wall surface.

v Story and action ·

The central figure is Christ. He is actually a little to the left of centre; this has the effect of pressing him towards us, making us encounter him a little more urgently. The thirteen figures surrounding him are his twelve disciples plus the man in doublet and hose, who stands with his back to us. He represents 'they that received tribute money', i.e. those charged with collecting a tax from visiting Jews for the running of the Temple. His clothes are those of Masaccio's world; the clothes of ordinary Florentines. Of course Florentines would have known this, and would have felt that this figure represented themselves in some measure, challenging and questioning Christ. Christ is gesturing towards Peter, and is thus shown to be speaking to him, and Peter gestures towards the sea and his own reappearance by it. It is Peter again who appears on the right, giving

35

the coin to the same tax collector. The sequence in which I have suggested we register these groups and actions, is not the sequence in St Matthew's account. The scene of Peter finding the coin is in itself relatively marginal to the story. The main points of what happened are two: Christ claimed that, as the Son of God, he should not be asked to pay the tribute, but nevertheless, 'lest we offend them', he arranged it should be paid. This is the first occasion in the Gospels that Christ claims a special status for himself and his immediate followers. You may have noticed that Masaccio gives Christ and most of the disciples golden haloes (tilted to accord with perspective), symbols of spiritual radiance used in many parts of the world. The four men on the right do not have them; these may be portraits of members of the Brancacci family. To show them with haloes, even when they were on stage in the role of disciples, would be sacrilegious.

Now look at the whole painting again. Does it strike you now that your eyes tend back again and again to the head of Christ? Mine do, and it is partly because of his position and because he is to a carefully limited degree more prominent than the others (note for instance the strong, eye-catching contrast offered by pinky-red and slate-green robes). But it is also due to the fact that what perspective lines the painting has running into the picture space—along the steps, the little tiled roof over the porch, the moulding under the windows—all meet in Christ's face. The pictorial construction and the intellectual focus are congruent. Although the painting as a whole suggests events following one another, Christ is the beginning and end, metaphorically and also literally as our eyes return to him. The tax collector in the middle group links with the space in which we stand and to which his heel seems to belong. This use of what might be thought of as merely a technical device—for making space seem realistic—underlines the meaning of the work, and is characteristic of Renaissance art at its best.

Masaccio was concerned with making a representation that would seem real to us, a *possible* representation if not an actual witness account. He made his figures stand firmly on the ground, gave them roundness and a sense of weight; made real also the intervals between them and between them and the distant trees. But this is sometimes made to seem more innovatory than it was. There was a great deal of reality in the art of the great Florentine painter Giotto, working a hundred years earlier, and there was a good deal of realistic detail in the work of Masaccio's older contemporaries. We see this, for example, in the work of Masolino, with whom Masaccio collaborated on the painting of the Brancacci Chapel. In Masolino's painting of Adam and Eve in Paradise (Plate 3) the bodies are quite convincing, though slight; details of hair and flowers are very accurate. Masaccio got some of his feeling for solemn figures in paint from sculpture, the sculpture of another contemporary, Donatello, in particular. He did not, as is sometimes implied, go out into the streets of Florence and find his figures ready-made amongst his fellow citizens.

Masaccio brings a new gravity and concentration into painting. Perspective, which others came to use as a way of putting interesting additional material into their paintings, is for him one of several elements by means of which to unify and dramatize his scene. Colour is another such element, and so, of course, is the whole composition or arrangement. Repeating the figure of Peter, openly having three scenes in one composition, is not an innovation but adherence to a tradition; that is how medieval artists coped with the problem of sequential narrative, and it was still used by Masaccio's contemporaries. But it became old-fashioned after his time since it worked against the logical coherence of paintings composed to appear as of one place and one time. For all that, Masaccio's fresco coheres strongly in itself, and works powerfully well in the chapel itself. The end wall, with the altar and window, is at a right angle immediately to the right of the painting. Masaccio's painted house seems almost a continuation of the plane of that wall, and Peter and the tax collector serve in part as a bridge to the next painting. I also believe that Masaccio planned his picture so that it makes a strong impact on anyone entering the chapel and so seeing it obliquely from the left. Try holding the book so that you see the reproduction angled away from you to the right: it remains clear and effective. Now, if you will, try something odder: look at the reproduction in a mirror, close to so that you can still read every part. Seen in reverse, Peter, the tax collector and the house behind them dominate the whole picture; the rest is left oddly short of space, and much diminished in importance.

One last point. The Brancacci were bankers, like the Medici and other leading families in Florence. Spending money on art of this kind was for the greater glory of God, of the order of monks to whom the church belonged, the Carmelites, and also of the name of Brancacci. That they should ask for the subject of *The Tribute Money* to be raised so prominently on the wall of their chapel indicates a lack of Anglo-Saxon delicacy. They knew they were money men and that everyone else knew it too. They reminded their fellows that they were also good sons of the Church, and willing to put some of that money towards the service of God. And everyone will have known the relevant parts of the Gospel. Many a sermon dealt then, as now, with the Christian's duty to Church and State. Moreover, the Florence of the 1420s was much intrigued by a dispute between the rulers of the city and the Church authorities over money questions. Masaccio's painting is both topical and specific to his time and location, and it reaches out beyond that to the wider issue of Church and State, and further, to the issue of conscience versus law and authority. It had meaning then and it has meaning now, and these two meanings overlap in the Gospel text. Nonetheless, someone unfamiliar with Christianity and its history and continuing issues would need to be told what this painting was about. The painting can shape the story and highlight particular aspects of it, give it both an immediate link and a general resonance, but it cannot, by itself, tell it.

HISTORY PAINTING

Masaccio's painting is a key example of a type of narrative painting that was considered, in the Renaissance and for centuries afterwards, *the* kind of painting for a serious artist to aspire to and to achieve. We, in the twentieth century, have lost their emphasis on the genres (see Glossary) of art, and do not feel that one is necessarily more valuable than another, so this category needs explaining.

Renaissance art theorists, often artists themselves, had no doubt that some kinds of painting were more demanding than others for the artist to produce, and more satisfying for the art consumer to look at. At the top of the list they put History painting. The word 'History' echoes the Italian word *istoria* which means 'story' as much as history or chronicle; it does not mean history in our present sense of the word, but in an older sense when, in English too, it means narrative, even a personal one. To avoid confusion I use a capital letter for it.

History painting meant not only painting subjects from history but any truly significant subject taken from a worthy source and treated in a suitably informative and serious manner. There are three main points here: significant subject; honourable source; proper manner. Each is important.

Subject

It was difficult to distinguish what we call history from what we call legend. History in our modern sense has become a relatively scientific, fact-based thing; in Renaissance times it would have been foolish to ask whether Homer's account of the fall of the city of Troy was fact or fiction. Hand on heart, they might have felt that the way Homer tells it, with the gods intervening, it could not be taken as pure, certifiable fact. On the other hand, where should they draw the line between hard fact and poetic and meaningful invention, handed down through centuries? Was it necessary to distinguish between them? They did not have our passion for fact and our reluctance to value anything not wholly secure. We lack their confident use of the past as something full of lessons for the present. If they could turn the stories of the past into object lessons for themselves, that justified their past, its history, its legends, its myths, its relics of all sorts.

Sources

The famous authors of Greece and Rome were honoured as representatives of a great culture that barbarism had obscured, which was being rediscovered as the true voice of civilized mankind. The Middle Ages were named thus as a dark and difficult period in between two ages of culture, and the Renaissance sought to build on the best qualities of the classical tradition and harmonize it with its newer base in Christianity. Ovid, the poet exiled to the shores of the Black Sea and Virgil, the successful and lavishly honoured poet of Rome who read parts of his *Aeneid* before the Emperor and his circle, both roughly contemporary with Christ, were found particularly rich in pre-echoes of Christianity. Plutarch,

Livy and other historians provided stories of human greatness and valour. The dramatists of Greece and Rome had turned history and legend into affecting stage actions; they served as a source and also as models for the creative use of given material, for making a particular narrative into an examination of mankind's aspirations and weaknesses. There were many other ancient writers whose texts were rifled by Renaissance and post-Renaissance scholars, poets, clergy and artists, and were found to yield ever fresh images and ideas. To them was added the Bible, and the apocryphal texts which were not thought worthy of Bible status. The stories of saints, the commentaries of the leading theologians of the Church and other religious material were also available. Great 'modern' writers such as Dante were enrolled as apt sources for serious art. Over the centuries the list grew. It was never a defined list, and it varied a little from country to country. But the general point was clear and accepted; these sources provided themes that mankind was well advised to consider deeply and apply to itself at any time and in any place.

Manner

That important matters should be treated as such seems self-evident. But how does one evolve a manner that is, and is recognized as being, important? The ancients provided some examples for artists to learn from, mostly single carved figures and low-relief sculpture (from tombs and buildings). The latter at times represented an action of some sort, and so could guide a Renaissance artist in his attempt to create a significant narrative art form. There was little in the way of ancient painting to study. When the ancient cities of Pompeii and Herculaneum were discovered in the eighteenth century, paintings found there were reproduced in books in the form of line engravings. These had an immediate influence, and about that time too Greek vase paintings became known. In other words, the art of Greece and Rome served as a basic model, but in time this model grew until it was a number of not quite congruent models, not one language but a range of styles.

There were also the ancients' writings about art and literature. The basic method of artists, they said, was to combine an ideal sense of beauty with the study of nature; nature by itself was too rough and varied, so artists would look for a perfect specimen or deduce a perfect example from whatever nature had to offer. They would go behind the particular phenomenon to the intellectually more valid ideal image. In this way close observation of nature and the abstract ideal of perfection together formed the basis for the classical art of Greece and Rome. It was for the purpose of presenting actions convincingly, i.e. in order to make art narrative, that the Greeks abandoned the immobile, unperforming art of the Egyptians and other Near Eastern civilizations.

The Renaissance inherited both the theory and a small but growing number of works of art testifying to its effectiveness. There was great excitement whenever a major piece of sculpture was dug up or ancient ruins were cleared and revealed traces of their original decoration. A major instance of a sculpture find

FIGURE **3** THE LAOCOÖN GROUP, Hagesander, Athenodorus and Polydorus of Rhodes, c. 125 BC
Marble, height 183 cm, 72 in, Museo del Vaticano, Rome

40

was the discovery, in January 1506, of the *Laocoön* group (Figure 3). Here was an ancient sculpture of which ancient authors had spoken with praise, and one related to a famous ancient text. It represents, in its three figures ensnared by serpents, the fate of the priest Laocoön and his sons as recounted in Homer's *Iliad*.

The Renaissance had the self-regard not to be overwhelmed by this growing inheritance but to add to it. It was recognized in Rome and Florence that recent and living artists, notably Raphael and Michelangelo, were worthy to stand beside the ancients as models for those that followed. The art academies that were set up as centres of artistic debate and teaching, first in Italy and then in most countries of Europe, supported and propagated the ideals of ancient classicism. That is what they taught; that is what they rewarded with prizes and with prestigious and profitable commissions. As time went on academic practice widened, but for centuries no one seriously challenged the basic conviction that History painting, with its high ideals and ancient lineage was *the* art form to which artists and an art public should give their attention and praise.

Let us now return to Masolino's treatment of the Adam and Eve scene in the Brancacci Chapel (Plate 3). Opposite it in the chapel is its partner, another Adam and Eve scene showing the next stage in that story, painted by Masaccio (Plate 4). The source is of course the first book of the Bible, the Book of Genesis; the subject of the two paintings is the perfect happiness prepared by God for man and woman, their rejection of it by the first act of disobedience, and their punishment for that rejection. We shall look more particularly at the manner in which the two painters presented these all-important moments in the history of the human race, and how that manner affects the meaning of each.

Masolino and Masaccio

We noted earlier the fine and attractive details Masolino gave to his painting, which was characteristic of Florentine painting at the time. This is true also of the elegance of the figures: their slim silhouettes and the way they are posed. That sweetness of manner brings out the beauty that God had given mankind, creating man 'in his own image', and hints at the happiness and even glamour of life in the Garden of Eden.

Masaccio's manner is quite different. His part of the story is different too of course. Masolino's painting shows us Adam and Eve just before or as they yield to temptation, symbolized by the apple which, persuaded by the serpent, Eve has taken from the tree. Masaccio shows us quite unambiguously the moment at which, expelled from Eden, mankind enters on its life of labour, pain and conflict. So the subject invites a different manner. It is tempting to speculate how Masaccio would have handled Masolino's subject. I think he would have brought out the drama of it more, and hinted at the punishment more than at the happiness that was being thrown away; we should have had a stronger painting but one that told us less about God's goodness. As they are, the two scenes together give us a broader portrayal of the story, and to some extent this reflects the character of the two painters.

Masaccio sets his scene of the *Expulsion* on a very bare stage. On the left is a narrow gateway, not very imposing but effective as a framing and space-making device. The background is quite plain: the Vale of Tears that mankind enters is a desert. We see three figures. The angel driving Adam and Eve out of the Garden of Eden hovers about them, grave rather than warlike. His calm contrasts with the howls of Eve and the silent horror expressed by Adam. Having Adam hide his face is a theatrical masterstroke. Eve's face is almost a mask, its smooth forms showing very little detail but conveying without reserve her total agony. The two human figures are evidently a pair and at the same time they contrast with each other. They move as one. (Masolino would probably have

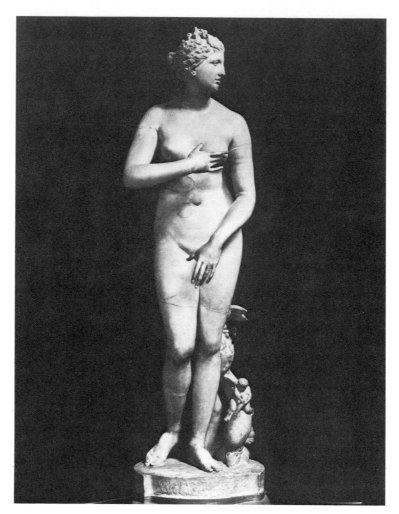

FIGURE **4** MEDICI VENUS (VENUS PUDICA), Artist unknown, c. 200 BC
Marble, height 153 cm, 60¼ in, Uffizi, Florence

wanted to give them poses that produced more of a contrast between them.)
Eve's open, clamorous reaction to what is happening tells us unambiguously
what she is feeling; Adam's more in-turned response suggests the burden of pain
and longing that will be everyman's.

If we look from the Masaccio to the Masolino, Masolino's figures seem unreal
in comparison and also inexpressive. To use words sharper than Masolino de-
serves, his Adam and Eve look like dummies in a shop window, arranged to
depict a biblical charade. Masaccio's strike us as much more real. Insofar as
they are not the actual Adam and Eve, they are actors identifying completely
with their roles. Masaccio, the producer, has picked them not for their good
looks but for their ordinariness, and set them on a stage that supports their
action well.

But, as I said before, Masaccio did not simply find this reality in the world

FIGURE 5 PRUDENCE (detail of Pisa pulpit), Giovanni Pisano, 1302–10
Marble, height 118 cm, 46½ in, Pisa Duomo (Cathedral)

about him and put it into his painting. The nineteenth century is full of painters proud to find a beggar in the streets when they need to represent a beggar, sketching him there and then or bringing him into the studio to copy his appearance. Masaccio was certainly aware of the world about him, and his art reflects that awareness, but he would have thought it a curious limitation to copy actual people in his painting. Perhaps he might have found a woman capable of expressing misery as his Eve expresses it, but this would have reduced the meaning of his Eve in two respects. First, to have used a particular model would probably have made his image less universal—one woman, not all womankind. Secondly, the model he did use, taken from art and not from life, brought with it elements of meaning which enrich the content of his staging of the scene.

His Eve is a quotation from the Greek. Greek sculptors, from the fifth century BC on, had made sculptures of the goddess Aphrodite in a range of poses. These are known to us mainly through Roman copies, and some of these copies were known to Italian artists of medieval times as well as to Masaccio's generation. A famous type of Aphrodite sculpture was what the Romans called the *Venus pudica*, modest Venus (Figure 4). She shields her body from our eyes with her hands. The original thought was probably to show the goddess surprised by an intruding male; to medieval eyes her guarded pose hinted at the moral dangers associated with nakedness. Adam and Eve had discovered nakedness through their act of disobedience; in sinning they had burdened themselves with shame. Using the pose of *Venus pudica*, Masaccio is able to add this loss of innocence to the meaning of his painting. But there is more to this borrowing of a pose-with-meaning. Obviously he is associating Eve with Aphrodite/Venus, a goddess much worshipped in the ancient world and associated with generation and fertility as much as with physical and intellectual love: Eve is the mother of all mankind. He is also reflecting theological commentaries that see, especially in the naked Eve, an antetype or pre-echo of Mary the Mother of God who is sometimes referred to as the New Eve. The ivy leaves you can just see in the reproduction were added after Masaccio's time.

People who saw these paintings were of course familiar with the story told in Genesis. Today most of us know it in outline. But many of them will also have recognized Masaccio's use of this quotation, and probably they were thrilled by it. They had seen other *Expulsions*, painted and carved, but here was one that brought a new vehemence to the subject and, in addition, brought out meanings in it by linking it with an honoured ancient theme and form.

Many of them will actually have known the specific source for Masaccio's figure. Pisa is not far from Florence. Two outstanding sculptors had worked there over a century before Masaccio's day. Nicola and Giovanni Pisano, father and son, had brought into Gothic sculpture a firmness and grandeur of style that reflected their interest in Roman remains. Among their most famous works were and are Nicola's elaborate pulpit in the Baptistry of Pisa and Giovanni's equally complex pulpit in Pisa Cathedral, a few steps away from each other. Part of Giovanni's pulpit is a figure representing the virtue *Prudence* (Figure 5). Giovanni aptly shows her in the guise and pose of *Venus pudica*. It may also be worth noting that she has the slightly squat, inelegant proportions that Masaccio gave to his Eve; the classical models, Greek and Roman, would have been rather more harmoniously proportioned. (For a more elegant interpretation of the *Venus pudica* type, done by a painter whose taste was more *à la* Masolino, see Botticelli's famous *Birth of Venus*.) It would not have been difficult for an evidently serious artist like Masaccio to go to Pisa to look at the work of the two Pisani. In any case, we know that he himself worked in Pisa, just before he began his paintings in the Brancacci Chapel, producing a multi-panelled altarpiece for the Carmelite church there. We have its centre panel, a *Madonna and Child with Angels*, in the National Gallery.

It looks as though Masaccio did not have as certain a model for his Adam. We can imagine him wondering how to represent man *in extremis*. He probably thought of a Crucifix made by Donatello for the church of Santa Croce in Florence in 1406. Masaccio certainly knew Donatello and admired his work. Donatello's figure is that of a man breathing painfully and crying out, his chest noticeably inflated. He had chosen to represent Christ at the moment of death, when he 'cried with a loud voice, and gave up the ghost' (Mark 15: 37). It seems likely that Masaccio had this figure in mind. As is the case of his Eve, the association brought additional meaning into his painting. Theologians saw in Adam an antetype of Christ: the first man, made by God, foreshadows the Son of God's life on earth; the Fall of Man from grace is a precondition for Christ's death on the cross and man's Redemption.

It is interesting to see Masaccio again deriving his ideas from sculpture. The sense of physical weight and presence that we get, for example, from the main group in *The Tribute Money* suggests a sculptural feel for forms. It is also likely that some of the heads in that group were taken from ancient sculpture. The young Michelangelo, studying Masaccio's paintings in the 1490s, was preparing himself for a career in sculpture. Masaccio's art was a major factor in developing Michelangelo's feeling for awesomely powerful, and powerfully expressive, figures—for what contemporaries were to call his *terribilità*; it taught him to interpret the ancient sculpture he could study in the Medici collection in similarly vehement terms. When the *Laocoön* group was discovered this added a further range of expressive forms to Michelangelo's repertory.

History Painting and the Network

Masaccio benefited from the Pisani and from Donatello; Donatello had learned from the Pisani and from other predecessors, and had sought out ancient sculptures in Rome and Florence; Michelangelo based his art on that of Masaccio and Donatello as well as on the work of the ancients, constantly enlarging his artistic range through new experiences, as in the case of the *Laocoön*, and through new insights. These examples illustrate, in summary form, how artists work and see themselves as members of a great association of artists that can span centuries and (in modern times) over the whole globe. They work with a language which is the accumulated mass of art. They are linked, consciously as well as unconsciously, by what I see as a kind of network that lies across space and time and works against the limitations of a particular place and moment. Anyone who wants his art to have more than momentary and local significance can plug into this network, but only those who contribute to it by creating new elements from its material can become part of the network.

To some extent this network existed in ancient times and served medieval art, but the fifteenth and sixteenth centuries saw great efforts being made to deepen and to systematize knowledge of ancient and modern art through the formation of collections like that of the Medici and the production of theoretical and historical accounts of art. With ever-increasing archaeological and historical research, something like total knowledge has become available. Perhaps this has tended to weaken the network composed of outstanding models: the weight of accumulating knowledge has borne down on the canon of models of excellence. Our knowledge and appreciation has become global, encompassing African sculpture, Japanese calligraphy, prehistoric cave paintings, and we have easy access to them all in museums and in illustrations. Yet I believe that the network operates to this day, helping the artist to work effectively and helping us to engage with art, and I mean to provide some evidence of this before the end of this section.

Originality or Imitation?

The network could not exist, of course, without imitation being an accepted and normal part of artistic creation. I emphasize this because modern art journalism, sometimes even professional accounts by art historians and art critics, make too much of the notion of originality and uniqueness. That a work of art should have a general flavour or particular characteristics that are the artist's own and make his work in some measure different from that of others, was noticed and valued by the ancients and also by the Renaissance from at least the sixteenth century on. Romanticism, around 1800 especially, put much greater emphasis on artistic individuality. The Romantic artist was often praised for his unconventionality, that is for not adhering to the principles taught in the academies and valued by society at large. The more art became a commercialized product, individual works to be sold in shops in competition with each other, the more insistence there was on the real or pretended originality of the merchandise on offer.

Everyone who becomes an artist is to some degree accepting a part of the great field of art as his working area. Even if he then develops away from that patch, perhaps forcing us to recognize as art something that in theory we might have considered as falling outside that capacious field, he is still linked to his starting point. Certainly art has grown as some artists have leapt over the fence that others erected and want to defend. Anyone who has observed the development of art in the last hundred years will have noticed how readily old conventions adapt in order to embrace striking idiosyncracies, and also of course how rapidly today's invention becomes tomorrow's routine.

Until Romanticism imitation was an honoured part of the process of artistic creation. I referred earlier, very briefly, to the ancients' principle of studying nature but adjusting what nature showed in terms of ideal and perfect forms. I also discussed the way a producer might stage his version of a given play as an analogy for the way History painters worked. I have shown, using Masaccio's work by way of example, how a painter might pay all possible respect to the text he has been commissioned to represent in visual form, and borrow or adapt forms from the work of others, and yet be strong enough to become a model for others after him.

I should like to give here two examples of writers about art in whom we find the principle of imitation clearly stated, one from the fifteenth century and one from the eighteenth. Leone Battista Alberti was the first great theorist of art in Renaissance times. He was an outstanding scholar, but he was also an artist and an architect. His treatise *On Painting* (the Latin original was circulated in manuscript in 1435; Alberti's own Italian version came out in 1436) is an impressive mixture of theoretical discussion and practical advice. His main concern is with History painting. He suggests how such paintings should be organized, how colour should be deployed, how many figures make an effective ensemble, and so on, but he also emphasizes the importance of finding worthy subjects, primarily in the writings of the ancients, and of finding worthy models to adapt to one's own purposes. He places great importance on making every action, position and gesture in a painting contribute to the meaning of the History painting. To show what he means he refers to ancient examples, and in particular to a relief carving

> . . . praised in Rome, in which Meleager, a dead man, weighs down those who carry him. In every one of his members he appears completely dead—everything hangs, hands, fingers and head; everything falls heavily. Anyone who tries to express a dead body—which is certainly most difficult—will be a good painter if he knows how to make members of the body flaccid.

47

Alberti probably did not know Masaccio personally but he certainly knew his work. In his book he ranks Masaccio with the renowned artists of ancient times, implying that this modern artist is as worthy of emulation as they.

The other author is Sir Joshua Reynolds, painter, founder member of the Royal Academy of Arts in London in 1768, and its first president. Most years during his presidency Reynolds lectured at the Academy on art in general and on the work of individual painters. His *Discourses* are an attractive mixture of classical ideas forcefully expressed and of personal and markedly eighteenth-century opinions more hesitantly fed into the classical framework. But again, like Alberti, Reynolds has no doubt that it is History painting that alone is great art; everything else, even the portraiture at which he himself excelled, is secondary. And imitation of the right models is the true road to good History painting. It is the painter's duty to prepare his mind as well as to develop skills of eye and hand, by studying the great modern masters he recommends to them, and the best works of the ancients:

> A mind enriched by an assemblage of all the treasures of ancient and modern art will be more elevated and fruitful in resources in proportion to the number of ideas which have been carefully collected and thoroughly digested. There can be no doubt but that he who has the most materials has the greatest means of invention.

Invention comes from using the best models, not from turning one's back on them. By Reynolds' time it had become normal for artists aiming at success as History painters to spend months and perhaps years in Italy, especially in Rome where there was the greatest concentration of ancient sculpture and modern paintings to be studied and drawn. He himself had been there, and if English patrons subsequently failed him by commissioning only portraits from him, he hoped nonetheless that the existence of the Academy, and his teaching in it, would lead his country into appreciating and supporting the more elevated art of History painting. He could not know that the great tradition he was doing his best to establish on English soil would soon be retreating under the pressure of Romantic individualism.

Reynolds invited his students to learn from, above all other masters, Raphael who (he said) had himself learned the grand manner of History painting at its most elevated from Michelangelo. As for the Venetian painters who were their contemporaries, Reynolds clearly had a deep affection for their sensuous, colour-ful art but thought them less reliable as models for his own time. He warned students against the sensuous delights of rich colour painting: form must come first, for the sake of clarity of communication, whereas colour is likely to diminish the intellectual appeal of the subject and satisfy merely the senses. Even Titian, whose work he evidently loved deeply, could thus lead the unwary painter away from the most elevated ideals of art.

48

Raphael and Titian

Let us now look at the way Raphael and Titian handled the same, or much the same subject. Please study Plate 5. Did you recognize its subject? If your eye went straight to the caption did the title *The Entombment of Christ* give you all the information you needed?

It would take a longer title to tell fully what the painting represents. We see Christ being carried across the front of the pictorial stage. On the left is the entrance to the cave which will be his tomb. In the background, on the right, we can see a hill with three crosses; there is still a ladder leaning against the central one, on which Christ died. Nearer us, on the right, is a group of women; one of them is Mary, his Mother, fainting with anguish. Among those carrying the corpse is another woman, Mary Magdalen, the once sinful woman whose repent-ance and devotion Christ recommended as a model to all.

There are, in effect, three actions. Christ's body has already been taken down from the cross but we are reminded of that part of the story by the distant scene. The second happened just a few moments ago, when the men laid the corpse down on the ground and the women gathered round it to lament Christ's death. Now, thirdly, most of the women have risen, and the men are straining to carry the body the last few feet of the way. There is sequentiality in the painting, but this is managed without the repetitions and the anachronistic representation of three separate moments that we found in Masaccio.

This is a relatively early work by Raphael, who started young, developed quickly and died in his thirties. He had studied in Perugia; the landscape background in this painting represents the delicate, slightly sweet style he learned there under Perugino. The figures and the composition as a whole show the influence of the years Raphael spent in Florence, and especially of the more vigorous and dramatic art produced there by Leonardo da Vinci and by Michelangelo.

The *Entombment* was commissioned when Raphael was twenty-two and was on a visit to Perugia. A lady of Perugia, Atalanta Baglione, wanted it as an altarpiece for the Baglione family chapel in a local church. Her son Grifonetto had been murdered in one of those Italian family feuds that Shakespeare drew on for his *Romeo and Juliet*. Atalanta Baglione had tried to stop the feuding and had refused to shelter Grifonetto from his enemies after he had killed one of them, and in this way had indirectly caused his death. The altarpiece should in some way commemorate these terrible events as well as serve as an expiatory offering to God. You will see that this background information is necessary if we are to understand what Raphael did.

Leonardo's example had taught Raphael to make detailed drawings for his paintings. From Raphael's drawings we know that his first intention was to paint a *Lamentation*: the group of Mary and other women weeping over the dead Christ. The painting he envisaged would have been dominated by that group, harmoniously and symmetrically presented. But then he reconsidered the matter, and, very probably under the influence of Michelangelo, produced this less harmonious but more energetic and more fully narrative work.

None of the figures is static; all but Christ and Mary are positively active, carrying, lifting, supporting. Facial expressions, as classical taste required, are not very strong but I see a hint of Masaccio's Eve in the face of Mary Magdalen, almost mask-like and with much the same emphasis on the turning plane of the forehead and the nose as an extension of it. (There is evidence that Raphael studied the Brancacci Chapel paintings.) The face of Christ certainly echoes that of Laocoön. The seated girl on the right, turning to support Mary, is taken from a recent painting by Michelangelo. The athletic young man who occupies so much space and our attention in the foreground has much of Michelangelo about him.

The body of Christ, in character and pose, is taken from a recent sculpture by Michelangelo, and in this indebtedness especially we have a telling example of the network in use. I quoted earlier Alberti's description of the relief sculpture of the dead Meleager. Raphael's painting derives much of its drama from the contrast between the inert weight of his Christ and the effort exhibited by the men carrying him, and it is likely that he was here responding to Alberti's implied challenge. He was certainly also responding to the *Pietà* Michelangelo had carved a few years earlier for a cardinal (Figure 6). A *Pietà* is a representation of the dead Christ and his Mother; a condensed version, in effect, of the *Lamentation* theme, reducing the narrative element and concentrating on the

FIGURE **6** PIETÀ, Michelangelo, 1498–9
Marble, 174x195 cm, 68¼x77 in, St Peter's, Rome

affecting image of the Mother with her dead Son. Michelangelo had not invented this formula; it had existed since medieval times, especially north of the Alps. But he had given it a new character and meaning by invoking the Meleager theme. There was a Roman relief that showed Meleager in a pose very similar to that of Michelangelo's dead Christ, and this was probably also the relief Alberti had been describing. The cardinal and his friends will certainly have known the relief too and will have recognized this association of Christ with Meleager. In fact, theologians saw in Meleager a prefiguration of Christ the Redeemer, so that the connection Michelangelo was making was not merely a matter of invoking the classical manner of the sculpture but also as an enrichment of the meaning of his Christian image.

Raphael adopted Michelangelo's Christ, with its pagan background. The story of Meleager, told by Homer and Apollodorus, is complex but includes his love of a woman named Atalanta, his hunting and slaying a fearsome boar that had wounded her, his awarding her the spoils (head and hide) of that victory, normally kept by the victor, his subsequent fight with his fellow hunters, rendered jealous by that act of generosity, and Meleager's own premature death—a death associated with acts of valour and self-sacrifice. By referring to Meleager in his painting Raphael was indirectly commemorating the modern Atalanta who had commissioned the painting. Mary's great sorrow, vividly expressed in the painting, is also Atalanta Baglione's sorrow. The young man in the centre of the painting represents St John, for whom Christ had a special affection and whom Christ from the cross offered to his Mother as her new son. He is clearly a reference to Grifonetto.

Raphael's painting is in oil on panel, a method which permits strong colours and a broad range of tones from light to dark, as well as fine detail where the painter wants it. The Brancacci Chapel paintings are frescoes, you will remember, painted with a watery medium into fresh wet plaster; this technique calls for relatively swift and broad brushwork, clear decisions, and unfussy forms, and does not allow for very bright colours or extreme tones. So some of the differences between Masaccio's manner and Raphael's must be attributed to technical questions, but it is clear also that, in this early work, Raphael has not been able wholly to control the complexity of the action in his picture. There are perhaps too many heads and legs claiming our attention, too many movements this way and that. If you look at the reproduction in a mirror, you will I think find that the group of women is much diminished in importance, and the hill with the three crosses is almost lost altogether, so that much of the narrative complexity is lost too. But it seems to me that the group carrying the body of Christ is enhanced by the reversal, and that there is now a greater and more affecting emphasis on Christ's face.

When Titian painted his *Entombment* (Plate 6) he used this reversed arrangement. He may have known Raphael's painting, but it is more likely that he started with the Meleager relief. Like Raphael's painting, his is done in oil paint, but on canvas and not on wood. Titian, like other Venetian painters of the sixteenth century, gave less attention to drawing his figures very precisely and much more to sonorous colours and a rich overall effect.

How do you think the two *Entombments* compare? I do not mean do you prefer one to the other (if you have a strong preference ask yourself what occasions it), but rather in what ways do they function similarly and differently. The basic message is much the same in both, though of course the Titian focuses on a more limited action than the Raphael. I find the Titian involves me more, and that on the general human level of someone being carried to his final resting place. This greater involvement has something to do with Titian's colour and light and dark, but it may also stem from the composition itself. The whole group is very harmonious, is expressive without stridency, and Titian's concentration on one group focuses also my feelings. I personally find the left-to-right movement more involving than Raphael's right-to-left, and I wonder whether you agree. I

51

feel I move with and into the group, and that the group is hollow, almost cavernous, with Christ's face darkly shadowed, enveloped by the others. Raphael's world of art, in central Italy, would probably not have approved of this obscuring of the divine hero's face; it would have seemed sacrilegious to them as well as unsatisfactory. Alberti had called for clarity, and Raphael had been able to combine clarity with rich and dramatic effects of colour and tone. The sensuous was at the service of the intellectual, and not allowed to become dominant. This made Raphael the best of all models for the young. Nonetheless, the greatest painters of succeeding centuries learned from both schools, the Venetian and that of Florence and Rome.

The narrative content of the Titian, as also of Michelangelo's *Pietà*, is very limited compared to what Raphael offered in his painting. Both Titian and Michelangelo on other occasions produced complex narratives in paint, but here they were creating images for private devotion, not a large altarpiece for a chapel which, though associated with a particular family, is open to the public at large. The altarpiece is much more a public statement; the Titian and Michelangelo's two-figure sculpture are images for contemplation more than edification.

The same applies to Titian's small *Tribute Money* (Figure 7), painted about the same time. This shows even greater concentration. Painted on a panel, it was to serve as the door of the Duke of Ferrara's cabinet housing a beloved collection of ancient coins. No doubt the Duke proposed the subject; it is obviously apt. Titian shows two half figures, Christ and the tax man. The latter holds the coin; we do not see Christ giving it or receiving it, and the message is quite clear: 'Render therefore unto Caesar the things which are Caesar's; and unto God the things that are God's' (Matthew 22:21). Titian makes much of the contrast between the two heads and the two hands: dignity and gentleness versus somewhat sharp features and a tight hold on the coin. And that contrast is heightened by the rich colours of Christ's robes, and the two points of radiance coming from his head (a diminished version of the cruciform radiance often used to designate the head of Christ).

We have here a contrast similar to that between a *Pietà* and a *Lamentation* or a *Entombment*: the narrative is signalled rather than told. In a similar way, the birth and childhood of Christ are signalled in the *Mother and Child* formula. To us it has something of the close-up character, familiar in photographs and films. We have, on the one hand, a public image and, on the other, something often smaller in scale and certainly more intimate in feeling and usually intended for domestic use. North and south of the Alps there was an increasing demand for devotional pictures for people to have in their homes. It is not surprising to find that close-up enactments of this sort bring with them an interest in facial types and facial expression, and this the next example shows particularly clearly.

The increased psychological interest produced by Titian's emphasis on the two heads is found also in a painting executed in Venice by a visiting German painter about ten years earlier (Plate 7). The story of *Christ among the Doctors*

FIGURE **7** THE TRIBUTE MONEY, Titian, probably 1516
Oil on panel, 75x56 cm, 29$\frac{1}{2}$x22 in, Staatliche Kunstsammlungen, Dresden

FIGURE **8** CHRIST AMONG THE DOCTORS, Butinone, c.1500
Oil on panel, 25x22 cm, 10x8¾ in, National Galleries of Scotland, Edinburgh

54

FIGURE **9** THE FINDING OF THE SAVIOUR IN THE TEMPLE,
William Holman Hunt, 1854−5 and 1856−60
Oil on canvas, 86x141 cm, 33¾x55½ in, by permission of the Birmingham Museum and Art Gallery

comes from the Gospel of St Luke (2:41–51). The twelve-year-old has been brought
to Solomon's Temple in Jerusalem for the Passover; when Mary and Joseph set
off for home they find that their child has disappeared; after much searching
they discover him still in the Temple, debating with the Jewish scribes there:
'And all that heard him were astonished at his understanding and answers.' The
narrative has obvious anecdotal attractions: the wise child astounding the
scholars. But it is also of great theological importance. Not only is Christ announcing his future role as the great teacher, but the ancient and the new world
are confronting each other, the Old Testament and the New. Probably the same
theme is conveyed in the symbolism in an Italian painting, done at much the
same time. Butinone's panel in Edinburgh shows the boy Christ seated on a
stone spiral (Figure 8). This gives him prominence in the picture. In addition the
spiral is a symbol of cosmic forces. The man-made stone spiral suggests spiritual
and intellectual law. Here it may also refer to the Tower of Babel and the disunity
occasioned when that was built. Through the doorway at the back of the room
we glimpse a spiral mound of earth and grass, topped with a tree in blossom; this
is nature's law of creation. Inside the room we see the doctors, the learned men,
turning to each other with amazement, their hands signalling their surprise and
heated discussion.

Dürer's composition focuses on a close up of heads and hands, to such a degree that he omits all else. The result is quite disconcerting: the details tell us almost more than we should wish to know. We observe cunning and arrogance in the heads of the scholars, as well as growing respect and honest puzzlement. Christ stands among them with quiet confidence, his small hands meeting those of the man to his left in something like a knot pattern in the visual centre of the picture. Dürer's interest clearly lay in physiognomy as characterization. Leonardo had been exploring that field just recently in the north of Italy, and it is possible that Dürer, visiting Venice and in close touch with the leading artists there, would have heard something of that.

Holman Hunt, attracted by the same story in the 1850s, thought first to represent only the reunion of the young Christ with his parents. The painting as he completed it (Figure 9), combines that moment with what may seem at first sight a merely stage-filling appearance of the doctors and others, backed by a lot of ornamental detail of an exotic sort. But Hunt was a painter with high ambitions in the area of didactic art, and believed that in this he had matched the Old Masters' achievement in History painting. There is little in this busy painting that does not support his priestly purpose. The frame made for this picture is inscribed both with its title and with key fragments of the second chapter of St Luke. In the painting itself, above and within the wheel pattern on the door of the temple, in Latin and in Hebrew, is a text from the Old Testament, from Malachi 3:1: 'and the Lord, whom ye seek, shall suddenly come to his temple'. The entire picture, apart from illustrating the story of Christ being found by his parents, is filled with references to Christ's coming and teaching, and of the confrontation of that new teaching with the old represented by the doctors and their scrolls and Torah. Doves, associated with the Holy Spirit, fly into the temple to be chased out. In the back of the temple a lamb has just been sold to be slain in sacrifice. Outside, to the right, we look towards the Mount of Olives, where the man Christ, not long before his Crucifixion, was to prophesy the destruction of the temple. The interior of the temple was taken from the Alhambra Court in the Crystal Palace reconstructed at Sydenham, but altered to accord with descriptions of Solomon's Temple. The costumes were as accurate and effective as the ever-painstaking Hunt could make them, and he put much effort into finding the right physical types to pose for the various figures.

The painting was bought at a substantial price by Gambart, an art dealer and impresario. He exhibited it around the country in and after 1860, soon recouping his outlay by means of the one-shilling entrance charge. He also made a good profit from selling an engraving made after the painting in large numbers. With it purchasers got an explanatory text by Hunt, but this did not spell out the meaning of each element of symbolism in the picture and on the frame. That they had to puzzle out for themselves. In 1857, when he was still working on the picture, Hunt wrote to John Ruskin, the great writer on art and society, that 'to me my "Finding" is as important [as] Da Vinci's Last Supper was to him'. He was heaping telling detail upon telling detail in his desire to present a convincing narrative, and then he added explanatory words lest his public should miss any one of the ideas he had built into the picture. The result is a worthy work, but it is unfortunate that he should have evoked the name of Leonardo.

Leonardo da Vinci

The subject of Leonardo's famous painting *The Last Supper* (Plate 8) was a familiar one. It was often represented in just such a location as that of his version, the refectory of a monastery, reminding monks of both the institution of the Sacrament of Communion and, in the betrayal of Christ by Judas, his imminent Passion and Death. Judas had usually been shown a little apart from Christ's other companions; often on the other side of the table, picked out by his isolation. Leonardo decided to have all the disciples and Christ on the same side of the table, facing their audience, so to speak, and to distinguish them by means of the language of face and gesture. His painting appears to portray a precise moment, the moment when Christ announces that one of the company is about to betray him. All but one react with amazement. Christ's words hang in the air, like those of Yeames' imagined anecdote, but Leonardo implies also that there are words coming back, exclamations of various sorts, and Christ's hands indicate the later moment when 'Jesus took bread, and brake it, and gave to them, and said, Take, eat: this is my body' (Mark 14:22). Once again we feel we are at a stage performance, an unusually thoroughly rehearsed one. The stage itself is both large and surprisingly bare. Leonardo's painting goes right across the end wall of the refectory, and seems to continue the walls with its own. So the pictorial space echoes that of the room itself, giving additional presence to the enactment shown at the front of the stage. The table goes almost across the full width of the painted space; we are not invited to penetrate the deep space behind it. The daylight seen through the far-off door and windows appears to come forward towards us, silhouetting most movingly the pyramidal form of Christ. As in Masaccio's *The Tribute Money*, the light in the front of the painting takes account of the actual light in the room which comes from windows high up on the left wall.

57

This is one of the great network paintings. Countless artists have been indebted to it. Copies of it started to be painted and also carved almost the moment it was done. There have been many engravings of it. Today we are offered plastic low-reliefs casts of it as souvenirs. The Spanish film director Luis Buñuel, quoted it directly in a scene of his film *Viridiana*. In many different ways it lives on, at several levels of use and abuse. Holman Hunt's painting, by contrast is not part of the network. He took from art only the tradition of exact and laborious imitation of the appearance of things. He was aware of Leonardo's painting, and it is just possible that he would not have striven so hard to make each of his line of doctors register a particular character and attitude to Christ's challenging questions if he had not had Leonardo's row of disciples in mind. But it was very much part of Hunt's conscious aim, and that of his fellow Pre-Raphaelites, not to be guided by the network, not to accept any of the lessons it had to offer, feeling, perhaps rightly, that these had been routinely repeated and worn thin over the centuries. In spite of Hunt's immediate success, his picture has not taken any hold on art or on people's minds, whereas Leonardo's lives on. Even its dreadful deterioration, the result of Leonardo's attempt to improve on fresco, has done nothing to diminish its status.

It would be a useful exercise to analyse *The Last Supper* using the headings employed for *And When Did You Last See Your Father?* and for Masaccio's *The Tribute Money*. I commented on some aspects of the Leonardo above, but unsystematically. There is much more to be noticed in this great painting. The headings should help you to examine it quite closely, but they do not cover everything and they should not stop you from giving your attention to the work as a whole. They help me, but I also know that one of their functions is to keep me looking at the painting. Studying a work of art takes time.

More on the Subjects of History Paintings

We have been looking at a sequence of History paintings, all of them representing biblical texts. The only non-biblical painting we have looked at was Yeames' historical-romance-without-a-text. That is certainly a narrative painting, but it does not qualify as a History painting because of its lack of a text and because the characters in it are anonymous. The action is only hinted at and can never be known, and does not involve anyone known to history or literature.

I used paintings with biblical subjects in the hope that their narrative will still be familiar, in outline if not in every part. This is less likely to apply to the texts supplied by Homer, Virgil, Ovid and other classical authors, so much part of intellectual life in the Renaissance and until the nineteenth century. In Victorian times, members of parliament and journalists could still come out with lines of Latin and sometimes Greek as quotations with which to add point and pomp to their homilies. In the twentieth century one would hesitate to do this even if one could. Homer and the others are on the shelf, respected but remote.

Or am I exaggerating? They are readily available to us if and when we want them, in paperback, with helpful notes and maps or whatever. We do not acquire them automatically, the way we do, say, reading and writing skills and basic mathematics. But there they are. What is more, we keep being referred to them in lots of ways. Modern writers use them. Poems, plays and novels use the ancient texts as themes, structures, background. James Joyce's *Ulysses* is perhaps the most famous instance, its title announcing Joyce's use of Homer rather than the fact that his subject is a day in the life of Leopold Bloom, citizen of Dublin. When Sigmund Freud needed a name with which to identify an aspect of sexuality he chose the term Oedipus complex and probably felt that the reference to an ancient myth strengthened his argument; he did not add a footnote referring his readers to Homer's *Odyssey*, Aeschylus's *Seven against Thebes* and Sophocles' *King Oedipus*. All around us the classical past is invoked at several levels of seriousness and fun.

Nevertheless, we have to recognize that this material no longer occupies the foreground of our culture the way it once did. History painting ceases to function fully when it cannot rely on a common ground of knowledge. Holman Hunt's explanatory text to go with the engraving of his *Finding of the Saviour*, is not unique. Painters of his time found that they had to issue instructions for use, so to speak, if they wanted to be sure their work would be understood. Or they could take their chance and risk their work getting its message across only to a more restricted public. In the pages that follow I want to offer you examples both of History painting continuing and of a new sort of narrative painting coming in to compete with it, as well as examples of the network of images and meanings being tapped for new purposes.

Rubens: Religious and Mythological History Painting, and an Allegory

Peter Paul Rubens was one of the most successful painters of all time. He was very much a painter, thoroughly trained and experienced, well born, well educated and well endowed with skills of eye and hand. He proves Reynolds' point about the best-equipped painter being also the most inventive. Rubens lived the life of an international diplomat, and this caused his work to be in even greater demand. His home was Flanders (now part of Belgium). He lived in Antwerp and established a busy workshop there, sending out commissioned works to most of the countries of western Europe, and he also spent time in France, Italy, Spain and England. Amongst the honours heaped on him was a knighthood bestowed by Charles I, the last British monarch to have a true appetite for art.

I offer this information partly to make the point that Rubens' art, which looks so personal to us, was something close to an international art language in his day. Not the only such language. His lively forms and colours and sometimes brisk brushwork had their answer in the more staid, and severe art of his French contemporary Poussin. (See Figure 79, *The Body of Phocion Carried out of Athens*.) Both had their artistic following, and later generations tended to place them at opposite poles. But they shared a lot of ground, and that included their experience of the classical tradition *and* of Titian and the Venetian school. And their subjects, whether they were painting to commission or not, covered the same wide range.

Plate 9 shows the three-part (triptych) altarpiece Rubens painted in 1611–14 for the altar of the Guild of Gunsmiths' chapel in Antwerp Cathedral. In the centre panel we see Christ being taken down from the cross. The left shows *The Visitation*, i.e. the visit of Mary to her cousin Elizabeth, when Elizabeth was carrying the future St John the Baptist in her womb and Mary was carrying

Christ in hers. The right is *The Presentation in the Temple*; the infant Christ brought to the Temple in Jerusalem by his parents, and held by Simeon, the devout old man who had been told he would not die until he had seen the Messiah. In all three scenes Christ is being held or carried. The guild's patron saint was St Christopher. His name means 'Christ-carrier': he had carried a child across a stream, and, though a giant of great strength, had nearly failed in the task since the child he was carrying was Christ and with it he was carrying also the weight of all the sins of the world. He is shown on the outside of the triptych, i.e. on the surface displayed when the two side panels are closed over the main panel. His massive form and pose are related to a famous Roman statue of Hercules, at that time in a collection in Rome.

In *The Descent from the Cross* we see eight men and women lowering and receiving the body of Christ. Christ is very much the visual centre of the composition, on a diagonal emphasis which is stabilized by the ladder on the right. Only two of the figures are actually touching Christ: the man top right holds his arm, and, at the bottom, the kneeling Mary Magdalen holds and supports the foot that earlier in the story she had anointed and wept over (Luke 7). She is the model penitent: a sinner who has repented and now devotes all to the service of Christ; she represents all sinners coming to Christ, and you will note that, not unlike the tax collector in Masaccio's painting, she is placed so as to form a link with our world outside the painting. It was on her feast day, 22 July 1614, that the triptych was consecrated.

In this very brief account I have stressed the Christian meaning of the composition. But again antiquity is invoked. Can you see where? What model served for the body of Christ? It is the body of Laocoön, reversed and slightly amended, as in the realistic depiction of blood oozing from his side. Laocoön was a priest, so the association is not improper. And whereas Laocoön and his sons were killed by serpents, Christ may be said to have been killed by the sins of the world. The dark figure to the right of Christ, standing on the ladder, is Nicodemus in the pose (unreversed) of one of Laocoön's sons, almost escaping the serpents' coils.

Soon after he completed this very large and complex work, Rubens painted the monumental canvas of *The Abduction of the Daughters of Leucippus by Castor and Pollux* (Figure 10), renowned horse tamers, the twin sons of Zeus and Leda. There is some doubt today that this is indeed the subject of the painting and not another mythological subject. Study the reproduction to see how this amazing group of two men, two women, two horses and one winged child (who may be Cupid) is arranged and displayed, and what narrative effect the arrangement has; then compare your thoughts on this with those elicited by studying *The Descent from the Cross* in the same terms. Both show Rubens at the height of his powers.

So does a small oil sketch in the National Gallery (Plate 10), in which mythological references are made to serve a seventeenth-century purpose in a way very characteristic of both the painter and his world. Rubens had been asked to

FIGURE **10** THE ABDUCTION OF THE DAUGHTERS OF LEUCIPPUS, Peter Paul Rubens, c.1616
Oil on canvas, 222×209 cm, 87½×82 in, Bayerische, Stadtgemäldesammlungen, Alte Pinakothek, Munich

provide a canvas for the ceiling of the entrance hall of the Duke of Buckingham's London house. He made this sketch to represent his ideas for the large painting. The lightness and life of the sketch is quite brilliant; we must assume that the ceiling painting, had it been done, would have been more solid, though Rubens would have known better than anyone how to keep that lively too.

It is not strictly a narrative painting: it is an allegory presented in narrative terms. An allegory is an image or a set of images chosen to convey a meaning, not a direct account of something. We see a warrior drawn up into the sky, towards the Temple of Virtue, by the helmeted Minerva and by Mercury. Minerva

=wisdom, Mercury = eloquence; Envy clutches at the warrior's boot in vain, for, on the left, the Three Graces smile upon him and award him the crown of eternal fame.

The warrior represents Buckingham, a general of Charles I's fleet and army. The painting is intended to persuade us of his outstanding virtues and achievements. A special favourite of the King's, he was in fact deeply hated and mistrusted. What view Rubens took of him we do not know, and it is not relevant. The painting was to function as a major public relations exercise. It belongs to the age of the Divine Right of Kings, when monarchs were held to derive their status and power directly from God. Much seventeenth-century art was created to celebrate greatness and also to confer it by giving it visible form.

Ours is an age of debunking, though we do celebrate lavishly our temporary heroes, pop and music stars, 'celebrities' of various sorts, and on occasion even politicians, roughly Buckingham's category. We see him here undergoing the process of apotheosis, being lifted up to the heavens to rank among the gods. The philosopher Francis Bacon, Rubens' older contemporary, said it was 'the supreme honour which man could attribute unto man'. Shakespeare, of the same generation as Bacon, said 'All the world's a stage, / And all the men and women merely players.' No one can have expected Buckingham to make such a glamorous exit; he was in fact assassinated by one of his many enemies, and Rubens' sketch is perhaps the best thing associated with him.

So realism, even in the sense of a convincing stage enactment, is not called for here. What is required is an effective orchestration of praise through symbolic characters. The associations brought by each of them—such as Minerva's special status as a child of Zeus, sprung directly from his head, honoured for her outstanding wisdom and knowledge of all the arts including medicine, and for her total virtue—are attributed to the hero. In effect Buckingham is being treated here like a saint, except that whereas the Virgin Mary was lifted to heaven by the angels and awaited there by Christ, Buckingham is being drawn up by pagan deities, surrounded by fluttering putti, little winged children associated with Cupid and love. So the formula is still a religious one, only the celebrants and the rites are pagan. The whole is a polite fiction, a piece of rhetoric characteristic of the age, of higher quality than most; a very public statement for the most public part of the mansion.

The Choice of Hercules

It is of course a simple thing to turn a portrait into a polite fiction, by putting into it symbolic objects that represent the sitter as something he or she is not and perhaps not likely to be. Reynolds had a line in upper-class portraits that involved a lady being portrayed as a pagan priestess making a sacrifice; Gainsborough portrayed a young gentleman in seventeenth-century finery, and we know him as *The Blue Boy*. In other portraits sitters could be given a fictional

62

FIGURE **11** THE CHOICE OF HERCULES, Annibale Carracci, 1595—7
Oil on canvas, 167x237 cm, 66x93¼ in, Museo di Capodimonte, Naples

staging to add interest to them. The process is not basically different from our having a photograph taken in a seaside booth after sticking our heads through openings in panels that thereupon identify us as a fat lady or a gorilla or the pilot of a plane.

An allegorical subject much used in seventeenth-century Italy and given topical interest in England in the eighteenth century is that of the Choice of Hercules. The Greek hero Heracles was said to have undergone a series of twelve exacting labours, and to have been outstandingly strong and virtuous (as well as on other occasions, angry and sexually potent); Hercules was the Roman version of his name and he was widely worshipped in the Roman Empire. No ancient author speaks of his hesitating between a life of self-indulgence and a life of self-negating service to others, yet the notion of his making his commitment served as a theme for discussion and for representation in the Renaissance. It clearly echoes the commitment asked of Christians, and more especially the vows taken by the clergy.

The influential painter Annibale Carracci painted a visualization of the moral issue (Figure 11). The picture presents a situation, not a story. Hercules stands between two females, wondering whose invitation to follow. One represents pleasure, the other virtue and self-denial. Poussin did a painting of the subject too, a very economical composition consisting of the three figures and little else. This painting is lost; we know of it through engravings done from it.

FIGURE **12** THE CHOICE OF HERCULES, Paolo de Matteis, 1711
Oil on canvas, 198x256 cm, 78x101 in, Ashmolean Museum, Oxford

64

The Earl of Shaftesbury, whose early eighteenth-century writings on ethics and aesthetics were widely read, used the theme of Hercules' choice to illustrate his contention that mankind had an innate inclination to virtue. He discussed at some length how a painter should represent it and commissioned Paolo de Matteis to produce such a painting (Figure 12). It is now in Oxford. Shaftesbury had an engraving done of it to illustrate his text, published the year the painting was done. In discussing it his main concern was what moment should be represented to give the image the greatest moral force. He pointed out that a painting, though showing one moment only, can portray change, can show the mind moving ahead of the body, and thus exhibit past and future. He required the painter to show Hercules still hesitating yet indicating that his mind was turning towards a decision in favour of virtue: the pregnant moment.

The painting shows us the mighty Hercules, looking very much the Georgian squire, leaning upon the massive club which is his trade mark or attribute. To his left a lightly clad lady appears to be asking him to join her in a well equipped picnic. To his right a sterner, more substantially robed lady holds a sword and points the way up a rocky path. It is to her that Hercules is turning. Contemporaries would have noticed that Virtue looks very classical, the sort of woman you would find playing an important role in a Poussin. Pleasure is altogether more modern in appearance, an attractive woman of the period.

We do not know whether it was Reynolds' desire to paint a portrait of the actor Garrick, or whether Garrick asked him for one. In any case the two men

FIGURE **13** GARRICK BETWEEN TRAGEDY AND COMEDY, Joshua Reynolds, 1762
Oil on canvas, 148x183 cm, 58½x72 in, private collection, United Kingdom

were friends, each eminent in his field. I suspect it was Reynolds' idea to treat the portrait as a parody of the Choice of Hercules theme; certainly it fits his way of combining History painting with portrait painting.

He shows us Garrick beset by two ladies, or perhaps by a lady and a girl (Figure 13). The serious lady is taken from a painting by one of Annibale Carracci's best pupils, Guido Reni, greatly admired in the eighteenth century. Another painter especially admired then was Correggio, Titian's contemporary, and from him came the cheerful girl. Reynolds refers in one of his Academy talks to Correggio's 'Exquisite grace' but stresses that this quality is as nothing beside the 'sublime in painting' which is the art of Raphael and Michelangelo. The particular Correggio Reynolds borrowed from is, aptly enough, a representation of Virtue triumphant over Vice. It is however an entirely serious, dark girl, part of a group that symbolizes Virtue, that he used, not a figure associated with Vice. Reynolds made her blond and a good deal more wanton looking. The two contrasting female faces refer us to the masks of Tragedy and Comedy inherited by the Renaissance from the theatre of Greece and Rome, still used today to symbolize drama.

The moment shown comes a little later than Shaftesbury recommended. Garrick, it is clear, has made up his mind. He may have hesitated between Tragedy and Comedy, but it is clearly Comedy that he will follow and he makes an apologetic gesture towards Tragedy. Was Reynolds, who so much wanted British painting to lift its sights and ambitions to the highest goals, commenting

FIGURE **14** MRS SIDDONS AS THE TRAGIC MUSE, Joshua Reynolds, 1784
Oil on canvas, 239x147 cm, 94x59 in, by permission of the Governors, Dulwich Picture Gallery, London (replica)

on the likely fate of the British theatre? One of his most powerful monumentalized portraits is one he did of another stage personality, *Mrs Siddons as the Tragic Muse* (Figure 14). The image is cleverly derived from the Prophets and Sybils on Michelangelo's Sistine ceiling in Rome.

So well known was his Garrick picture, and so well understood its point, that when Garrick opened a new theatre in 1775, he could start the first evening's entertainment with a musical prelude that parodied his parodistic portrait. He appeared as Harlequin in *The Theatrical Candidate*, pulled this way and that by the demands of tragedy and the promises of comedy. Harlequin, one of the chief characters of the Italian commedia dell'arte tradition, is the reverse image of Hercules: unique physical and moral strength in the antique hero, and charm laced with guile and two-faced villainy in the modern.

DECLINE OF THE GENRES SYSTEM

Reynolds' mixing of the History and Portraits genres is symbolic of a general weakening of the genres system. Proper History painting, known subjects of elevated meaning treated in a properly elevated manner, continued to be produced, especially in Italy and France. Producing such a painting was still the final test undergone by students in the academies, the best of them rewarded with the fortifying prize of a period of study in Rome, at the heart of classical art ancient and modern. History paintings still tended to be given the best positions in academy exhibitions; these exhibitions were normally hung very densely, frame to frame, all the way up the wall, and those who decided which paintings should be hung at eye level, and which 'skied', determined also what should be noticed most.

The best talent still went sometimes to History painting, but often into other genres. The mixing of genres went on and was generally taken for granted. A particularly telling instance is Turner's *Snow Storm: Hannibal and his Army Crossing the Alps*, a landscape painting of great power injected with dramatic but almost invisible historical reference (see Plate 37, and the discussion of this painting on pages 214–16). Occasionally, though, it produced a response that suggests how strong the tradition of History painting's special status amongst the genres still was in the middle of the nineteenth century. In 1850 the French painter Courbet sent to that year's Academy exhibition in Paris his *A Burial at Ornans* (Plate 11). It shows a crowd of country people, most of them dressed in black, attending a country funeral. The priest is saying prayers over the open grave; some of the women are weeping. It is an ordinary event, momentous for those intimately connected to the dead person, but normal. The painting is rather dark. The landscape background shows accurately the chalk ranges of that area of eastern France, between Dijon and the Swiss border, but it is late afternoon on a grey day and there is little light in the picture. Rarely has a painting been so roundly attacked by critics. They said it was stupid and ugly; worse still, it was socialist. If you wonder why it was attacked on political grounds when all it shows is someone ordinary being buried amongst ordinary people, the answer lies primarily in one particular aspect of the painting that reproductions make us forget: its size. Courbet—who knew very well what he was doing–had given those country folk the status of heroes by painting them life-size. That, combined with his realistic manner which excluded any thought of idealizing them in the painting, let alone introducing any hint of this being an event watched over by divinity, made it wholly improper. He was claiming the status of History painting for a Genre scene. The same painting on a much more modest scale would not have caused an outcry.

Breaking the hold of the genres hierarchy sounds like a liberation. In some respects it is. The system did, for example, tend to make a poor History painter (of which the nineteenth century produced many) look more important than a marvellous landscape painter. The modern view tends to be that you must judge each work of art on its own merits, not start with preconceived scales of value.

Do you share that view? Do you judge each work of art with an open mind? I rather suspect that a *wholly* open mind is an empty mind, and that we all come to works of art, just as we go to the cinema or sit down to dinner, with some expectations and hopes. The genres system eased communication. Approaching a large History painting, people knew they were about to confront something major in the sense that it contained important ideas, had been thought out and presented through long study and effort, intellectual as well as technical, and called for full consideration of its visual and mental message. You could say that the difference between a History painting and, say, a still life is like that between a symphony and a song. Whichever we might prefer, we know on the whole that one is intended to carry more weight than the other. Above all, it helps us to know which of the two to expect; we can prepare ourselves for the encounter. It is characteristic of late eighteenth- and nineteenth-century culture that the small, minor formats were often given the importance and sometimes also the scale of the major formats. The late quartets of Beethoven, the song cycles of Schubert and Schumann, can be said to be exceeding their mandate by aiming at the highest seriousness when the occasion called for something closer to decent entertainment. We can welcome this. It certainly demonstrates mankind's insatiable need to construct significant monuments. But it also leaves us without a secure framework. Should every work of art be, or try to be, an earth-shattering masterpiece? Or is there room for major and minor works to fit major and minor occasions? And, if so, does it not help us to know at once what class a work belongs to, what role it is intended for?

The Death of Marat

(Plate 12) One factor that certainly contributed to the breakdown of the genre system was the French Revolution and the social pressures that caused it and continued to produce political crises and instability throughout the nineteenth century. The French Revolution also produced a painting that is of especial significance to our subject.

The painter Jacques-Louis David became known in the mid-1780s as a History painter of exceptional moral seriousness and stylistic purity. He had spent time in Rome. His work sounded a call for a chaste, very controlled idiom and the highest idealism in content. His sympathies were with the Revolution, which started in 1789. He became a member of the National Assembly and was one of those who voted for the death of the king in 1793. He also became, in effect, the leading figure in French cultural life. He designed the festivals through which the new republic sought to give itself a strong and high-minded character; he turned the Louvre palace into the world's first public museum (it opened late in 1793); his teaching influenced generations of French artists and found echoes also outside France.

1793 was also the year of *The Death of Marat*. Marat was an ardent revolutionary. He too was a member of the National Assembly. He was also busy as a journalist, writing and publishing a paper called *The People's Friend*, through which he sought to rid France of anyone he considered an enemy of the Revolution. He suffered a skin condition which required him to spend long hours in a bath filled with a saline solution and to swathe his head with cloths dipped in the solution. Always busy in the cause in which he so passionately believed, he was accustomed to working and to receiving visitors whilst in his bath. On 13 July 1793 he was thus visited by a young woman, Marie-Anne-Charlotte Corday. She had written to say that she could name some people working against the Revolution in her part of France. What she in fact brought was not a list of names but a dagger. She stabbed him in the chest. The blade penetrated his lung and he died soon after. We are told that Corday was not impelled by hatred of the man so much as by a sense of duty. She had been reading Plutarch's *Lives* of great Greeks and Romans, an anthology of moral excellence which had been the source book for many a History painting since the Renaissance.

David and his radical colleagues in the Assembly decided that this assassination of a revolutionary leader had to be recorded in a special way. There were fulsome speeches in celebration of the dead man. David was publicly asked to paint a picture memorializing Marat's death. Deeply moved, he replied there and then 'Yes, I shall do it.'

Plate 12 shows the result. Figure 15 reproduces a broadsheet of the time, describing the assassination through the image and a long caption in which Marat is equated with the great social critics of imperial Rome, Cato and Juvenal. Let us look at these two pictures, both of them done to record the event and to honour the dead man. The painting is large and will have lost more in reproduction than the woodcut. In so far as you can, I suggest you try to analyse the painting and the woodcut in the terms we used earlier.

I shall be relatively brief. The woodcut first. It shows Marat dying and probably crying out, Corday in the centre pointing towards her handiwork with apparent pride, and, stage right, the entrance of a second man. He is Robespierre, leader and most ardent of the radicals. His inclusion in the scene is a piece of dramatic invention. He was nowhere near at the time. Otherwise the account may be more accurate than we would perhaps expect after that: the wallpaper, for example, is more or less correct. The whole looks like a scene from a play or opera of the time. The painting is almost shockingly empty. There is almost no enobling visual detail: only the Roman lettering on the box signals high cultural values. It says with startling simplicity: 'To Marat. David.' The rough wood crate that serves as Marat's bathside table could not be humbler. Green baize lies over the board that forms his desk. The sheet lining the bath is patched. The knife lies on the floor. Marat's hand rests near it, still holding the quill with which he has been working for the people. His other hand still holds a sheet of paper on which he has been writing. He is not quite dead, though life seems to have ebbed from his face, turned towards us and lit from an invisible window to

FIGURE **15** BROADSHEET ANNOUNCING THE DEATH OF MARAT, 1793: 'Robespierre entrant dans l'appartement de Marat Assassiné' (Robespierre entering the rooms of the assassinated Marat), 13 July 1793
Woodcut, Collection Bulloz (as reproduced in F. Furet and D. Richet, *La Révolution*, vol. 1, Réalises Hachette, Paris 1965, p. 305, fig. 4)

the left. Much of the rest of the painting is plain background; no wallpaper but a soft grey-blue-green that seems to melt where it is touched by light.

It is amazingly still. But because it concentrates our attention on the dead man it is also resonant with meaning, passionately communicated.

Did you see David plugging into the network? Marat = the dead Christ = Meleager. The revolutionary activist = the Son of God = the ancient hero, slain out of envy. I put it this baldly because I feel that the normal phrases ('A is in the pose of B,' 'A echoes depictions of B' etc.) would understate David's intention. His painting was given to the nation and was hung in the Assembly where members sat on stepped benches arranged in a semicircle, the high back of the bench in front serving as a desk for the row behind. These desks and backs were covered with green baize, and the painting was hung on the wall facing them. Marat, a member of the Assembly, had given his life for his people. He is a hero, a god. David was addressing a Roman Catholic world, even though he and others were rejecting the Catholic Church. Those who saw the painting when it was finished later the same year will have understood the message. It has been described as 'a lay *Pietà*'.

But where is the woman? If this is a *Pietà* we cannot help feeling her absence. David has achieved a masterpiece of painting, that is at once stark and gentle in manner. We confront the bath and the corpse with a frontality that is quite unnerving. The painting seems devoid of sweetness—except for the light that falls on the scene like a blessing. The face could be called an affectionate likeness; it resembles Marat's but we have to guess at what that busy politician looked like asleep, with something almost like a smile on his lips. I cannot help feeling that the woman is, so to speak, we who are looking at the painting. Or, to put it more exactly, the French people whose son and friend Marat was and claimed to be. The people will shelter this martyr in its bosom.

David's painting is an outstanding piece of pictorial propaganda. It is a portrait, a History painting (he was not the first to turn a contemporary event into a History painting but this was still an exceptional and bold act), and, in its concision and in spite of its large scale, it is a devotional image giving a feeling of intimacy. In theory, depending on one's view of the Revolution and especially of Marat, one might argue that David has gone too far. In front of the painting it is difficult to withhold total surrender.

The Third of May 1808

(Plate 13) David's contemporary and in some respects counterpart in Spain was Goya. He served as court painter to the king, but portrayed the royal family with a truthfulness that brought out their physical and moral limitations. From 1808 until 1814 Spain suffered the so-called War of Independence. Napoleon had forced the Spanish king to abdicate, had imprisoned the natural heir in France and had imposed his own brother, Joseph Bonaparte, as Spain's new king. For years Spain was a battlefield, with the British under Wellington confronting the French, and with Spaniards fighting on both sides. This experience elicited the first trenchant anti-war statement in art, Goya's eighty engravings entitled *The Disasters of War*, not published until 1863. A particular uprising against the French in Madrid, and its aftermath, was the subject of two paintings by Goya, done six years later. One of them shows a guerilla action against the French in the streets of the capital. The second shows the execution of a large number of Spaniards in the outskirts of the city early the following morning, *The Third of May 1808*.

Out of the darkness looms, first of all, the man in the white shirt and yellow trousers. The lantern on the ground illuminates him starkly, and also, as we then see, the dead figures on the ground closer to us, as well as the other people who with him are now being shot down. More wait their turn. The soldiers are faceless death-dealers. The bareness of the mound behind the victims is a little like that of the minimal landscape behind Masaccio's *Expulsion*; this and other aspects of the composition make one wonder whether Goya was interested in the art of the early Renaissance in Italy. He certainly visited Italy, but in his day it was normal to think of the early Renaissance as the uncouth beginnings of something that became important only with the work of Leonardo, Raphael and Michelangelo.

Like Leonardo, Goya has individualized the victims: they show different responses to their situation, from outright panic to, in the most prominent of them, angry defiance. He raises his arms as though challenging the bullets to do

71

their worst, and thus he takes up the position of Christ Crucified. To underline that identification Goya shows in the palms of the man's hands the holes made by the nails fixing Christ to the wood. Perhaps it is only a coincidence that the light colours he wears, because of which he so much dominates our reading of the composition, are also the colours of the lantern and the light it gives. He seems to be the sacrificial Christ and also light amid the darkness.

If we allow History painting to concern itself with contemporary and very recent events, then this is a History painting. As I have said already, this use of topical material was not unprecedented though still rather new. It can be defended on the grounds that a topical event can be alive in people's minds and thus function like a familiar moment in the Gospels or in ancient literature. The crowd of Spaniards and the faceless soldiers give the painting something of the Genre character, and one could argue that it should be set beside Courbet's *A Burial at Ornans* (Plate 11) as a Genre painting elevated by size to History status. But we should probably not assume that those faces we see are anonymous: Goya was close enough to the event to have known some of the people executed at first hand, and certainly to have had individual information about them. The execution made them heroes, martyrs, and thus they make this a History painting. Goya's painting is a particular event translated in a universal image of human bestiality and fortitude.

Odd, how short the road from Masaccio to Goya seems, how long the road from Goya to Yeames and Hunt.

72

THE TWENTIETH CENTURY

Art since Impressionism generally seemed too involved in stylistic experimentation to have concerned itself with the high-minded manner and messages of History painting. In fact, much twentieth-century art has based itself directly on that tradition, with varying degrees of success. The fascist years in Italy and Germany saw the classical idiom, its references as well as its forms, raided to glorify the state and its leaders. In less crude terms, Soviet Russia has required art to celebrate Lenin and other great figures in the history of Communism in terms that lie somewhere between History painting and filmic realism—terms not unlike those of Yeames, whose painting is only a short step away from Hollywood. During the 1920s, Mexican schools and other public buildings were decorated with murals contrasting the good convivial life of the people under a Socialist regime with the hardship and oppression they had suffered before. Wherever art is made to deliver a particular message, memories of History painting surface.

In another sense, the tradition of serious discourse through art led straight into abstraction. Painters such as Kandinsky, Malevich and Mondrian, removed recognizable imagery from their paintings in order to move from particular phenomena to universal truths about humanity and the cosmos. I cannot illustrate or argue this development here, but it would be wrong to end this introduction to narrative painting, especially narrative painting of this religious or quasi-religious sort, without suggesting that it persists in other forms.

But I am also convinced that art cannot, and perhaps does not wish to, escape what I have called the network. I end with just a few examples of modern art that derive their weight from conscious and unconscious input from the History tradition.

i George Grosz, *Pillars of Society*
(Figure 16) Part of Grosz's art training had been under a German painter of altarpieces. This picture, like many of Grosz's prints and drawings, is an indictment of German leadership during the Weimar Republic. In his view the government elected after the end of an appalling war and the abdication of the Kaiser who had led Germany into it, had totally failed to prevent reactionary forces from controlling the country. In his painting he shows us, in almost caricature terms, the old militarists, false priests, and money-grabbing tycoons who, he claims, are running everything as before.

Can you see any links between this and the paintings we were looking at earlier? The picture is an allegory rather than a narrative, but it uses a formula noted earlier—in fact a formula associated with a German painter whom Grosz and his friends greatly admired. I am thinking of Dürer and *Christ Among the Doctors* (Plate 7). Shortly before he started work on his picture, in March 1926, Grosz had expressed his desire to produce 'modern History paintings'. In May

FIGURE **16** PILLARS OF SOCIETY, George Grosz, 1926
Oil on canvas, 200×108 cm, 79×42½ in, Nationalgalerie Staatliche Museen Preussischer Kulturbesitz,
West Berlin

1927 he referred to *Pillars of Society* as one of his favourites.

ii Picasso, *Guernica*

(Figure 17) In January 1937 the republican government of Spain commissioned Picasso, living in Paris, to paint a large picture for their national pavilion in the Paris World's Fair, to open that June. Picasso rented a large studio to be able to do this work, but for long did not seem able to think of a way of fulfilling the commission. Then, on 26 April, German aeroplanes bombed the Basque town of Guernica in support of Franco's fascist rebellion against the elected government. The event was unprecedented and was widely reported and discussed in the press. It was the first time bombs had been dropped on arbitrarily selected civilians and a town destroyed. The news and the photographs accompanying it enabled Picasso to start work, and in mid-June what is perhaps the most famous twentieth-century painting was in place.

It is a painting almost without colour: black and white predominate, but there are also ivories and dark-blueish-greys. This harshness must have been quite striking amid all the visual self-glorifying that exhibitions of this competitive sort attract. It offers an allegory of war. There are elements of narrative in it—the woman on the right falling from a burning building; on the left the powerfully depicted woman with a dead child (another lay *Pietà*?); in the middle the wounded horse screaming with pain. There are also symbolical elements whose meaning is disputed: the bull on the left, especially; the electric light in the middle; the woman's head and arm coming out of the window on the right and holding a candle beside the electric light. The general meaning is abundantly clear; particular meanings were put in but got lost as Picasso worked and reworked his painting.

It warrants careful analysis. I will point just to a few of the factors that seem to me most important and effective. The hints of architecture left and right establish a space in which the horse and everything else can exist, but nothing is made emphatically three-dimensional. The painting has a graphic character rather than the feel of a realistic representation. Distortion in fact plays a major expressive role: compare Picasso's way of representing the woman with a dead child with whatever mental image you can call up of an actual woman with a dead child. Yet this is a large painting and it is constructed like a large painting. Indeed, I think it is constructed like a triptych altarpiece. The Rubens we looked at earlier (Plate 9) is scarcely a run-of-the-mill example, but it is typical in its division. The Picasso is all one canvas, but compositionally divides into two vertical rectangles—bull + woman with dead child on left; burning house + falling woman on right—and a square middle section in which forms are grouped into a pyramid rising under the two lights.

Modern painting is often judged obscure and thus ineffective, but this work has been wholly successful. It keeps alive the memory of an event. At the time, however, people were disappointed with it; they had hoped for a much more realistic portrayal. But would that have lasted as well?

iii Fernand Léger, *The Constructors*

(Figure 18) Léger, much of whose art reflects city life and industrial work, had seen men erecting electricity pylons in the countryside near Paris and was struck by the sight of these men and their construction against the blue sky. He decided to make a very large painting on this theme, and did many drawings and paintings before he arrived at the final version illustrated here. The colours are very strong and affirmative, and so is the organization of the painting, with its great metal beams and the more malleable but also strong forms of men, clouds and rope. One man is sitting astride a beam near the top; another is up a ladder; four men together carry a short girder.

The whole has a resonance which reference to the way it is painted and what it represents does not quite explain. Again, it seems to me to strike an echo in what we have seen earlier. A vertical/horizontal structure, a ladder, men collaborating in carrying something weighty; ever since it first struck me that this image is a kind of optimistic answer to the sad image of Christ taken down from the cross, I have not been able to discard the idea, for all the many differences between this painting and any *Descent from the Cross* I can find. The Rubens version we saw (Plate 9) is in any case much richer and more complicated than Léger would wish his work to be, but of course there are countless other pictures of this time-honoured and important subject. Léger liked and got some of his stylistic ways from folk-art prints of the sort produced in France during the eighteenth and nineteenth centuries. Perhaps among them is a *Descent from the Cross* that contributed to this painting.

iv Reg Butler, *Maquette for a Monument to the Unknown Political Prisoner*

(Figure 19) This is a sculptural sketch for a monumental sculpture, and yet in a way it is a very graphic work, more line than mass, more space than surface. It

FIGURE **18** THE CONSTRUCTORS, Fernand Léger, 1950
Oil on canvas, 300×200 cm, 118½×78½ in, Musée National Fernand Léger, Biot

NARRATIVE PAINTINGS

FIGURE **19** MAQUETTE FOR A MONUMENT TO THE UNKNOWN POLITICAL PRISONER, Reg Butler,
1952. Height 223 cm, 88 in, Tate Gallery, London

was prepared by a British sculptor, a recent convert from architecture, as his entry for an international competition to commemorate the many persons who, during the preceding decades, had been imprisoned for political reasons and were never seen again. There were some very eminent names amongst the sculptors sending maquettes to this competition, and there was much surprise, a scandal even, when Butler was awarded the first prize early in 1953.

Few modern monuments are truly successful. Perhaps we lack the confidence, in heroes as in the multiplicity of art idioms that surround us, to know how to achieve a great one. I rather suspect that Butler's work would not have looked impressive on the cliffs of Dover or on a hill in West Berlin, close to the border with East Berlin. But why, do you think, did it win the first prize? I am going to leave you struggling with this one, confident that what we have been looking at and discussing in these pages will have enabled you to cope with this riddle. If you want a helpful hint, have another look at Plate 5. If you don't want a hint, don't even look to see what that is.

PORTRAITS

Alistair Smith

Section Two

PORTRAITS

Portraits form part of the collection of almost every art gallery in the Western world. I have stood in front of many, some of which are illustrated in this book, thinking to myself, 'What a marvellous portrait.' Of course, on many occasions I may have been ill-equipped to make that judgement, since it is very seldom that I have known what the sitter looked like in real life, and consequently I have almost always been unable to judge whether the portrait achieved a good likeness. Indeed, since most of the portraits in the National Gallery in London, the Louvre in Paris, or the Metropolitan Museum in New York are of people who died many years ago, we have no way of directly comparing the painting or sculpture with the original. Thus, we describe a portrait of an unknown person as 'marvellous', not because of its accurate rendering of the sitter, but for some other reason.

We have a firmer basis for judgement in the case of portraiture at its most basic level. Most of the family photographs which stand on mantelpieces all over the world are portraits made in a very direct way. All of us have played the part of sitter, artist or critic. We are able to decide, without limitations, how well the photograph renders the sitter.

Essentially we demand two things of a portrait. One, a good likeness—that is that the portrait conforms to the image we have already formed of the sitter. Two—and this applies particularly to portraits of those unknown to us and about which we have no expectations—we ask that it projects a heightened image of humanity.

Consider for example, the case of the *Portrait of a Man* by Titian (Plate 14). Today the sitter is officially described as unknown, and it is suggested that the picture might be a self-portrait. At one time it was believed to show the famous Renaissance poet Ludovico Ariosto. However, unless we are historians and have preconceptions about the appearance of Titian or Ariosto, we come to the portrait having no means of determining the accuracy of its 'likeness'. Nevertheless, we may decide that the portrait is 'marvellous'; in my experience, this is quite a common reaction. We do so because the painting presents such a powerful sense of life, portraying the man as if he were actually alive.

In perceiving this and judging the portrait 'marvellous', we are exercising no specialist knowledge. We apply to the painting only critical habits which we have formed elsewhere, in our own daily life. We may subconsciously compare Titian's richly-coloured, life-size painting with our smaller family photographs, or with fuzzy newspaper photographs, finding Titian's carefully-composed, highly-charged image to be much more powerful in its effect. We may think that the painting is simply more like a person, although this may seem at first unlikely since a photographer can ostensibly record reality, while a painter has to labour hard to invent it. In any case, while not being historians of portraiture, we are all able to pass judgement on portraits of other eras in certain ways, bringing to our consideration what often amounts to a personal psychology. I have heard Titian's sitter described variously as 'a dandy', 'an extraverted, open personality', 'probably a bit sly'. These judgements are based on the personal experience of the observer, and they serve to demonstrate the ease with which we project our own feelings on to a portrait. I think we are liable to do this more readily with portraits than with any other kind of art, simply because we are so used to making judgements of people in real life, judgements at least partially based on appearance. This is something we should be wary of, yet I think we should also be conscious of the value of our day-to-day experience both of individuals *and* of the art of portraiture.

While preparing this text, I have talked to many friends and colleagues about portraits. More often than anything else mention is made of the 'power of the portrait', of the fascination which the image can exert. This feeling seems to have a considerable history, and part of this text is concerned to exemplify if not explain it. I do not aim to provide a developmental scheme, detailing when, in any particular period of time, hands were introduced, or when and why it came to be acceptable for a lady to be shown dressed as a shepherdess, since these variations belong to a much more detailed account than this. Instead, I propose to concentrate on particular episodes which are important to our perception of portraiture as a potent form of communication. One has only to think of the *alter ego* of the portrait—caricature—to realize that there still exists a form which is designed to affect the life of the person it portrays. Portraiture has often had this as its aim in a positive sense, and has been successful partly because of the artist's ability to portray his sitter with credible accuracy, and partly because of public belief in the genuinely representative role of the portrait.

THE CREATION OF A PORTRAIT

I begin with a detailed 'case study' of the creation of a portrait and the reactions, almost superstitious in some cases, which it aroused.

Graham Sutherland, *Sir Winston Churchill*

It is valuable to consider a portrait about which a great deal is known. This is interesting for two reasons—one, it will allow us some insight into the type of information which is available to us in other cases; two, we can test our reaction to the painting *before* summarizing the relevant facts, and compare it with our understanding of it afterwards. While this book was in production, the thirty-year rule regarding this case came into force on 1 January 1985; thus when you read this new material may be available.

Sutherland's portrait of Winston Churchill (Plate 15) no longer exists for reasons which will become clear. Having a photograph of it before us, we come as close to the original as anyone can today. Naturally, it cannot carry the force of the painted image which measured 5 feet by 4 feet, but it is sufficient for us to consider for a moment whether we judge it 'marvellous', and whether we consider it 'a good likeness', and to think about whether these feelings are aroused by the painting or by our opinion of the sitter or the artist.

In 1954, Churchill was Prime Minister, having become so after the election of a Conservative government in 1951. His eightieth birthday was to fall on 30 November 1954 and a Birthday Presentation Fund was organized by an all-party committee of the House of Commons. It was suggested that the eightieth birthday present from the House be 'a good likeness' and it was decided that a portrait should be painted by an artist eminent in the genre. The name of James Gunn was discussed, best known for his painting of the royal family at Windsor Lodge of 1950, but it was thought that his fee might be too high. A committee member, Jennie Lee, suggested Graham Sutherland, and this was agreed by the committee.

The decision to commission a portrait could be said to have made assumptions about the vanity of the sitter. There seems to have been no serious thought, however, that Churchill might not wish to have his portrait painted. Certainly, he was not known to object to having enduring likenesses of himself made.

Of the possible alternatives, a sculpture might have brought with it the problems of siting, but, more significantly a time problem, since a sculpture is liable to take longer to complete than a painting and discussions were still going on in July. A photograph would probably have been thought not grand enough. Several important photographic sittings had in fact been given in the past (e.g. Figures 20 and 23) and it was hoped that the new portrait would supersede these. A painting would be more fitting for the traditional interiors of the Palace of Westminster.

FIGURE **20** PHOTOGRAPH OF SIR WINSTON CHURCHILL, Karsh, 1941
The Sketch, 11 March 1942

FIGURE **21** PORTRAIT OF LORD BEAVERBROOK, Graham Sutherland, 1951
Oil on canvas, 175x94 cm, 68½x36½ in, collection of Lady Beaverbrook

FIGURE **22** PORTRAIT OF SOMERSET MAUGHAM, Graham Sutherland, 1949
Oil on canvas, 137x64 cm, 54x25 in, Tate Gallery, London

PORTRAITS

Graham Sutherland seemed an inspired choice. His reputation as an artist was considerable, but he had turned to portraiture only in 1949 and had completed only two portraits, both of very famous sitters. Thus a portrait by him would possess a certain cachet because of its rarity alone. Lastly, and this may well have been a clinching factor, he had recently completed, to the satisfaction of the sitter ('It's an outrage but it's a masterpiece') a portrait of Lord Beaverbrook, himself a great admirer of Churchill (Figure 21). Thus Sutherland's track record as a portraitist was conveniently short and establishment-orientated. Both the Beaverbrook portrait and his only other to that date, of Somerset Maugham (Figure 22), had been shown at the Tate Gallery. The committee seemed to disregard the fact that neither was overtly flattering.

Sutherland's credentials for the job were also acceptable in a sense other than artistic: he was what one might describe as an 'official' British artist, a friend of Kenneth Clark (later Lord Clark), the then guru of the art establishment and former director of the National Gallery. Sutherland had been one of the Official War Artists, and had been a trustee of the Tate Gallery from 1948. In 1951, at the age of forty-eight, he had had a major retrospective exhibition at the Institute of Contemporary Arts in London.

When approached about making the portrait of Churchill, Sutherland showed some reluctance, but he agreed and the commission was officially given by letter on 14 July 1954. It decreed that the finished portrait be presented on Churchill's birthday. 'The portrait required will be full length,' wrote Charles Doughty, the Secretary to the committee, 'the details of it—costume, location and other matters—to be arranged between Sir Winston and yourself. We would not attempt to interfere in a technical matter of this kind.' Sutherland's fee (1,000 guineas) was to be collected by subscription from Members of Parliament. At the time of the commission this was not assured, but Sutherland made it clear that, should there be any difficulty in achieving this amount, he would nevertheless complete the commission.

Our knowledge of the circumstances of the commission is somewhat enlarged by Sutherland's memory of his attendance at a meeting of the commissioning body. They wished Churchill to be shown in his normal parliamentary clothes. The picture was to be given to Churchill for his lifetime, and, after his death, was to revert to the House of Commons. 'I was even', said Sutherland, 'shown places where it might hang in the Palace of Westminster.'

This might be a convenient moment to make some kind of summary of the sitter's biography, which is, of course, important to the making of a portrait, and to our perception of the relationship between sitter and artist.

The entry for Churchill in *Who's Who* for 1954 is far too lengthy to quote here. He had received the freedom of forty-four cities, was an honorary citizen of a further twenty and the honorary mayor of one. He possessed a dozen foreign decorations and twenty honorary degrees, and had won the Nobel Prize for Literature in 1953. In a way, his career had come to a height in the Second World War. The caption to a photograph of Churchill by Cecil Beaton (Figure 23),

FIGURE **23** PHOTOGRAPH OF CHURCHILL, Cecil Beaton, 1941
The Illustrated London News, 4 January 1941, courtesy of Sotheby's, London

published in the supplement to the *Illustrated London News*, summarizes the sitter's achievements at that time,

Britain's great war leader: the Right Hon. Winston Churchill, MP

Soldier, orator, statesman, writer and historian—such epitomises the versatile career of Britain's Prime Minister. Only son of Lord Randolph Churchill, the famous Victorian statesman, Mr Churchill, born in 1874, was educated at Harrow and Sandhurst, and joined the Army in 1895. After seeing active service in India, attached in 1898 to the 21st Lancers, he fought in the Battle of Khartoum under Kitchener. In the Boer War, then the 'Morning Post' war correspondent, he was taken prisoner, but escaped and subsequently fought in eleven actions, including Spion Kop and Pretoria. In 1900 he was elected M.P. for Oldham, became Home Secretary, and successively First Lord of the Admiralty, 1911–15, Minister of Munitions, 1917, Secretary of War, 1918–21, for the Colonies, 1921–22, and Chancellor of the Exchequer, 1924–29. At the outbreak of the present war he was reappointed as Prime Minister and Minister of Defence in May last, since when his stirring leadership has inspired the nation and the world.
(*ILN*, 4 January 1941)

One can understand Sutherland's hesitation when confronted with the ageing national hero, especially since he considered the time available for the portrait rather short. He himself was in Venice until early August, and the first meeting of artist and sitter took place at Chartwell, Churchill's country home in Kent, on the twenty-sixth of that month, Churchill having proposed by letter that the first sitting take place after Sunday lunch and that Sutherland install himself in the studio. Churchill himself was a conscientious 'Sunday painter'.

At the first meeting the sitter made it clear that he wished to be shown wearing the robes of the Order of the Garter. While he had not been painted wearing them before (he had received the honour only in 1953), this would have produced a very different image from that which the commissioning body had in mind, with Churchill in the guise of parliamentarian dressed in striped trousers, black jacket, waistcoat and spotted bow tie.

Different formats were tried out. Some years later, Sutherland was to describe how, when they first met, Churchill asked, 'How are you going to paint me? As a cherub, or the Bulldog?' Sutherland replied, 'It entirely depends what you show me.' One study shows Churchill smoking a large cigar. The artist found this gimmicky and rather ostentatious and it was abandoned 'by joint agreement'.

The final pose, Sutherland recalled (in 1978), was eventually chosen by the sitter, 'It was Churchill who wanted to look powerfully down from his dais: I didn't ask him—he insisted.' On another occasion, during a television interview made directly after the presentation of the painting, he said, 'I wanted to give a kind of four-square look to the picture—Churchill as a rock.' Curiously, these words echo a statement which he attributed to Churchill. Trying to account for Churchill's final view of the painting, Sutherland explained that the sitter was in a particularly insecure mood 'amounting almost to paranoia. He knew his party wanted to ditch him as leader—it did the following year—and he desperately wanted to stay. "But I am a rock, am I not" he would say. . . . I think he thought I was an instrument of denigration from the beginning.'

Churchill's health had been in question for some time, and he had suffered a second, if mild, stroke in June 1953. Recently it has been revealed that the exact nature of his condition, 'a disturbance of cerebral circulation, resulting in attacks of giddiness', was made known to only a few members of the Cabinet, and that the Cabinet collectively and, of course, everyone else, including the general public, remained uninformed. It is more than likely that, while sitting for Sutherland, he was not only concerned about the image of him which the portrait would present to the world, but also about his physical state in general.

In any case, the pose was decided upon, with Churchill sitting as shown in the final portrait. Many studies of the head were made (Figures 24–8). One sheet which concentrates on the mouth and eye has a particularly long note, which serves to exemplify the nature of the artist's concentration on detail (Figure 28).

FIGURE **24** STUDY FOR CHURCHILL, full face, Graham Sutherland, 1954
Oil on canvas, 43x30·5 cm, 17x12 in, National Portrait Gallery (No. 5332), London

FIGURE **25** STUDY FOR CHURCHILL, three-quarter facing to sitter's right, with colour notes,
Graham Sutherland, 1954
Oil on canvas, 40x30·5 cm, 15¾x12 in, National Portrait Gallery (No. 5331), London

PORTRAITS

FIGURE **26** STUDY FOR CHURCHILL, three-quarter facing to sitter's right, squared-up,
Graham Sutherland, 1954
Chalk, 54x42 cm, 21¼x16¼ in, National Portrait Gallery (No. 5333), London

92

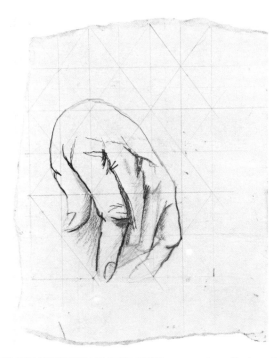

FIGURE **27** STUDY FOR CHURCHILL'S LEFT HAND, squared-up, Graham Sutherland, 1954
Pen, ink and pencil, 21x16·5 cm, 8¼x6½ in, National Portrait Gallery (No. 5334), London

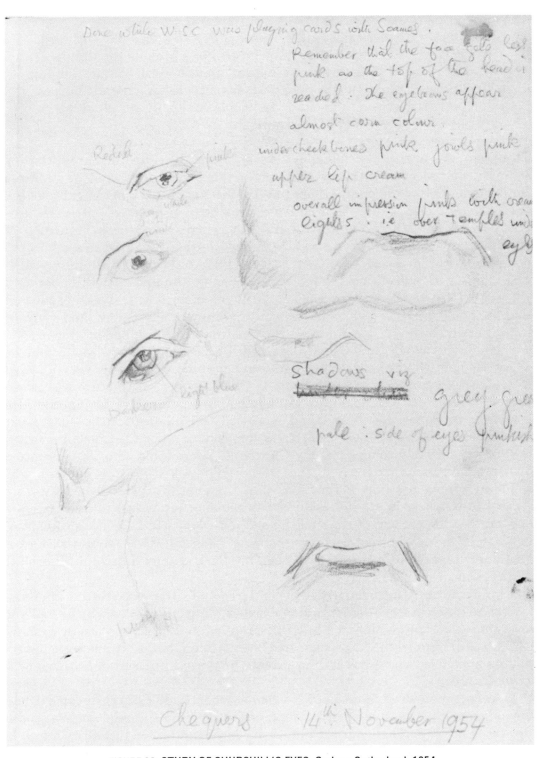

FIGURE **28** STUDY OF CHURCHILL'S EYES, Graham Sutherland, 1954
Pencil on paper, 37x25 cm, 14½x10 in, Gift of the Artist, The Beaverbrook Foundation, Beaverbrook Art
Gallery, Fredericton, N.B., Canada

PORTRAITS

The inscription reads:

> Chequers. 14th November 1954. Done while WSC was playing cards with Soames. Remember that the face gets less pink as the top of his head is reached. The eyebrows appear almost corn colour—under cheekbones—pink—jowls—pink—upper lip cream. Overall impression pink with cream lights i.e. over temples under eyes—shadows viz grey-green—pale ·. side of eyes pinkish.

This study was made only a couple of weeks before the scheduled presentation. It had been preceded by many similarly detailed drawings; and in addition, Sutherland invited the photographer Felix Man to photograph the sitter's head from different angles, since Churchill was proving to be a restless sitter. He used one in particular to help him work on the canvas in his own studio (Figure 29).

Sutherland explained his procedure. Since Churchill wanted to see how the portrait was progressing after each sitting, 'I had to be a bit dishonest, really, and juggle with something I didn't mind showing him and something which I was really doing.' Churchill was prone to advise alterations, stressing the fact that he should be shown as a 'noble' person. On one occasion, Sutherland returned to the version he had left at Chartwell to find that Churchill had altered it.

The canvas which Sutherland prepared for the final image was 5 foot by 4 foot. He painted one head on it, which was admired by some who were allowed to see it. He removed it and began again. On 9 October, the picture was transported to Saltwood Castle so that Kenneth Clark could give his opinion. He compared it to a late Rembrandt and expressed deep admiration. On 10 October it was seen by Churchill's only son, Randolph, and his wife. The former remarked that it was unlikely to please Lady Churchill. Randolph's wife, Jane, wrote a few days later to the artist saying that the portrait looked so alive that 'he might suddenly change position and say something—something pretty beastly'.

About two weeks later, Sutherland stretched another canvas in order to start another version of the picture, since he had sensed a certain lack of enthusiasm in some of those who had seen his painting. This putative version was soon abandoned in favour of the original seen by Clark and by Randolph Churchill and his wife.

A kind of altercation occurred between artist and sitter when Sutherland was invited to lunch at Chequers in mid-November. Churchill asked why he had not brought the portrait with him; Sutherland replied that he was not ready to show it. Churchill implied that a promise had been broken, but relations were nevertheless amicable, with Churchill preparing to paint a portrait of Sutherland's wife, Kathleen.

The crucial viewing came on 20 November when Lady Churchill came to see the painting. She was moved by it, wept, praised it and expressed her gratitude. On the same occasion, Somerset Maugham saw it and liked it. Lady Churchill asked for a photograph of it. Sutherland gave her one and she took it away to show her husband.

FIGURE **29** PHOTOGRAPH OF CHURCHILL'S HEAD, Felix Man, 1954
Collection F. Man

Next day, a letter arrived from Churchill, expressing his views on the photograph. He gave his opinion that the picture was bound to be controversial, and that therefore it would not be suitable as a presentation from members of parliament; thus it could not be part of the birthday ceremony at Westminster Hall. Churchill also proposed that he and Sutherland concoct a joint statement to cover the circumstances.

Shortly after, Churchill was persuaded by the Secretary of the committee to accept the portrait. He nevertheless referred to it with dissatisfaction on several occasions, saying it seemed to show him sitting on the lavatory: 'Here sits an old man on his stool, pressing and pressing.' He is also quoted as saying, 'It makes me look half-witted, which I ain't.'

These events served to make Sutherland extremely nervous about the public reception of the painting. When it was photographed for the press by *The Times*, he disliked the results so strongly that he made attempts to have them substituted with prints made by his friends John Underwood and Elspeth Juda. Not all the newspapers agreed to this.

The presentation ceremony was televised, with the painting on display on the platform (Figure 30). A commemorative book was handed over by D. R. Grenfell, the 'Father' of the House of Commons, and the painting was presented by Mr Attlee. Churchill received it with the words 'The portrait is a striking example of *modern* art. It certainly combines force with candour. These are qualities which no active member of either House can do without or should fear to meet.'

FIGURE **30** THE PRESENTATION TO SIR WINSTON CHURCHILL AT WESTMINSTER HALL, 30 November 1954
The Times, 1 December 1954

After the presentation, reactions were both positive and negative. The most outspoken attack came from Lord Hailsham: ' . . . we have all wasted our money. . . . It is bad-mannered; it is a filthy colour. . . . Churchill has not got all that ink on his face—not since he left Harrow, at any rate.' The members of the presentation committee were, however, all satisfied with the portrait.

The *Daily Express* of 1 December talked of the 'storm' over the Churchill portrait. There was some discussion in the Commons, with support mainly from the Socialist members. That night at a reception at 10 Downing Street Churchill declared that he and Sutherland could still be friends. Yet the painting was not on show. An inspection of the painting on 3 December by art critics proved mainly favourable. Benedict Nicolson, a respected art historian, lauded it in the *New Statesman* (11 December 1954). The painting was transported to Chartwell. Thereafter, requests to reproduce or exhibit it were consistently refused.

As might be expected, the popular press relished the whole incident, and a cartoon in the *Manchester Guardian* (3 December 1954) encapsulates the situation, which was inevitably simplified into factions of 'for' and 'against' (Figure 31). In it Lord Hailsham (then Quintin Hogg) and Sutherland face up to each other. In Hailsham's corner is Sir John Rothenstein who had a short time before struck the art-historian and collector, Douglas Cooper, during an altercation. (Cooper is in Sutherland's corner with Lord Beaverbrook.) Sir Thomas Monnington commentates. The captions are self-explanatory, save for Sutherland's nickname 'Golden Mustard', which refers to the colour of the background in the Churchill portrait.

PLATE **1** AND WHEN DID YOU LAST SEE YOUR FATHER? William Frederick Yeames, 1878
Oil on canvas, 131x251 cm, 50x97 in, Walker Art Gallery, Liverpool. See page 28

PLATE **2** THE TRIBUTE MONEY, Masaccio, c.1427
Fresco, 255x598 cm, 100x235 in, Brancacci Chapel, Santa Maria del Carmine, Florence. See page 33

COLOUR PLATES

PLATE **3** THE TEMPTATION IN THE GARDEN OF EDEN, Masolino, c.1427
Fresco, 208×88 cm, 82×34½ in, Santa Maria del Carmine, Florence. See page 41

PLATE **4** THE EXPULSION FROM THE GARDEN OF EDEN, Masaccio, c.1427
Fresco, 208x88 cm, 82x34½ in, Santa Maria del Carmine, Florence. See page 41

COLOUR PLATES

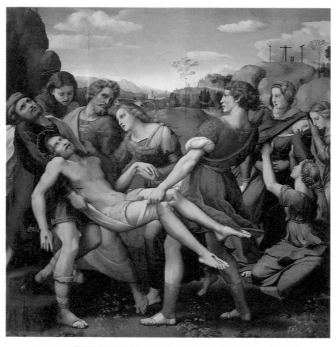

PLATE 5 THE ENTOMBMENT OF CHRIST, Raphael, 1507
Oil on panel, 184x176 cm, 72½x69½ in, Galleria Borghese, Rome. See page 48

PLATE 6 THE ENTOMBMENT OF CHRIST, Titian, c.1516
Oil on canvas, 148x215 cm, 58x85 in, Musée du Louvre, Paris. See page 51

PLATE **7** CHRIST AMONG THE DOCTORS, Albrecht Dürer, 1506
Oil on panel, 65×80 cm, 25½×31½ in, Thyssen-Bornemisza Collection, Lugano, Switzerland. See page 52

PLATE **8** THE LAST SUPPER, Leonardo da Vinci, 1495—8
Mixed media on plaster, 429×910 cm, 169×358 in, Refectory of Santa Maria delle Grazie, Milan. See page 57

COLOUR PLATES

PLATE **9** THE DESCENT FROM THE CROSS, Peter Paul Rubens, triptych, 1611—14
Oil on three panels, 420x610 cm, 165x240 in, Antwerp Cathedral. See page 59

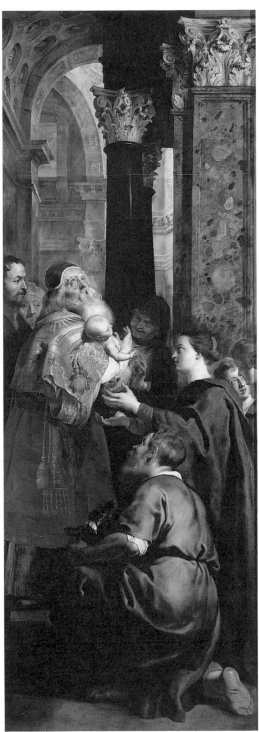

left and right panels above
centre panel opposite

COLOUR PLATES

PLATE **10** THE APOTHEOSIS OF THE DUKE OF BUCKINGHAM, Peter Paul Rubens, c.1625
Oil sketch on panel, 64x64 cm, 25x25 in, National Gallery, London. See page 60

PLATE **11** A BURIAL AT ORNANS, Gustave Courbet, 1849–50
Oil on canvas, 315x668 cm, 120x272 in, Musée du Louvre, Paris. See page 67

PLATE **12** THE DEATH OF MARAT, Jacques-Louis David, 1793
Oil on canvas, 165×182 cm, 65×72 in, Musées Royaux des Beaux-Arts de Belgique, Brussels. See page 68

PLATE **13** THE THIRD OF MAY 1808, Francisco de Goya, 1814—15
Oil on canvas, 266×345 cm, 105×136 in, Museo del Prado, Madrid. See page 71

COLOUR PLATES

PLATE **14** PORTRAIT OF A MAN, Titian, c.1508
Oil on canvas, 81 x 66 cm, 32 x 26 in, National Gallery, London. See page 83

PLATE **15** SIR WINSTON CHURCHILL, Graham Sutherland, 1954
Oil on canvas, 147x122 cm, 54x48 in, destroyed. See page 85

COLOUR PLATES

PLATE **16** SELF-PORTRAIT, Rembrandt, c.1660
Oil on canvas, 114x94 cm, 45x37 in, by courtesy of The Greater London Council as Trustees of the Iveagh
Bequest, Kenwood, London. See page 136

108

PLATE **17** MAN IN A RED TURBAN, Jan van Eyck, 1433
Oil on oak panel, 25x19 cm, 10x7½ in, National Gallery, London. See page 146

PLATE **18** THE ARNOLFINI MARRIAGE, portrait of Giovanni Arnolfini and Giovanna Cenami,
Jan van Eyck, 1434
Oil on oak panel, 82×60 cm, 32¼×23½ in, National Gallery, London. See page 146

COLOUR PLATES

PLATE **19** THE AMBASSADORS, portrait of Jean de Dinteville and Georges de Selve,
Hans Holbein the Younger, 1533

Oil on oak panel, 207x209 cm, 81½x82½ in, National Gallery, London. See page 149

PLATE **20** POPE JULIUS II, Raphael, c.1512
Oil on wood, 108x81 cm, 42½x31¾ in, National Gallery, London. See page 151

PLATE **21** SELF-PORTRAIT IN CONVEX MIRROR, Parmigianino, 1523
Oil on wood, diameter 24 cm, 9½ in, Kunsthistorisches Museum, Vienna. See page 152

PLATE **22** CHOPIN, Eugène Delacroix, 1838
Oil on canvas, 45x38 cm, 18x15 in, Musée du Louvre, Paris. See page 155

OLD LOW'S ALMANACK   *PROPHECIES FOR 1955*

FIGURE **31** 'OLD LOW'S ALMANAC' Cartoon by Low, the *Manchester Guardian*, 3 December 1954
Cartoon by permission of *The Standard*

Churchill died in 1965, eleven years after the Sutherland portrait was painted. The portrait had not been seen by the public. Lady Churchill died in December 1977. On 11 January 1978 her executors revealed that the painting no longer existed and that Lady Churchill had destroyed it shortly before her husband died because they both hated it so much.

The circumstances of the destruction were amplified by an article in the *Sunday Telegraph* of 12 February 1978:

> A former employee at Chartwell, Mr Ted Miles, 62, now retired and living in a council house, not far from Chartwell, Kent, said in a statement to the *Sunday Telegraph:*
>
> 'Lady Churchill smashed the painting in the cellars and gave it to me to burn. I watched her do it. Another close member of the family was there too.'
>
> Mr Miles who has 14 children, told us:
>
> 'I was called to the cellar one day in the autumn of 1955 to help clear out some rubbish. It was part of my regular duties to do so for burning and to collect swill from the kitchens. I already knew the painting was kept in the cellar behind the boiler. Lady Churchill and another member of the family were there in the cellar. They had already put aside a big pile of rubbish. They both reached behind the boiler and

pulled out the painting. Lady Churchill then smashed it to the floor. The frame broke up and they threw it on the pile. I was told to take the whole lot out and burn it immediately. I put it all in the trailer of my tractor and took it down to the incinerator pit behind the house. I tipped it all in and set fire to it immediately. The whole lot burnt quickly as it always did. There was a lot of thick black smoke this time.

It was a horrible painting. I told Sir Winston as much. They all hated it, they really did. They never walked past it without expressing their dislike.'

Sutherland voiced his reaction in different ways at different times. The day the news broke he said: 'I am not distressed. I think it is an odd sort of thing to happen, but these things do happen.' On another occasion, he talked about the problem of being a sitter: 'Only those totally without physical vanity, educated in painting, or with exceptionally good manners, can disguise their feelings of shock or even revulsion when confronted for the first time with a reasonably truthful painted image of themselves; there is a quilted atmosphere of silence as when it snows.'

The cartoonists, again, had a field day—'I don't know much about art, but I do like a good fire'. The views of the general public, or perhaps of the more concerned part of the public were made apparent in two principal ways—through the correspondence columns of *The Times*, and in interviews with visitors to the National Portrait Gallery. A couple of examples from *The Times* should be cited. One correspondent rejoiced that Sir Winston and Lady Churchill had managed to strike 'yet another blow for the freedom of the individual'. Another expressed a view that must have been in many minds, namely that an image of Churchill as he was in 1946 would have been a more natural expression of his contribution to the nation.

The general sense of the reactions was in a condemnation of the painting's destruction since it had in fact been intended to become public property. It was felt that the sitter himself and the work of Sutherland had, in any case, become public property in an intellectual sense.

Those interviewed in the National Portrait Gallery affirmed the view that the painting should not have been destroyed, and they sensed a certain malice in Lady Churchill's treatment of the painting which 'she could easily have donated to the Portrait Gallery'. However such views underestimated the depth of super-stition which portraits are capable of stirring. It would not have been enough for the portrait to be elsewhere. In order that it cease doing what Lady Churchill felt to be its malign work, it had to be destroyed. The nature of its effect on the sitter was said to be that 'he looks in the glass all day at his neck'. The folds of flesh around the neck and the other physical signs of age had depressed Churchill.

Thus the object which had evoked his anxiety had to be destroyed, the uncon-scious hope being that its psychological power would be destroyed with it. We have, in other words, an example in sophisticated modern society of the kind of 'sympathetic magic', which Frazer observed in primitive groups (J. G. Frazer, *The Golden Bough*, 1890, abridged edition 1922).

The history of the painting includes another example of iconoclasm, quite different in intent and procedure. In the years between the creation of the portrait and its destruction, the Churchill family refused all requests for loans to exhibitions and enquiries about photography and illustration. The result was that the public was unable to see the painting, either the original or in reproduction, for the remaining eleven years of Churchill's life. Essentially, the family attempted to exercise a control over the images of Churchill which were available to the public.

This ban was instituted by the family when Churchill was still Prime Minister and needed to present an image of power and competence to his party. To preserve his political status, he felt he had to expunge the evidence of the physical decrepitude that the painting detailed. So, in 1978, when the destruction of the painting was announced, the newspapers had difficulty finding a colour negative of it. The *Sunday Times* of 12 February 1978 eventually published a colour reproduction which had been taken by Larry Burrows (best known for his war photographs) who had died in Vietnam in 1971. Others existed but this was the only satisfactory colour rendering of the whole painting (Plate 15). A colour negative is also in the archive of the National Portrait Gallery and has attached to it strict instructions limiting its reproduction. Churchill's desire to control his public image has its ramifications even today.

The story of the Churchill portrait is not only fascinating in itself, but also extremely useful to the student of portraiture. Being so well documented, it presents a valuable insight into many important aspects of portrait manufacture in the twentieth century. Of course, it reverses the usual situation whereby we have a portrait but no information about it. Here we have what amounts to a surfeit of information and no portrait. In the former case, the lack of information generally results in the painting being assessed in something of a vacuum as a beautiful or rare object or as a 'work of art'. In the latter case, the richness of detail may have the effect of obscuring the portrait as an object—we view it not so much as a work of art, but as one element in a historical situation, an episode in the social history of portraiture. If we want to take portraiture seriously we have to be aware of the limitations of using either of these approaches separately. We should be clear that the art historian has a duty to consider the totality of the situation, while the social historian must take account of the way the painting is composed and executed including what the artist has 'meant', or signified, by pose, colour and brushwork.

We probably find that our original attitude to the painting has been altered somewhat by the information now available. But before passing final judgement, if such a thing is desirable, it is wise to consider how the portrait was judged or understood when first made.

The statements about it show that it was expected to be both a piece of fine painting, *and* an act of homage to the sitter. The major criticisms were that it failed in the latter (although surely there is a case to argue—the portrayal of weakened body but unbowed spirit is surely flattering). The audience for the portrait had certain expectations. The M.P.s, for example, would have had their own preconceived image of Churchill, probably a fairly complex one. The public at large knew him through newsprint and other portraits: photographs, busts, statues and other paintings (Figures 20, 23). His immediate family would have known the private man—the husband, the father, the painter. Expectations were undoubtedly various, each section of the audience having its own view of the man.

But expectations were also created by other factors. M.P.s would have compared Sutherland's portrait to other portraits hung at the Palace of Westminster. Thus we have already a dual expectation—one in regard to sitter, the other to the 'object'.

Finally, there is some kind of expectation about the 'art' of a painted portrait. It is the general expectation that it should display the care taken by the artist and the reverence of the artist for his sitter, as do most historic portraits. It should be, most obviously, a work of art, in the sense of displaying its craft openly, being either very detailed or brilliantly executed in some other way—with free, dexterous brushwork or dazzling colour, for example.

Generally speaking, the audience of the portrait expects it to elevate or ennoble the sitter, to emphasize the more significant or worthy aspects of his life, and to suppress the less happy.

Sutherland's portrait of Churchill shuns the overtly glamorous use of colour or brushwork. It does not glamorize the sitter's physique: through the display of areas of sagging stomach and neck, it reveals Churchill as an old man, weak in physique but with great spirit. The painting is illuminated by the Kenneth Clark comparison of it to a late Rembrandt (Figure 32), which it resembles in pose and focus, and to me, it is as ambitious and serious a work as the Rembrandt, its statement, similarly, as much about mortality as achievement. My own view is that Sutherland's revelation of the physical weakness of the national hero (which was, after all, a fact) was unacceptable to those who expected a less complex, more laudatory image. M.P.s clearly expected something like an updated Karsh or Beaton photograph—a stereotype of Churchill which would simultaneously enhance the image of the Conservative party, parliament in general or even Britain as a whole. Their shock was quickly rationalized in various ways: they pointed out how 'unlike' the painting was, or how it was badly painted (with unpleasing colour, unglamorous pose and no legs). In fact, the inclusion of the feet might simply have served to distract from the very alive and determined spirit visible in the head.

We should, I believe, feel some pity for the portraitist, when we consider the varied expectations of his audience and the number of personalities that he must please with his production, for portraiture differs from most types of art in that the product is made partly to be compared with the original. Would the

FIGURE **32** MARGARETHA DE GEER, Rembrandt, c.1661
Oil on canvas, 130x97 cm, 51½x38½ in, National Gallery, London

commissioning body not have done better to commission a photograph, or a measured sculpture in the manner of Mme Tussaud? The answer is two-fold. While they wanted a fairly accurate document, they wanted an 'up-market' one. In this day and age, *anyone* can have a photograph. As for the wax-work, it is a curious fact that the productions of Mme Tussaud's staff, while accurate in many details are unsatisfactory since they do not present the illusion of life. Paintings, although themselves static, seem to achieve this illusion more readily as we will discuss later.

The commissioning body, however, declared itself satisfied and indeed may have had more vision than the remainder of the subscribers. Looking back in time, how do we view the portrait? How *should* we view it? A historian might prefer to describe without judgement, but it seems to me that we must do more than this in the face of powerfully emotive material like Sutherland's portrait. Further, we habitually make judgements about almost everything in spite of ourselves. In many fields—politics and religion for example—we are compelled to make decisions on relevance, quality and so on, based on insufficient information—and portraits are no different.

An assessment of historic paintings requires us to be conscious of the limitations or bias imposed on us by several factors. These include our own personalities—in the case of the Churchill portrait, for example, we may admire the sitter or artist so deeply that it colours our view to the exclusion of other factors. Then there is the change in values which time effects.

We must, however, make ourselves aware of the limits of our information about any portrait we look at, as when we examined the Churchill portrait *before* being aware of the background of its commission and production. It should be emphasized that our response will not be an ignorant one, for we will be bringing with us a wealth of experience of ourselves, other people, photographs, television and other communication media. When we know all the details of the situation we are, however, more able to make an *informed* judgement of the portrait. In order to help us become aware of just *how* informed that judgement is, we should consider the main variables of the portrait situation, as follows:

i The Commission
Who commissioned the portrait and for what purpose?
What were the requirements?

ii The Sitter

iii The Artist

iv The Method of Creation
How did i, ii, iii interrelate? How was the format or costume decided? Were sketches or photographs used?

v The Result
Normally a finished portrait, but how does it relate to the commission? Did the artist change the nature of the commission? If a pair was required, were both carried out? Is the portrait used as envisaged by the parties involved? If intended for the board room, for example, is it hung there?

vi Contemporary Reactions to the Portrait
From commissioning body, sitter and artist.
From those intimately connected with the above and having a commitment to one or other of them.
From 'experts' (either in the art world or in the sitter's field of activity).
From anyone else.

vii Later Reactions
Is the portrait still used as intended?
Is it viewed as a document of the sitter, or as a work of art?

Given the amount of information we have about the Churchill portrait we could fairly easily complete a checklist based on the above. Our only difficulty might be in answering question vii. This would, however, be the exception rather than the rule when considering historic portraits.

DEFINITIONS

In the 1830s, a photographic image was first fixed almost simultaneously by M. Nicéphore Niépce and M. L.J.M. Daguerre in France and William Henry Fox Talbot in England. Others were working on the same lines in various parts of Western Europe.

Although the first blurred image reproduced by Niépce was a landscape, this was an important event in the history of portraiture since soon afterwards a great part of the population could afford to have an 'accurate' image of themselves. The invention and development of photography should be understood, however, as only one part of the history of Western image-making which has, unlike the art of the Orient and other cultures, been particularly obsessed with the accurate reproduction of visual appearances.

Because of this enduring concern, it is hardly surprising that at least one of the Western accounts of the origin of portraiture fuses it with the origin of painting itself. Pliny the Elder, in the first century AD wrote a lengthy account, *Natural History*. In the section dealing with the uses of various stones and pigments, he writes an account of the history of art from its beginnings up to his own day. His two versions of the origin of portraiture are:

> ... modelling portraits from clay was first invented by Butades ... owing to his daughter, who was in love with a young man; and she, when he was going abroad, drew in outline on the wall the shadow of his face thrown by a lamp. Her father pressed clay on this and made a relief.

> The question as to the origin of the art of painting is uncertain ... but all agree that it began with tracing an outline round a man's shadow and consequently that pictures were originally done in this way. (Figure 33)

119

If we analyse this according to our schema (page 118), we arrive at several fundamental points:

i The Commission
None. But we are informed of the reason the portrait was made.

ii The Sitter
No supplementary biographical details necessary beyond the fact of his relationship with the girl.

iii The Artist
Detail adequate to the situation.

FIGURE **33** L'INVENTION DU DESSIN (THE INVENTION OF DRAWING), J. B. Suvée, 1799
Oil on canvas, 256x128 cm, 100$\frac{3}{4}$x50$\frac{1}{4}$ in, Groeninge Museum, Bruges

iv The Method of Creation
Described.

v The Result
Described.

vi Contemporary Reaction
Not described.

vii Later Reactions
Pliny reacts, not to the portrait itself, but to its technical and chronological importance. His attitude to it is very different from that of the parties involved.

Happily for the girl, she was creating the image primarily for her own satisfaction, and did not have to worry about any other views.

The actual technique involved—the tracing of a line around the shadow, is reflected in the English word 'portrait' itself, which derives from the French *trait pour trait*, meaning literally 'line for line'. The definition thus emphasizes the act of tracing or precisely copying in some manner. (The Italian *ritratto* carries the same meaning.) The supplementary meaning of the word 'trait' completes the significance of the word 'portrait'. It suggests the way a line can convey character and defines the portrait as something which should render character as well as documenting appearance. Of course, the closeness of the two meanings indicates that this could be almost the same thing.

The essential feature of the portrait is that it begins by aspiring to record a particular person. We should always be aware of the difference between a portrait and the generalized heads which appear in narrative paintings. The latter are normally invented by the artist in order to represent a particular 'type' (representing, say, bravery or poverty) instead of a particular individual. In such a case, the artist seeks to portray an abstraction by means of a personification or, better, characterization. In a true portrait, he seeks to define the particular rather than the general. Naturally, the situation is not always so clear. Very often an artist will make a portrait likeness of his sitter but will conflate this into a generalized image based on the sitter's most important characteristic. This is fundamental to the act of portraiture, and history is littered with examples. Think how Verrocchio made a portrait of Bartolomeo Colleoni into a symbol of military power (Figure 34); and his contemporary Laurana in his commemorative portrait bust of Eleanor of Aragon has given us a personification of female beauty, as seen through the eyes of someone with geometric ideals (Figure 35).

Here I think we should make clear two important functions of the portrait. There are two modes—one retrospective, the other, for want of a better word, active, or prospective. Very often a portrait is designed to have both functions.

For an example of a retrospective function, we can do no better than cite the Greek girl tracing the profile of her lover. This portrait was designed to remind

FIGURE **34** EQUESTRIAN MONUMENT TO BARTOLOMEO COLLEONI, Verrocchio, 1479–88 (unveiled 1496)
Bronze, height 395 cm, 155½ in, Campo SS. Giovanni e Paolo, Venice

122

FIGURE **35** PORTRAIT OF ELEANOR OF ARAGON, Francesco Laurana, c.1468
Marble, height 43 cm, 17 in, Galleria Nazionale della Sicilia, Palermo

her of his face and personality, and their life together. It is nostalgic or retrospective in function. Essentially, Giorgio Vasari referred to that mode when he wrote, 'Portraiture is the art which keeps the images of men alive after their deaths.'

Although Vasari emphasizes the retrospective function, he also implies that portraits are in the business of creating reputation. There exists a more active function which seeks less to commemorate than to promote or propagandize. We are all familiar with the way that film actors and actresses are careful to control the photographs of themselves which are available to the press; and of how, for example, the image of Hitler was spread throughout Europe. Perhaps one of the problems with the Churchill portrait was the fact that Sutherland was working with a retrospective or commemorative function in mind, portraying Churchill for eternity, while Churchill (and members of the Conservative party) were all too conscious of the possible active or propagandist use of the painting—and of the damage it might do to Churchill's credibility and that of the Conservative party in general.

There is some overlap between the two differing functions, each giving evidence of a belief in the essential representational role and power of the portrait. Little is written about the way portraits in general are to be thought of, but we do have plenty of evidence about how they were used. Pliny's shepherd girl might almost have been born in the Victorian era, for she seems to have thought of the image of her lover very much in the same way that a young lady of the nineteenth century might have sighed over a keepsake given her by an admirer. The same may be said of miniature portraits in, for example, Renaissance times and after, for not only are poems of the time stiff with references to 'my lady's picture' but the portrait miniature itself was often worn close to the heart (Figure 36), and was often incorporated in jewels like the locket still in use today.

Naturally, there are many other uses for portraits. Heroes stand in important town squares. Country houses often have portraits of members of the owning family, past and present, hung in a line in chronological order. Almost every country has its own national portrait gallery in some form or other, where portraits of famous women and men are displayed as 'representations of genius'.

Despite the many uses to which portraits are put, all of them are assumed to represent the sitter in a very essential way. Many examples show how the feelings aroused by the sitter are transferred to his portrait—the portrait of the Queen is accorded respect in officers' messes the world over; many portraits of St Thomas à Becket were deliberately defaced. In fact, in the modern world where likenesses of individuals are spread abroad cheaply and in large numbers, it is common for people to project emotions on to portraits of people whom they have never seen.

This habit, of giving reverence to an object rather than to a person aroused the anxiety of St Augustine as early as the fifth century. Augustine addressed the problem of the religious image. He was particularly concerned that the prayer and thoughts of a suppliant who knelt before a painting of the Virgin and Child, be addressed not to the image but to the true force to which the painting

123

FIGURE **36** PORTRAIT MINIATURE OF AN UNKNOWN MAN AGAINST A BACKGROUND OF FLAMES,
Nicholas Hilliard, c.1595?
Vellum on playing card (Ace of Hearts), 6x5 cm, 2½x2 in, Victoria and Albert Museum, London

124

was but a convenient bridge. Portraits have acted, throughout the ages, as a focus for emotions akin to the religious. The early portraits of holy men and women (e.g. St Louis, St Francis and St Clare) were objects of considerable veneration. One has only to think of photographs of the Ayatollah Khomeini being brandished in procession, of posters of Marx and Lenin presiding over May Day processions, or of vast cinema hoardings with gigantic images of film stars, to realize how far human emotions can be transferred to, and aroused by, the portrait.

I think this is easy to understand. A fine portrait does seem to achieve a distillation of the personality of the sitter, and it is small wonder that we are prepared to accept the premise that the portrait, in some way or other, 'represents' the sitter. Just how it represents him is a question which might have as many answers as spectators, yet it seems possible to make a number of relevant generalizations.

In the field of 'sympathetic magic', the little doll into which pins are stuck can have some connection with its original. It will often wear a hat like the original, or bear a relevant facial scar. But it will be all the more powerful if some actual item of clothing (or nail-parings, or spittle) belonging to the prospective victim is incorporated in the little fetish. Frazer gives many examples of the lengths to which primitive people go to stop their hair-cuttings, extracted teeth etc., falling into the hands of enemies who might use them to create evil. Ultimately the figure is not a likeness but is sufficiently like to attract the spirit of the original which is then thought to be controllable.

FIGURE **37** RELIQUARY OF ST EUSTACE, c.1210
Silver-gilt, height 32 cm, 12½ in, British Museum, London

This may seem to be a far cry from the representational aspirations of a modern-day portrait, but there is enough supplementary evidence for us to construct further analogies. Still within the mystical or religious field, we might consider the question of miracle-working objects.

The importance placed upon relics by some religions is evidence of the belief that something of the personality of the original person pertains to the relic which 'represents' him or her—or which provides the 'bridge' to that person's spirit, as St Augustine would have it. Portions of the True Cross on which Christ is thought to have suffered; dried drops of the Holy Blood; pieces of garments thought to have belonged to the three magi; bones from the martyred bodies of St Ursula and her 11,000 virgins—these have all been accorded deep reverence. Frazer described this kind of belief under the heading of 'contagious magic'.

Christian relics were preserved, and displayed, in various ways. They would be mounted in crosses, monstrances, caskets, clasps, brooches. If a piece of a saint's foot was being preserved, it might be preserved in a foot-shaped reliquary; if his arm, in an arm-shaped one. A part of his head would be mounted in a portrait bust. This form was, indeed, so popular as a representational image that even other parts of the body were preserved in a head or bust reliquary (Figure 37). Certainly, this form of image would seem to substantiate the idea that quasi-religious emotions could be transferred to what amounts to a portrait. The process of preserving the ashes of the deceased within a funerary urn shaped

FIGURE **38** ETRUSCAN BURIAL URN, second half of the 7th century BC
Clay, height 74 cm, 29 in, Florence

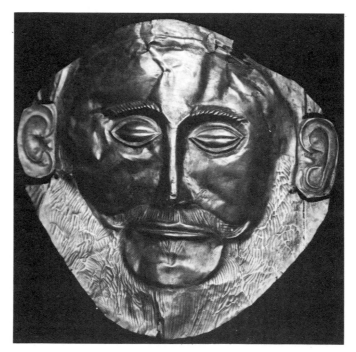

FIGURE **39** FUNERARY MASK FROM THE ROYAL TOMBS AT MYCENAE, GREECE, 1600–1500 BC
Gold, height 32 cm, 12½ in, National Museum, Athens

FIGURE **40** PORTRAIT STATUE OF A ROMAN HOLDING BUSTS OF HIS ANCESTORS, 1st century AD
Marble, height 180 cm, 71 in, Museo dei Conservatori, Rome

like the dead man's head is recorded as early as the seventh century BC; Etruscan examples are particularly apt (Figure 38).

Pliny gives what may be close to a factual account of portraiture, unlike his more poetic passages about the Greek maid and her lover. The first death masks were formed by pressing thin skins of gold or silver or wax on to the face of the deceased (Figure 39). Pliny lamented,

> The practice has died out . . . in the old days wax models of faces [death masks] were set out each on a separate side-board, to furnish likenesses to be carried in procession at a funeral in the clan, and always when some member of it passed away the entire company of his house that ever existed was present.

Here, therefore, we have an object which is so close to being a part of the body of a dead person that it can be construed as a relic (just as are parts of saints' bodies); it also documents the appearance and therefore constitutes a portrait. In fact, the use of these death masks is a model for both. Death masks were carried through the streets on ceremonial occasions just as sacred relics are today; and they were displayed on the sideboard as are family photographs. Like sacred relics, they gave evidence of authenticity. A Roman patrician was seen to have ancestors (Figure 40); a medieval church similarly justified itself by the display of its relics. The reverence accorded to these portraits is documented by

FIGURE **41** LIFE MASK OF WILLIAM BLAKE, taken by J. S. Deville, 1823
Fitzwilliam Museum, Cambridge

Pliny, and it goes some some way to explaining the awe and reverence which we are still prepared to give to portraits of famous men and women.

At times, a death mask has a certain genuine documentary *raison d'etre*. It surely is of interest to preserve the features of Napoleon, William Blake (Figure 41) or Lorenzo the Magnificent, in the form of a life or death mask, even if it scarcely summons up the achievements of the man. (Indeed, Albrecht Dürer's famous portrait of Erasmus is inscribed to the effect that the sitter's works provide the better image.) Additionally, there is some point in preserving, for example, a cast or photograph of the hands of a famous musician, although of course his technical resources are only a part of his artistic make-up. But it would be fatuous to make a cast of Chopin's feet, rather than of his hands, since these would not be 'representative' of his unique quality.

The example of 'Chopin's feet' is really of great relevance to our judgement of portraits, for a portrait is flawed if it displays only an insignificant aspect of the sitter's life and omits to refer to his most important achievements. It is here that we begin to approach a central fact about portraiture. A portrait is, inevitably, an interpretation, and it may well over-emphasize one feature to the detriment of others. Its final form is, therefore, like all other pieces of reportage (or like works of art), dependent partly upon its producer (i.e. the artist, in the case of a painting) and partly upon its medium. The history of portraiture is thus partly the history of a genre whose form is to an extent pre-conditioned by its use.

FUNCTION AND FORM

The aim of all portraits is to create an image which will acceptably 'represent' the sitter. At times it is also meant to *identify* the sitter. We are, for example, identified by the photographic portraits on our passports. On occasions, the possession of a portrait will identify someone who is known to the sitter. Thus, in ancient times, a messenger carried documents which were often sealed with a likeness of the man he served. It need scarcely be said that, at one time, the ability to have a portrait made and to have it reproduced was the preserve of the rich and powerful. Usually, a king would employ a 'king's painter' who would carry out varied works including the making of portraits. In general, the 'standard image' of the king would be designed so that it could be easily reproduced in various media, including coinage (Figure 42), postage stamps, even inn signs (all of which, of course, needed a royal licence). Thus most of the King's Heads are in profile, a pose which lends itself to easy recognition and which is less demanding on the portraitist than a three-quarter or foreshortened view of the head.

   While there was a good legal reason for the dissemination of royal portraits in this way, the propagandist value of the portrait should not be overlooked. It seems to have developed in several stages. Even if a local landowner did not

FIGURE **42** TETRADRACHM OF TYRE, 1st century BC–1st century AD
British Museum, London

FIGURE **43** THE DONNE TRIPTYCH, Virgin and Child with Saints and Donors, Hans Memling, c.1477
Oil on oak panels, 71 x 70 cm, 28 x 27¾ in (centre), 71 x 30 cm, 28 x 12 in (wings), National Gallery, London

have his own coinage, he would certainly have had portraits of himself and his family made. These would be produced in several versions, and the landlord would make presents of the cheaper versions to his adherents. In feudal times, the practice would have had a highly practical aim, namely to familiarize the peasantry with the face of the man to whom they should accord respect, and whom they should protect in battle when the need arose. In modern times, now that the reproduction of a likeness in the form of the printed photograph is fairly cheap, it no longer advertises even the financial resources of the sitter, but simply aims to ensure recognition. In our overpopulated, urban society, the mere fact of being recognized is its own form of status, and often constitutes an aim complete in itself. It is also important to those for whom recognition helps to achieve 'fame'—film stars, politicians and other public figures.

Of course, the ultimate aspiration of the portrait is that which Vasari alluded to, it 'keeps the images of men alive after their deaths'. The more portraits a ruler issues, the more chance there is that his image will survive. In times when the majority of people believed in life after death (whether in heaven or hell), the rich spent time and money having images of themselves made, which might pre-empt their reception in heaven. How many of them were painted kneeling before the Virgin and Child in their heavenly throne-room with their patron saints interceding for them? Often sons and daughters were also included (Figure 43). It was the duty of the rich to decorate the family church or chapel and the opportunity was taken repeatedly to show oneself with those achieving salvation.

Perhaps the most astonishing example of this aspiration is the *Tempio Malatestiano*, the Christian mausoleum which Sigismondo Malatesta created to the memory of his wife and himself in Rimini (Figures 44–5). It involved the refurbishment of an earlier building. The name of Sigismondo appears on the exterior;

FIGURE **44** TEMPIO MALATESTIANO, Alberti, c.1450
San Francesco, Rimini, view of the exterior

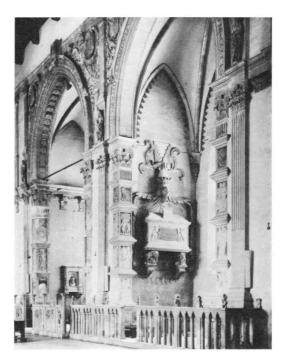

FIGURE **45** TEMPIO MALATESTIANO, Alberti, c.1450
San Francesco, Rimini, view of the Isotta chapel

PORTRAITS

FIGURE **46** PROFILE OF SIGISMONDO, Agostino di Duccio, c.1453
Marble, slightly more than life-size, Tempio Malatestiano, Rimini

FIGURE **47** SIGISMONDO MALATESTA BEFORE HIS PATRON SAINT, SIGISMONDO,
Piero della Francesca, 1451
Fresco, 257x345 cm, 101¼x135¾ cm, Tempio Malatestiano, Rimini

his coat of arms, initials and emblem (the elephant), appear everywhere—all of these representing him. Most important, his sculpted profile (Figure 46), geometric, formalized, and flatteringly youthful, appears too often to be counted. In the sacristy he kneels in fresco before his enthroned patron St Sigismondo (Figure 47).

One of the methods by which Sigismondo Malatesta ensured that we know him today, was to choose good artists and good materials to do the job. The painters included Piero della Francesca, and Agostino di Duccio was the principal sculptor; the architect was Leone Battista Alberti. The logic was this: not only would they produce good work, it would be recognized, revered and preserved—as has indeed happened.

THE ARTIST AND HIS PORTRAIT

This section deals with the 'artistic' aspect of portraiture, and outlines the factors a portraitist has to consider in his work.

The portrait is one of the principal genres of art. However individual the artist, he is the product of his era and is likely to produce a portrait which, while being an acceptable rendering of the sitter, is also identifiably made at a certain time and in a certain place. Thus, we are unlikely to confuse a portrait of around 1810 with one painted around 1510.

The reason for this is partly technical—at any one time in history there are only so many types of pigment, drawing materials or stone available to an artist. It is also partly conceptual—just as the artist is technically limited so, it has to be said, has he certain conceptual limitations. For example, it would have been impossible for an artist to paint an *art brut* portrait (Plate 25) in 1510.

Nevertheless, every portraitist has many possibilities open to him. Many of these would be discussed with the sitter, or with the commissioning body. The things which an artist must think about are:

i Medium
Two-dimensional or three-dimensional? If two-dimensional, graphic (for reproduction) or painted? A painting would cost more than, say, a pastel. If three-dimensional, is the portrait to be in terracotta, stone or bronze (quite a variation in cost)?

ii Function
Is the work for public use or private? For a specific board room or for a locket round the neck? (This also helps determine size.) Is it to be one of a series, or of a pair, a group portrait, double or single? A donor portrait?

iii Format
Is the sitter to be shown head only, bust length, bust length with hands, half length, three-quarter length or full length; life-size, over life-size, or on a reduced scale? Note that it was normal to charge less for a simple head than for any larger format.

iv Costume and Pose
The choice of costume depends on the function of the portrait. If it is to be a public image, or a state portrait, the artist will obviously be presented with some very precise requirements. Before the nineteenth century, the sitter or commissioning body would have been very clear about what type of portrait was required. The artist would have been specifically asked to provide, for example, a pair of betrothal portraits or a coronation portrait, a family group or an equestrian picture. Each of these types of image had a standardized type of costume

FIGURE **48** SELF-PORTRAIT, Albrecht Dürer, 1500
Oil on wood, 67x49 cm, 26¼x19¼ in, Bayerische Stadtgemäldesammlungen, Alte Pinakothek, Munich

and pose, though variations could be made. The artist would consider whether the 'type' of portrait required the sitter to be standing or sitting, on horseback or reading. The later the date of the portrait, the less liable it is to conform to a type, and the more free the artist: Whistler, for example, chose the costume for some of his sitters.

v Viewpoint
Profile, full-face, three-quarter? In the Renaissance, an artist using full-face would have been conscious that this format was associated with rulers and also used for Christ in his role of Redeemer (Figure 48). Today any professional painting a portrait in full profile would be making a conscious allusion to a fifteenth-century or antique mode (Figure 49).

vi Persona
All the preceding are linked to this consideration. The sitter is shown as some sort of recognizable ideal. The simplest example might be the case in which the sitter wishes to be shown as his patron saint (e.g. Giovanni Bellini, *Man as St Dominic*; Sebastiano del Piombo, *Lady as St Agatha*); or as a god or goddess (e.g. École de Fontainebleau, *Diane de Poitiers as the Goddess Diana* (Figure 50)). This may approach the propagandist image (e.g. *Hitler as a Medieval Knight*). Dürer showed himself with different personae, but managed to keep his self-portraits on the right side of credibility.

FIGURE **49** LORD CLARK, Graham Sutherland, 1963—4
Oil on canvas, 55x46 cm, 21½x18 in, National Portrait Gallery, London

vii Style
Clearly related to all the above. Note colour, brushwork and composition.

viii 'Effect'
There is no doubt that every artist considers what effect his portrait should
have on the spectator. Usually, the aim is relatively simple, most portraits being
designed to elicit sympathy, admiration, even love.

There are very many different kinds of portrait, but looking back from the
vantage-point of the twentieth century, we can decide which is the most prevalent type and concentrate our attention on one example of this. A painted
portrait showing one man at about half length is, I think, probably the common-
est type. I have chosen a self-portrait by Rembrandt (Plate 16). Look back to the
checklists on pages 118 and 134—6 and consider the portrait in relation to these
headings.
Since this is a self-portrait, the sitter and artist are one, and we can presume
that no commission existed. Rembrandt was free to paint himself exactly as he
chose, and all the choices which he made would have been of his own volition.
Some of his self-portraits are larger, some smaller, some head only, some painted
to a fuller length. Since he painted himself throughout his life, they show him at
various ages. This one shows him old. He has chosen to show himself at three-

FIGURE **50** DIANE CHASSERESSE (Diane de Poitiers as the Goddess Diana), École de Fontainebleau, c.1550
Oil on canvas, 191x132 cm, 75¼x52 in (original on wood, 180x100 cm, 70¾x39 in), Musée du Louvre, Paris

quarter length in a virtually square field. His face is the most focussed part of the composition, the rest being painted in much less detail. He has chosen to show himself as a painter holding his brush and looking outwards as if into a mirror. Behind him there are drawn shapes which have been variously interpreted. They perhaps allude to the perfect O that Giotto was said to be able to create freehand. He is dressed plainly, in his everyday work clothes, not having dressed up especially for the occasion. He is alone, as he would have been while working. The style is Rembrandt's own late style, making no overt allusion to anything else (i.e. he is not posed like an ancient Roman athlete, for instance). The persona adopted is that of the artist, struggling perhaps with a geometric technique which may be thought to hold some universal key.

The 'effect' is rather more difficult to gauge. Is the old man anxious, stoical or triumphant? It is surely difficult to judge and, unfortunately, we lack contemporary reactions to the painting. Yet Rembrandt was a master in defining expression. Why is he less than explicit here? Let us examine the possibilities. His late manner, with its lack of definition in areas such as space, hands and body, brings with it a certain imprecision in facial expression and consequently in emotion and psychology. But this does not quite explain *why* he chose to produce what amounts to an imprecise portrait. The lack of detail brings with it a relaxation of the need to 'describe' colour, and through this the increased possibility of using colour to define the emotional tone of the painting. In this case, colour and light seem as inexpressive as the face and we must therefore conclude that

Rembrandt deliberately worked towards a kind of imprecision which could be ambiguous, or allusive. That is, in expressing no one emotion, the face, pose, colour might suggest many. This is rather less far-fetched than it might at first appear to those who assume that ambiguity, or even inscrutability, in the visual arts is a twentieth-century invention. Seventeenth-century plays (think of *Othello*, for example) are full of actions which mean different things to different people. Indeed, we might recall a passage from *Hamlet* (III.ii) when the same visual material is interpreted in various ways.

> *Hamlet*   Do you see yonder cloud that's almost in shape of a camel?
> *Polonius* By th'mass and t'is like a camel indeed.
> *Hamlet*   Methinks it is like a weasel.
> *Polonius* It is backed like a weasel.
> *Hamlet*   Or, like a whale?
> *Polonius* Very like a whale.

One has the impression that Shakespeare is not only demonstrating the way courtiers will agree with anything their masters say, but also lampooning the type of speculation which one might have heard in scholars' studies. What is referred to is the way that meaningless shapes can take on different meanings for different people. (We should remember here a passage in Leonardo's notebooks, written 100 years before, describing how shapes on a wall suggested imagery to him.)

Thus it seems quite probable that Rembrandt intended a painting that would allow the spectator to read different expressions in it. We now find ourselves in a difficult situation. If Rembrandt deliberately produced an allusive portrait, in which we see various expressions—calculation, determination, anxiety and defeat—how can we tell which of these expressions are *meant* to be there, and which we are projecting on to the portrait from our own lives?

This is where historical knowledge might help. We are aware of Rembrandt's circumstances at the time. He was ignored by the art world, and bankrupted in 1656. Can we detect a certain melancholy in the expression, or are we imagining it? Perhaps there is no answer, but I believe, without having any real proof, that Rembrandt's allusiveness through lack of definition was his answer to a problem which had arisen when artists began to achieve a certain level of technical veracity in their portraits.

Before about 1500, artists did not show their sitters as if at 'one moment in time', 'as if they were alive'; they created an image of the sitter *as* a man of courage or *as* a woman of piety. When artists achieved the ability to render fleeting expressions, they were beset with the problem of which to select. To show him smiling would be to undermine his gravity; to show him glum would underemphasize his sense of fun. It is this problem that Rembrandt was attempting to solve, and one which every portraitist since about the year 1500 has had to consider. Rembrandt invented a style which was capable of hinting at the 'completeness' of the individual instead of stating only one facet of his personality. His innovation was, like all movements in art, part-technical, part-conceptual, and it is therefore interesting to summarize the technical and conceptual aspects of the type of portraiture to which he was reacting; this is done in the next section.

The remainder of this section of the book deals with three different periods in the history of portrait paintings:

1. The Renaissance, when art (and portraiture) reached, for the first time in the medium of painting, a high level of 'realism'. I put the term in inverted commas since within the field of the visual arts it is open to many different interpretations. Here I use 'realistic', 'life-like', 'naturalistic' to mean 'true to the facts of vision', as will be apparent from the context.

2. The period immediately following the invention of photography, which naturally had an immediate and telling effect on painters and painting. The greatest use of photography in the first years of its development was for documentation, which includes portraiture. The reactions of the artists and their establishment of a 'post-photographic' style are important in the development of a kind of portraiture which takes a more flexible view of documenting the sitter.

3. The years around 1900 and after. At this time new theories of human behaviour were advanced which were to have tremendous repercussions in all fields. For example, Freud's Theory of the Unconscious proposed that there was a vast substructure of internal life in everyone, not visible in an accountable form in their everyday behaviour. Thus the harmony between appearance and character which had previously been generally accepted, was called into question. In the field of visual arts, it became theoretically possible for a portrait to be painted which would be less recognizable as a documentation of the sitter's physical appearance and yet would be acceptable as being an adequate representation of the inner life of the sitter.

THE PORTRAIT IN THE RENAISSANCE

When in 1860, Jacob Burckhardt published his famous study, *The Civilisation of the Renaissance in Italy*, he entitled one of its sections *The Rise of the Individual*. He construed one of the main characteristics of the period to be the way in which society was controlled by brilliant individuals rather than by groups. He saw, as a corollary, that during the same period each person gained greater control over his fate. The visual manifestation of this he perceived in the way people in portraits gradually began to look different from each other, each sitter looking more 'individual' than before. Is it possible, however, that the portraits merely exemplify an increased technical facility, a developing ability on the part of the artist to portray the face and its expressions more realistically?

Well, there is no doubt that the genre did increase in realism, but this is not the whole story. In order to invent the means artists had to be able to conceive the end. In other words, the need to study the individual more precisely was the source of the techniques to do so. Thus, as we scan the illustrations (Figures 51–7) we have to be aware that each technical advance (the new vision of detail, the inclusion of telling hand gestures) is also conceptual.

It is interesting to try to define the main drift of this development. Consider first (remembering our checklists on pages 118 and 134–6) a small portrait of the

FIGURE **51** JEAN II LE BON, KING OF FRANCE, French School, c.1550–60
Oil on oak, 60x45 cm, 23½x17½in, Musée du Louvre, Paris

LOOKING INTO PAINTINGS

FIGURE **52** MEDAL OF CECILIA GONZAGA, Pisanello, 1447
Bronze, diameter 8.7 cm, 3½ in, obverse: portrait bust, reverse: girl and unicorn with crescent moon,
Museo Ambrosiana, Milan

PORTRAITS

FIGURE **53** BATTISTA SFORZA, COUNTESS OF URBINO and FEDERIGO DA MONTEFELTRO, COUNT
OF URBINO, Piero della Francesca, diptych, c.1472
Tempera on wood, each 47x33 cm, 18½x13 in, Uffizi, Florence

PORTRAITS

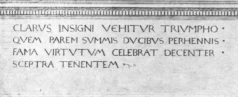

CLARVS INSIGNI VEHITVR TRIVMPHO ·
QVEM PAREM SVMMIS DVCIBVS PERHENNIS
FAMA VIRTVTVM CELEBRAT DECENTER ·
SCEPTRA TENENTEM ⸱⸱·

QVE MODVM REBVS TENVIT SECVNDIS ·
CONIVGIS MAGNI DECORATA RERVM ·
LAVDE GESTARVM VOLITAT PER ORA ·
CVNCTA VIRORVM ·

FIGURE **54** TRIUMPH OF THE COUNTESS and TRIUMPH OF THE COUNT, Piero della Francesca,
(reverses of the diptych, Figure 53)

144

French king Jean le Bon, by an unknown artist presumed to be French, or at least working in France (Figure 51). We have no details of commission, artist or reactions. The king is shown without any signs of rank, the emphasis being on his physique and personality rather than on his social status. This suggests that the portrait was intended to be used in a personal or informal way, and that it was not conceived as a state portrait. Its size, fairly small at $2 \times 1\frac{1}{2}$ feet, agrees with that assumption. As a record of the king's features and personality, it has the limitations of the profile format. One is allowed to see only one side of the face. Aspirations seem scarcely to have progressed since the daughter of Butades traced her lover's profile on the wall. In the meantime, however, the profile form had acquired an air of nobility due to the fact that it had become the standard way of showing a monarch's face on a coin or medal (Figure 42), the face turned away, almost haughtily, from the observer. Because of his lack of crown or sceptre, Jean's image is one of the least imperious of the type. One can construe it, rather, as having a familial rather than a regal function since the profile view generally emphasizes physical features common to most members of a family (shape of nose for example), and one may surmise that it was meant to take its place as one of a series of family likenesses. It is conventional in form, even unambitious, but it acts, nevertheless, as a noble ancestor to a great many portraits of the Renaissance period.

FIGURE **55** ARCHDUKE RUDOLPH IV OF HABSBURG, Austrian School, c.1360
Parchment on panel, 39x22 cm, 15½x8½ in, Erzbischöfliches Dom-und-Diözesanmuseum, Vienna

Notable among them, are those profile portraits which are on one side of a medal (Figure 52). The obverse of the medal is generally occupied by the sitter in bust-length profile, with his name around the edge, while the reverse usually shows an emblem or device associated with him, often his coat of arms or some allegorical representation of an attribute which he possessed.

This elegant form of personal propaganda is also seen in painting. Piero della Francesca's pair of profile portraits of Duke Federigo da Montefeltro and his Duchess (Figures 53 and 54) have reverses with each sitter shown in triumph with personifications of virtues which each was supposed to display. Although uncommunicative and of limited descriptive function, the profile possesses, even on a small scale, dignity and grandeur. (In this case, Piero used the profile with discretion, for the duke had lost his right eye in battle.)

Let us compare with the profile of Jean le Bon another virtually contemporary royal portrait, that of Rudolph IV of Habsburg (Figure 55). We find ourselves considering side by side the attributes of two different viewpoints. Rudolph is shown as a king, with his crown. While not an example of great skill, the portrait of Rudolph serves to show that the three-quarter view gives one much more information about the sitter's appearance—two eyes instead of one, the breadth of nose, mouth and forehead. In fact, it would now be theoretically possible for the artist to show some expression on the face of his sitter, although in this case the artist did not possess the skill to do so. Generally speaking, this is the essential difference between the three-quarter image and the profile, although some artists have achieved wonders of expression in profile portraits.

The next major development takes place in the Netherlands and is visible almost simultaneously in the works of artists like Jan van Eyck, Rogier van der Weyden and Robert Campin (also known as The Master of Merode or The Master of Flémalle). Early texts give Jan van Eyck the honour of having made a technical advance of prime importance for painting in general, and of great significance to portraiture. He was said to have been the inventor, or better, the discoverer of the oil medium. Now it is known that this is not strictly true. A manuscript written in the twelfth century gives the basic recipe, but Jan's portraits (Plates 17 and 18) certainly look very different from those showing Jean le Bon and Rudolph, and he is probably to be credited with 're-discovering' the medium or making some advance in its practical use. Certainly he seems to have developed an individual technique and to have used it consistently.

Before Jan's time the tempera technique was used universally for easel painting, and it continued to be the staple process in Italy until much later. Basically, the difference between it and oil is this. In tempera painting the pigments are mixed with egg and the resulting mixture is spread on the surface of the panel. In oil painting the pigments are mixed with oil produced from nuts of some kind. Tempera dries very quickly and is opaque. Oil drying times vary, but the artist has more time to work and more opportunity to make changes and erasures. Oil thus becomes capable of greater detail and also of more expansive effects. Most important of all, the results look different. Tempera paintings generally have a dry, powdery look with an even opacity. Since oil can be opaque, translucent or transparent, depending on how the pigments are thinned and handled, a greater range of effects is attainable. The painting is built up in layers, and one sees the opaque areas through the tinted transparent passages. The effect is rather like that of gazing through a glass-bottomed bucket at the bottom of the sea. Finally, oil paintings can have, certainly in Van Eyck's hands, a hard lustrous finish, like an enamel.

It appears reasonable to suppose that the oil medium was being developed simultaneously in several centres, yet Jan van Eyck certainly seems to have been the master of its potential. One might even see him as struggling to develop his technical apparatus in order that he could achieve the effects of detail and lustre that he had seen in his mind's eye, and the advance in realism attributable partly to Jan is truly remarkable. (Other artists at the time were interested in the achievement of a thorough-going illusionism. The Limbourg brothers, for example, who were employees of the Duc de Berry, are said to have made a *trompe-l'œil* apple which was selected by the duke in all seriousness from a bowl of fruit.)

There is a possibility, of course, that what we find 'realistic' in old paintings today, might not have been thought to be so when the originals were created. Was Jan's portrait of the *Man in a Red Turban* (Plate 17) thought to be realistic at the time? We have no really precise contemporary account of any of Jan's portraits, but we have other evidence which is telling. An almost contemporary

146

(1456) description of a landscape by Jan stresses its marvellous control of detail and in particular the way it showed distant objects so clearly—a kind of super-realism. Also, there exist documents which tell of Jan being sent to Portugal by his patron, the Duke of Burgundy, in order to make two portraits of a possible bride there, Isabella. To reduce the possibility of both being lost when at sea, the portraits were sent back on separate ships. When the duke looked at them, he liked what he saw and put the marriage in hand. This documented anecdote surely supports the notion that Jan's portraits were held to be extremely realistic. This is not to say that Jan's portraits are perfect reproductions of their sitters—he disregards, for example, the scale of hand to head, and of body to head—but they are significantly more informative than those of Jean le Bon and Rudolph. When we look at his *Man in a Red Turban* (Plate 17), we are immediately conscious of the force of documentation. Even the painting's frame carries information round its edges rather as a medal would. It tells us that Jan van Eyck made 'me' (i.e. the painting) on 21 October 1433. In the way it is painted (to look as if it had been tooled into a gold frame by a goldsmith), it proclaims a *trompe-l'œil* ambition. The painting itself informs us about the sitter in a supremely visual way. It tells us about the clothes he wore. It tells us about his age, via the texture of his skin and the gray stubble on his chin. His eyes and his gaze (directly into ours) tell us about his personality—extraverted, even challenging, and I suspect, adventurous. Jan has developed the portrait into something that can build a bridge to the spectator in the way a *Madonna* can. With the portrayed person we can share a common moment.

147

To me, this is one of the most significant developments in the genre. Like all great inventions, once achieved it was immediately imitated. Jan was a court painter most of his life and made only a few works which one might describe as truly public. Nevertheless, the main principles of his portrait painting were followed by Petrus Christus, his successor as the leading painter in Bruges. Although historians still differ in their views as to how it happened, Jan's style and technique permeated the centres of painting in Europe (Antonello da Messina is diagnosed as a carrier) including Umbria, Florence and Venice. Indeed, it is possible to write the history of fifteenth-century portraiture in terms of the influence of the Eyckian style.

Jan's production shows him to have worked empirically. He did not have available to him the scientific rules of perspective, as did his counterparts in Italy. The description of space in his interiors was achieved as much by the use of his eye as were the highlights in the eyes of his sitters. Because he was famous for painting what he saw, Jan van Eyck documented—as he did the appearance of Princess Isabella of Portugal—the marriage of Giovanni Arnolfini and his wife Giovanna Cenami (Plate 18).

This is one of the most famous and widely discussed paintings, partly because of its charm, which is compounded by seeing what appears to be a heavily pregnant girl taking her marriage vows. In fact, it is accepted by all modern historians that Giovanna was not pregnant and that her appearance was due to the fashionable clothing of the day. The painting is historically of considerable interest, not only because of the exactitude of its technique, or because it is an early example of a full-length double portrait. Its prime significance is that it is both a narrative and a portrait. It shows real people enacting a real event. Unlike Jean le Bon and Rudolph who seem to be doing nothing other than sitting for their portraits, the Arnolfini have been portrayed acting out a significant event in their lives. The exact significance of the event is detailed by the objects in the room, which have been interpreted in a famous passage by Erwin Panofsky (*Burlington Magazine*, 1934, and *Early Netherlandish Painting*, 1953):

> The sacrament of marriage is not dispensed by a priest but by the recipients themselves. Two people could conclude a perfectly valid marriage in complete solitude. The picture shows them taking the marriage vow in the hallowed seclusion of their bridal chamber—the picture is both a double portrait of Giovanni Arnolfini and Jeanne Cenami and a marriage certificate.
>
> This explains the signature—*Johannes de Eyck fuit hic. 1434.* (Jan van Eyck was here 1434) . . . The artist has set down his signature—in the flourished script normally used for legal documents—as a witness rather than as a painter. In fact, we see him in the mirror entering the room in the company of another gentleman who may be interpreted as a second witness.
>
> What looks like a well-appointed upper-middle-class interior is in reality a nuptial chamber, hallowed by sacramental associations: all the objects bear a symbolic significance.
>
> A burning candle was required for the ceremony of taking an oath, but also had a reference to matrimony: the 'marriage candle' was lit in the home of the newly-weds.
>
> The dog was an accepted emblem of marital faith.
>
> The statue of St Margaret invokes the patron saint of childbirth.
>
> The crystal beads and the 'spotless mirror' are well-known symbols of Marian purity.
>
> The fruit on the window-sill recalls the state of innocence before the fall of man.
>
> I would dare to assert that the observer is expected to realise such notions consciously. Jan's interiors are built in such a way that what is possibly meant to be a mere realistic motive can, at the same time, be conceived as a symbol. The spectator is not irritated by a mass of complicated hieroglyphs, but is allowed to abandon himself to the quiet fascination of a transfigured reality.

Of course, it is possible to quibble over the precise meaning of some of the objects—the mirror could be compared to that mentioned in the famous passage:

148

Now we see in a mirror in darkness, but later we shall see face to face. Now I know in part; but later I shall know as I am known.

There is a good reason to suppose that Van Eyck is not documenting the actual moment of the vows being sworn, but rather constructing a painting which depicts the marriage state in general. He treats a portrait with the seriousness and complexity normally given to a large religious painting. Yet this is not a major propagandist scheme for an important economic or political purpose, but the portrayal of two people of the merchant class who stood to gain nothing politically from the painting.

The Arnolfini Marriage elevates the portrait. We have to wait almost a century until another portrait of like ambition was painted. It is the large painting, signed by Hans Holbein the Younger and dated by him 1533, normally (if inaccurately) known as *The Ambassadors* (Plate 19). It shows two friends standing in front of a table on which are grouped a number of objects, selected to demonstrate the range of their interests (Figure 56). Those items on the lower shelf of the court cupboard show the men to possess the latest edition of hymns, the most up-to-date arithmetical system and considerable musical ability. The upper shelf is covered, not only with an extremely expensive Eastern rug but with objects used in astrology and astronomy. Some of these acted as calendars and time-keepers, and inform the spectator that the scene was visualized by the artist as taking place at 10.30 on 26 April 1533. The picture is painted life-size, the men being shown rich, self-assured and young (their ages are given: twenty-eight and twenty-five). But three things blight the scene. At the top left-hand corner of the painting, just visible at the edge of the green curtain is an ivory crucifix, which brings a more sober note to the composition. This is consolidated by the fact that one of the strings on the lute is broken—a well-known symbol of death; also by the shape which spreads itself over the ornate floor—it is a human skull rendered in perspective so that it is unintelligible when seen from in front of the painting, but easily discerned when the spectator stands near the frame to the right. These three objects classify the painting as being not only a portrait but a *Vanitas* picture, a subject most often used by still-life painters (see page 257), and conceived to demonstrate the vanity ('emptiness') of human life and the inevitability of death.

Without delving too deeply into the detail of Holbein's painting, I think it is possible to assert that the subject-matter must have been agreed between the artist and at least one of the sitters. The more swashbuckling of the two, Jean de Dinteville, wears a cap badge with a skull on it, which suggests that he may have had some personal interest in the *Vanitas* theme. The sitters deliberately had themselves shown as leading impressively full lives which will come to nought. Clearly, in having themselves portrayed by a great artist they have in a sense achieved immortality.

In this painting, Holbein combined a portrait with a more general statement on mortality. Equally important for the history of portraiture, is its precise

149

FIGURE **56** THE AMBASSADORS, Hans Holbein the Younger, detail of the table between the figures, see Plate 19

description of time which Holbein achieved not only through the conceit of the table-top sundial, but through the 'instantaneous' quality in the portrayal of his sitters. The painting can be said to be Holbein's solution to the problem that the instantaneous portrait brought with it. In order that such an elaborate solution should be sought, one would suspect that the problem had been recognized for some time. Can we date this particular event?

My own view is that many painters in the fifteenth century were grappling with this problem, which is so important for the veracious portrayal of a particular individual.

Leonardo's *The Last Supper* is certainly a painting which demonstrates an interest in defining time (Plate 8). The event it portrays took place at twilight. Leonardo's lighting of the scene reproduces the actual lighting circumstances of the room in which the picture is located, as at twilight. Each evening the low sun streams across the room from windows on the left (west) side of the room; in Leonardo's painting the light has a similar direction, height and intensity. There exists an account of how Leonardo would spend much time in front of his picture and then paint for only a few moments. Although censured for laziness, he may well have been waiting for the right moment to reproduce the light in his fresco.

In short, Leonardo was able to define a particular time of day by relating his treatment of light to location. He was able to intensify the experience of time by defining a precise action through a precise delineation of anatomy. *The Last Supper* is in poor condition, but Leonardo's drawings for the disciples give a real sense of dramatic reaction to Christ's announcement. Place could be described with precision by means of the recently perfected science of perspective. Leonardo, his contemporaries and his followers, ushered in an era where the three dramatic unities of time, place and action could be employed in the visual arts.

How is this relevant to portraiture? It means that in about the year 1500 Leonardo's absorption with light, shade and the definition of time could have a great influence on the portrait work of his contemporaries. It means that for the first time we begin to see painted portraits which are truly startling in their veracity. Suddenly the phrase 'looking as if he were alive' is actually applicable. Vasari describes Raphael's portrait, *Pope Julius II* (Plate 20) by saying that people who saw it were afraid—an indication of how the primitive fear of precise visual reproduction can surface in highly sophisticated circumstances. In this painting by Raphael the control of time, place and action is used for the purpose of giving the ultimate in life to a portrait. The sitter is seen to act in a credible physical space, and his action is also credibly described as taking place within credible time.

In my studies in the field of portraiture, I have always assigned great importance to these paintings of the High Renaissance, because of their achievement, for the first time, of a realism which still looks real today. This realism is quite clearly won through hard study on the one hand (anatomy and perspective), and through minute observation (of light effects) on the other. Nevertheless, I am

151

also aware that my perception is at least partly subjective and I think it wise to examine by what standards I judge realism. Ultimately, I suppose, in our century we equate visual realism with the documentary movie and with photographs. Raphael's *Julius II* has much in common with a photographic image (Figure 59). If you examine the painting carefully, you will find that there is no part of it which one could describe as being 'a line'. In other words, Julius' image is modelled in tone—or light—and is truly 'photographic' ('written in light'). It is just possible that we accept the realism of this portrait because of its resemblance to a photograph. Perhaps our concept of realism in art is not historically accurate; perhaps we should be conscious of the influence of twentieth-century media upon it.

Almost every era has its criterion for realism, and the High Renaissance was clearly no exception. No sooner had portraiture achieved such compelling veracity than portraitists began to expand the aims of portraiture beyond realism. Holbein, for example, produced in his *Ambassadors* a work which contrasts a vivid display of life's riches with the inevitability of death. One could list a number of portraits of the period which adopt an aim beyond (or to one side of) the 'simple' realistic characterization of an individual. Among them one would certainly include the self-portrait of Parmigianino, painted in 1523 (Plate 21). Here the artist followed the precepts of realism to their natural conclusion, and produced a self-portrait which paradoxically, does not render his day-to-day appearance. Vasari gives a good account of how this famous painting was made:

152

> Francesco took a piece of wood and modelled it into the convex shape of a barber's mirror and therein he set not only himself but everything he could see—his hand drawing etc.—all curved and distorted exactly as he saw them in his mirror. . . .

Parmigianino's self-portrait imitates visual reality so precisely that it produces a totally 'unreal', quasi-surrealist result—an abstraction, which neither documents the sitter's appearance nor tells us about his character. It is, perhaps, one of the most extravagant reactions to the 'portrait as realist document'.

Some other important examples should be quoted. Most intriguing are the self-portraits by Albrecht Dürer, who was principally active in Nuremberg, but whose journeys to Venice and the Netherlands kept him in touch with the main artistic events there. His series of self-portraits (Figures 48 and 57) are evidence of his perception of the variety of one man. In one he styles himself as a confident, composed gentleman; in another he becomes a kind of Christ-like figure. The latter is surely a sincere protestation about his desire to emulate Christ, for Dürer was a deeply religious man. Yet another self-portrait shows him as a witness to martyrdom.

Dürer grappled with the problem of the over-specificity of the realistic portrait by making many images of himself. Perhaps today we can make from the diversity of the self-portraits one complex but discernible character; perhaps not. As out-

FIGURE **57** SELF-PORTRAIT, Albrecht Dürer, 1498
Oil on wood, 52x41 cm, 20¼x16 in, Museo del Prado, Madrid

lined above, Rembrandt also painted himself many times in many guises, but it seems quite possible that in his late, wisest works, he was aiming at an accurate portrait which also had the advantage of being unspecific in certain ways. These great artists were some of the few to be troubled by a problem which was almost of their own devising. Most artists working in what one might term the 'age of realistic portraiture' (from about 1500 to about 1850) seemed to aim at little more than a realistic yet flattering image of their sitter, which grew easier to achieve in the years following 1500, as the techniques required became more available to everyone. After 1500 most first-class artists working in any of the main centres of art were able to produce a 'speaking likeness' at will.

THE PORTRAIT IN THE AGE OF PHOTOGRAPHY

It takes a revolution to change the habits of centuries. The revolution that brought an abrupt deviation in the history of portraiture was the invention of photography.

There are few disagreements about the basic facts of the development of photography in its early stages. What principally concerns us here is the availability of the photographic portrait. As one might expect, the portrait was one of the principal subjects for early photographers. Since the new medium was advertising itself as possessing previously undreamt-of documentary accuracy, the photographic portrait was naturally in heavy demand—as were pictures of exotic sites to which few could hope to travel. For the first time one could have reasonably cheaply 'automatic' views of the pyramids, of heads of state *and* of oneself and one's wife. After a few years when the daguerreotype reigned supreme, factory-like production took over and better-off people left calling cards with their portraits on them (Figure 58) known as 'cartes de visite'.

For painters who saw their art as being principally reproductive, the invention of the photograph was a shock. The words 'From today painting is dead' were supposedly spoken by Paul Delaroche, the Salon painter. They were certainly not prophetic, for painting took on a new life, partly because of the challenge provided by what at first appeared to be a rival medium.

Certain styles in the photography/painting relationship have been clearly defined. Photographers, many of whom had been trained as painters, initially made images which employed the compositions, subject-matter and poses of painting. It was only after a period that the new medium took on its own style and produced its own masters. By that time, the painters had adopted certain of the attributes of the photograph.

Photographic and Painted Portraits

It is instructive first to make a brief comparison between a photographic and a painted portrait. I will then discuss the major novelties introduced into painted portraits through a direct relationship with photography, this being principally visible in the work of Edgar Degas. My reason for concentrating on the painted portraits rather than the more numerous photographic ones will become clear below.

In 1848, a few months before his death, Frédéric Chopin, pianist and composer, was photographed (Figure 59). This is the only surviving photograph of Chopin, whose portrait was made many times in paintings, drawings and engravings—even on his death bed.

The most important artist to paint Chopin was Eugène Delacroix, with whom Chopin was extremely friendly. Delacroix painted his sitter, not alone as one

FIGURE **58** CARTE DE VISITE (visiting card), Disderi, 1860
Photograph of the Prince and Princess de Metternich, 8·5x5 cm, 3¼x2 in, Bibliothèque Nationale, Paris

might expect, but with Georges Sand, his friend and companion of several years, the cigar-smoking, trouser-clad writer who despised the conventions of society and conducted her many love affairs with little regard for what the public thought. This double-portrait was at some time split into two portions. That showing Chopin (Plate 22) is now in the Louvre, while the fragment bearing the image of Georges Sand is in the Ordrupgaard Collection in Denmark (Figure 60). Despite the fact that Delacroix's painting of Chopin is no longer in its original form, I think it still provides a viable comparison with the late photograph.

The photograph shows him clearly ill, with hair dark enough to be black, his features in an anxious scowl. He is posed uncomfortably, even by the standards of the medium which required sitters to remain still for up to two minutes. He looks cramped as if cold or shivering. The photograph has done its work as documentation. Delacroix's painting also has certain documentary aspects. Because it is in colour it can tell us, for example, that Chopin's hair was brown, as were his eyes. Yet, since the painter is, unlike the camera, not simply a lens, we see Chopin as Delacroix saw him. The portrait was painted quickly. In places it is almost sketch-like, the sitter's hair constructed by means of a few dashing strokes, almost like a run on the piano. One might describe it as an impromptu. There is no mistaking Delacroix's view of Chopin. The colour of the background sets a mood which is both rich and contemplative. In short, Delacroix shows a man who was capable of doing what Chopin did. The photograph shows Chopin as he was at one moment, but that moment bears no relation to the portrayal of

FIGURE **59** PHOTOGRAPH OF FRÉDÉRIC CHOPIN, L. A. Bisson, c.1849
20x14 cm, 8x5½ in

FIGURE **60** GEORGES SAND, Eugène Delacroix, 1838
Oil on canvas, 79x57 cm, 31x22½ in, Ordrupgaardsamlingen, Copenhagen

anything more than a physical shell—and a sick one at that. This was the limitation of a medium which pre-eminently documented physical appearance.

There are certain conclusions which we can draw from our comparison. The most obvious is that Delacroix had greater freedom of interpretation than the photographer. It was to be some time before the portrait became an equally creative art form in the medium of photography. At this time, however, we are able to see clearly that the tendency was for the painter to create an ideal or abstraction—to generalize—while the photographer seized the particular.

In the early days of photography there was discussion, in intellectual circles, about the degree of realism obtainable by the new medium, but soon the case had been won and photography was accepted as being a medium of startling veracity. As it showed the public at large just how horses *did* gallop, so it demonstrated the extent to which supposedly 'realistic' artists had altered the facts of vision (either consciously or unconsciously) to produce more 'artistic' effects. Painting came to be seen as a thoroughly interpretative medium; and Delaroche's supposed words can be interpreted to mean, 'From today *realistic* painting is dead.'

The invention of photography ultimately had the effect of releasing the painter from the need to reproduce visual reality, since this function was adequately carried out by the camera. The flood of photographic portraits also had the effect of imbuing the painted portrait with an increased social status but, ironically, with a decreased credibility as a realistic medium. In the hands of first

FIGURE **61** MARGUERITE DE GAS, SOEUR DE L'ARTISTE, Edgar Degas, c.1862—5
Etching 3/4, 12×8 cm, 4½×3½ in, National Gallery of Art, Washington, Rosenwald Collection

class artists the portrait became just another format, with no especially realistic aims.

One more effect of photography was the distortion of that type of subject in art known as Genre. The word is used to describe a picture populated with 'types'—a lady and her maid, an old woman with a cat, and so on. The essence is that the people in the paintings and the paintings themselves represent a generalized set of circumstances. Photography could produce only flawed Genre scenes, since each person came to possess the specificity of a portrait.

The responses to photography on the part of painters were extremely varied. One of the most 'concerned' of artists was Edgar Degas. He was a collector of photographs and is known to have taken photographs himself. He was also the artist who reacted most intelligently to the new medium and whose portraits most singularly bear the stamp of photography. One can cite numerous examples of photographic resemblances in his work in general, but it was never more crucial than in his handling of the portrait.

From early in his career Degas made tiny portrait etchings which are clearly related to the small daguerreotypes or tintypes which were then so fashionable (Figure 61). Yet this was the least important of the innovations he made in the realm of portraiture. Some of them were highly instrumental in extending the range of the portrait and increasing the 'art' of it to the detriment of verisimilitude.

Degas' 'tintype' style, mentioned above, conformed to the classical style of

FIGURE **62** ESTELLE MUSSON, MADAME RENÉ DE GAS, Edgar Degas, 1872
Oil on canvas, 65x54 cm, 25½x21¼ in, Musée du Louvre, Paris

PORTRAITS

FIGURE **63** PLACE DE LA CONCORDE (Vicomte Lepic and his Daughters), Edgar Degas, c.1876
Oil on canvas, 79x118 cm, 31x46½ in, ex-Gerstenberg Collection (destroyed), Berlin

portraits. The sitter was usually tightly-framed, and there can be no doubt about the subject of the piece being no more nor less than the appearance of the sitter. Other Degas portraits alter the portrait form substantially. One, for example, of the artist's sister-in-law Estelle Musson (Figure 62), shows her as if seen through the lens of a camera, with a vase of flowers looming immense in the foreground. The vase is freely painted, out of focus, while the sitter's face is the part of the painting rendered in the tightest detail. There is a distinct change in the nature of the portrait. In what other portraits to this date had the sitter taken second place to a vase of flowers? What other painting had given such homage, not to the reproductive faculty of the photograph, but to its latent stylistic traits?

Degas, in other paintings, delights in the bizarre effects of the new medium, as well as in its excellences. His *Bureau de Coton* of 1873 (Plate 23) and his *Place de la Concorde* (Figure 63), painted about two years later, show two distinct reactions to photography's tendency to translate the Genre subject into a group portrait. The first shows the office of the artist's brothers in New Orleans. The brothers Degas, Achille and René and their business acquaintances are shown. There can have been few less formal group portraits. In fact, the painting is as much Genre as portrait, as much narrative as both. It has, I suppose, an ancestry in Dutch group portraits of the seventeenth century showing numbers of men who belong to the same company. Degas' group are unified by their concern in common—cotton—its texture, and its market value. Despite the rigidity of the

FIGURE **64** CHANTEUSE DE CAFÉ (COFFEE-HOUSE SINGER), Edgar Degas, c.1878
Pastel and distemper on canvas, 53x41 cm, 20¾x16¼ in, Fogg Museum, Harvard University, Bequest—Collection
of Maurice Wertheim

composition, the painting is a milestone in the history of portraiture since it chronicles, not an extraordinary event, but an everyday scene.

The point is that Degas has been influenced by the formal aspects of photography rather than by its reproductive ability. This is perhaps clearer when we study his *Place de la Concorde* (Figure 63). In his *Bureau de Coton*, Degas produced a beautifully proportioned and precisely detailed interior. If it had been a photograph, it would have been taken with a large plate camera, in a carefully posed session. As a painting, it is no less formal because of its photographic aesthetic; it is a classic composition as if conceived in the life room. His *Place de la Concorde* (Figure 63), however, makes no attempt at a balanced, harmonic composition, or at a unifying psychology for that matter. The composition is delightfully gauche. The bottom half of his figures is missing and, more shocking still, the man on the left is sliced off at the top, bottom and on the left, his legs becoming little more than a sliver of paint. The aesthetic is that of the instantaneous photograph (the 'snap'), not the carefully-posed exposure. The 'shutter-speed' seems to have been fast enough to capture the faces of Degas' painter friend Vicomte Lepic and his daughters, but not to detail their clothing, and the focus of the background is relaxed. There is a great deal of wit in evidence: the girl and dog (both in profile) are made to have a certain resemblance, as are the hats of the father and children; father's cigar and umbrella assume like angles. Yet the most important aspect of this painting is that which can also be seen, if less clearly, in the *Bureau de Coton*, that is, the way that the formal device adopted by the artist becomes the most important thing about the painting. Suddenly, we are in the realm of Churchill's jibe 'This is an example of *modern art*'. We are in the era when the sitter's image begins to assume less importance than the work of art as a whole.

One more example might suffice to demonstrate the tilting of emphasis between reproduction and formalism. It revolves around one of Degas' firmly documented uses of a photograph. From the small carte-de-viste photograph of Princess Pauline de Metternich and her husband (Figure 58), he made a larger but still small ($16 \times 11\frac{3}{8}$ in) study of a detail of the princess (Plate 24). He made some changes to the photograph, supplying a pattern to the wallpaper. Most important, however, he relaxed the precision of the detail on the princess's face, showing her blurred, as if looking round while posing too quickly for the camera to freeze her. The effect is a visual transcription of movement.

In all probability Degas did not make this painting as a portrait on commission for the princess; yet it is surely significant that he chose a portrait head on which to carry out his formal experiment. (One could quote other examples: his *Chanteuse de Café*, which exists in several versions (Figure 64), shows a portrait subject frozen into a study of the bizarre.) Why then, do we think Degas used a portrait head for academic research? My own view is that it was because we are more sensitive to any slight changes being made to a head than to any other part of the body (or any other object for that matter). Thus, as he 'blurred' the head, he could observe how both the realism of the head became diminished, and also how the facial expression altered under the influence of the blurring. This is extremely relevant to the making and interpretation of portraits in the twentieth century.

162

THE TWENTIETH CENTURY

Since about 1900 the formal basis of art has come to be at a premium, and its reproductive aspect less emphatic. Thus almost any kind of art that is not totally abstract can produce a 'portrait', provided that we do not expect it to look like a photograph or a Raphael. This presupposes that the artist is intent on portraying something other than the outward appearance of his sitter.

What, then, is the aim of the twentieth-century artist involved in making a portrait?

I am not concerned with the painter who seeks to produce no more than a larger, more status-laden, coloured piece of photographic realism. That type of image—the 'board-room portrait', for want of a better term—seems to me to deny itself the possibility of being either art or simple perception. Why is this? How can a portrait by Raphael, made in the first years of the sixteenth century, be construed as both high art and deep observation while a painting with the same aspirations made 450 years later is classified as being devoid of either?

When Raphael made his painting, art was unified with science in a very specific way, in that all scientific experiment was conducted by the use of the eye, sometimes aided by one or two simple magnification devices little stronger than spectacles. Scientific experiment—dissection, for example—was therefore visually ascertainable. There was no way in which scientific fact was invisible. The cell, atom, electron and other literally microscopic materials had not been discovered. Raphael's *Julius II* was as much a scientific illustration of the most up-to-date understanding of musculature and light effects as it was a cogitated work of art. It thus possessed a greater veracity, and a greater confidence in the face of visual reality than can any twentieth-century portrait.

Let us examine the dilemma of the twentieth-century portraitist. He exists in a world in which visual truth, as it was accepted in the Renaissance, has been undermined. Biochemistry is only one of the sciences which has proved that the perception of the eye alone is severely limited. The artist can no longer be also the most advanced scientist as was Leonardo. He is still, however, capable of producing his personal world-view, although this will not be true to scientific fact. His world-view is his style. The twentieth-century artist, when making a portrait, treats his sitter as an expression of one aspect of his style. Some of the results, while deficient as portraits in the Raphaelesque sense, are magnificent. Consider an extreme example:

Jean Dubuffet, *Bertélé écrevisse au sinus*

(Plate 25) There could scarcely be a better example of the modern artist's disregard of the conventional aim of the portrait. Dubuffet was deeply influenced by the kind of graffiti found in bus shelters and public lavatories, which allowed him to achieve images very different from those usual in portraits. His portraits, therefore, some of which have been lauded as having a telling 'truth', are conceived in a primitive way, the raw power (*art brut*) of the untrained hand having been deliberately courted by Dubuffet. Their 'truthful' quality depends mainly on a linear expression and is close to caricature.

It becomes clear, then, that the appearance of the sitter is changed according to the precepts of the artist's style. One might say that this was always the case, but it is particularly so in our century, in which art has come to be more overtly about art itself than about the ostensible motif.

There are, in addition, other factors of which we should be aware. Few twentieth-century artists, for example, have attempted to invoke in their portraits the discoveries of biochemistry or of the electron microscope, but every serious modern portraitist must have considered to some extent the theories of analytical psychology and of relativity. Just as increasing microscopic knowledge made it seem naive to paint a 'straight' photographic portrait, it is equally untruthful to omit consideration of the theories of Freud and Einstein. While some aspects of the latter may have considerable relevance to the development and interpretation of cubism and other forms concerned with the space/object relationship, Freud's studies embodying a new theory of personality have greater significance for our study of portraiture.

164

PORTRAITURE AND PERSONALITY THEORY

Every portraitist tries to convey his sitter's personality to some degree. If we look back at the earlier illustrations in this book, we will see different methods artists have adopted to convey this relationship between appearance and personality. What we have not yet considered is something which could actually be described as a theory of personality. Indeed, did such a thing exist before the revelations of analytical psychology, and did it affect portraits?

Personality theories certainly did exist at most times in history. In the West, the most widely accepted theory was that of the four humours. According to this, personality was governed by a kind of body chemistry, namely by the particular balance of fluids or 'humours' within the body. This theory, which originated in classical times, enjoyed popularity until the eighteenth century.

Ben Jonson's *Everyman in his Humour* (1601) is probably the best-known piece of literature demonstrating the theory, while Burton's *Anatomy of Melancholy* (1621) is the most complete treatment to originate in English. In the field of the visual arts, one can cite Dürer's engraving of *Melencolia I* (Figure 65) which demonstrates brilliantly the attributes associated with that 'humour'. His famous *Four Apostles* (Figure 66) were also considered by Dürer's contemporaries to be embodiments of the four temperaments. Less well-known is

FIGURE **65** MELENCOLIA I, Albrecht Dürer, 1514
Engraving, 24x17 cm, 9½x6½ in, British Museum, London

FIGURE **66** FOUR APOSTLES, Albrecht Dürer, 1526
Oil on wood, 204x74 cm, 80¼x29 in, Bayerische Stadtgemäldesammlungen, Alte Pinakothek, Munich

Cranach's pair of portraits of a man and his wife (Figure 67) which show in the background iconographical references to the temperament of each. Dr Johannes Cuspinian is characterized as a melancholic and child of Saturn, while his wife Anna is shown with attributes of the sanguine temperament.

Many more examples could be given, but these suffice to demonstrate the desire to express a sitter's personality according to a particular ideology. We can see that the expression of a humour would most often be accomplished by giving the sitter a particular attribute or pose, rather as an artist would furnish a particular saint with his identifying attribute.

Another prevalent theory was allied to the science of physiognomy. This had influence from ancient times until the nineteenth century. One particular facet of it is of interest to us here. It concerns the theory of animal comparison and is admirably illustrated in the book by G. B. della Porta published early in the seventeenth century. Here della Porta gives visual form to the basic tenets of the theory (Figure 68). It says, simply, that if a person's features resemble those of a lion, for example, then he will be powerful and courageous. These theories were certainly current in the Leonardo circle and it is probable that Andrea del Verrocchio characterized the military Bartolomeo Colleoni (Figure 34) in this way, the folds of flesh and set of his head giving some support to this interpretation.

In the early nineteenth century, Charles Bell published a book on artistic anatomy which still subscribed to the basic theory of physiognomy although in a rather more rational way. Although physiognomical theory has now fallen into disrepute, the theory of somatotypes which was developed in our own century still subscribes to the belief in a direct and obvious link between physique and personality (Figure 69).

The most important influence on the perception of the personality in the twentieth century has been Freud's psycho-analytic theory with its exposition of infantile sexuality. It was being developed in Vienna in the last years of the nineteenth century. Parallels have been made between Freud's concerns and the contemporary work of Symbolist artists—the interest of both in dream states, for example—and it is generally accepted that Freud and the painters were imbued with the same general spirit with neither having a direct influence on the other at this particular time. It was only around 1910 that artists began to know of Freud's works which were until then available only to specialists.

It is instructive, nevertheless, to examine the portraits painted in Vienna ('the city of Freud') in the early years of the twentieth century, for although any direct influence of Freud on the principal artists can, in the main, be discounted, the Viennese portraitists are probably the first to articulate concerns analogous to Freud's.

It was one of the central precepts of Freud's theory that the everyday behaviour of a person bore a different relationship to the psyche than had previously been thought to be the case. He and a few colleagues were experimenting with ways of gaining insight into this behavioural fundament. Eventually, they developed the technique which came to be known as psycho-analysis. For our interest in portraiture, two points are important. First, the individual is not aware of the functioning of a deeper level of the self which conditions behaviour (i.e. the 'Unconscious'). Second, a trained interpreter was necessary to read the expression of the unconscious in the individual's everyday life.

The comparison between the psycho-analyst and the portraitist has been drawn many times, but it was in Vienna soon after 1900 that it was most justified. Some painters displayed a more overtly sexual style, which can certainly be seen as a parallel to Freud's belief in the primal influence of the sexual impulse on human behaviour. Others seemed to place less emphasis on external appearance, not so much describing their sitters' physiques as attempting to map their personalities.

The most obvious example of the first category is Gustav Klimt who caused a scandal in 1900 with his painting *Philosophy*, which displayed naked bodies floating in space rather than the expected comforting images of Plato or Nietzsche.

Klimt's interpretation of his sitters emphasized their sexuality. Even if we were not aware of his drawings of women in abandoned postures, we might be able to infer them from the way he arranged his sitters. He controlled the image of the model almost as much as Dubuffet some forty years later, producing a portrayal which documents the projection of his own feelings on to the sitter, rather than their own personality. From about 1905 to 1907 a number of well-to-do women were painted in Klimt's Byzantine style. The hairstyles (invariably

FIGURE **67** DR JOHANNES CUSPINIAN AND HIS WIFE ANNA, Lucas Cranach the Elder, 1503?
Oil on panel, each 59x45 cm, 23$\frac{1}{4}$x17$\frac{3}{4}$ in, Collection Oskar Reinhart, Winterthur

PORTRAITS

FIGURE **68** MAN AND LION Giacomo della Porta, 1598
Woodcut from *De Humana Physiognomia*

170

swept on top of the head), costume (Klimt insisted that the dresses be especially made by the dressmakers of the Wiener Werkstätte, one of whom was his mistress) and mosaic backgrounds reflect the artist's interests rather than the sitter's. They express nothing of the personal preferences of the sitter. Instead each becomes a 'Klimt'.

This can be very clearly seen when we compare Klimt's portrait of Adele Bloch-Bauer of 1907 (Plate 26) with his painting of the same sitter made five years later (Plate 27). Each conforms to Klimt's style of the time. In one, Adele Bloch-Bauer's face and hands hover in a mass of golden facets and curves. In the later painting, Klimt's tastes have changed and she stands like a totem in front of his Chinese wall-hangings. In Klimt's work, the sitter scarcely exists in her own right. She has been obliterated by the personality of the artist.

This exemplifies the general trend of twentieth-century portraiture in the hands of first-class artists. As in the case of Dubuffet, the formal element commands the image. The sitters offer themselves to become works of art in the manner of the artist. The analogy with the psycho-analytic process has been made. As Freud wrote, 'The treatment makes heavy claims upon both the physician and the patient . . . the latter must make considerable sacrifices, both material and mental.' With Klimt as portraitist, the sitter's everyday aspect disappeared and was replaced by a commanding sensual presence, a dream figure. The portraits are examples of the predominance of the artist over the sitter. Klimt described himself more than his sitters, and the aspect of himself

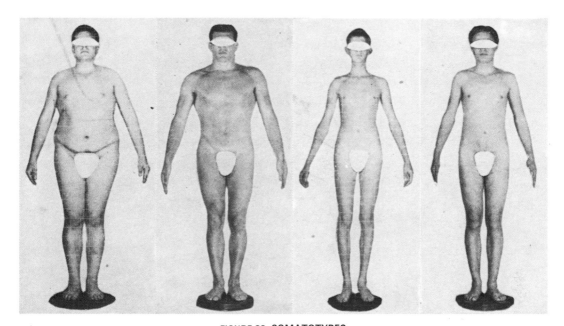

FIGURE **69** SOMATOTYPES
Photograph from W.H. Sheldon and S.S. Stevens, *The Varieties of Temperament*, New York (Harper) 1942, fig. 73

which came to the fore was that which also gained expression in his less public works, the sexual. In infusing his works with a greater sexual content, Klimt was in harmony with Freud's theory of the personality and with contemporary Viennese dramatists like Arthur Schnitzler whose *Reigen* (better known as *La Ronde*) was created in 1900.

Other artists appear to express different aspects of the cra, and, although parallels with the new psychology are hard to justify in a truly rational way, two developments can be discerned. One, that the artist now occupied a more decisive role in the making of the portrait than, say, one hundred years earlier. Two, as a consequence, the image of the sitter comes to be more a formal expression of the artist's style than in previous centuries. Because the artist seems to have found it less necessary to produce a particular 'type' of portrait (e.g. 'wedding' or 'academic'), he has greater freedom to concentrate on a prescribed type of image. Thus, many artists came to create portraits which are instantly recognizable as being Klimts, Dubuffets or Modiglianis.

In Vienna, another distinctive portraitist was Egon Schiele. Like Klimt, many of his drawings and paintings are overtly sexual in content. His expression of this subject-matter is always in the form of a portrait: the models whom he showed in sexually challenging poses always have their faces studied in recognizable detail. In Klimt's drawings they are usually more generalized. Thus it is perhaps to Schiele that we truly owe the portrait as an expression of sexually-based character.

Schiele portrayed himself in many guises, even masturbating (Figure 70), an act which was relevant to Freud's theory of repression. His self-images often

FIGURE **70** SELF-PORTRAIT MASTURBATING, Egon Schiele, 1911
Watercolour, 48x32 cm, 18¾x12¾ in, Graphische Sammlung Albertina, Vienna

172

proclaim him as a disturbed personality, releasing his self-obsession, loneliness and despair on to paper or canvas. His portraits of others convert them into so many Schieles (Plate 28); isolated in space, assuming twisted, restless or uncomfortable poses, they very much express a state of mind, often becoming credible as illustrations of hysteria or depression, the kind of neuroses which Freud hoped to explain and treat.

It would be quite possible to continue to plot the diversity of aims and styles with which the portrait has been invested in our own century, yet I think a few examples are adequate to exemplify the process, and I have selected them from works by Viennese contemporaries of Klimt and Schiele in order to demonstrate the variation which portraiture could attain now that the artist, rather than the commissioning body or sitter, was in control of the process; and now that 'photographic' reality was no longer expected.

Even before Schiele began to create his compelling series of portraits and self-portraits, another Viennese, Richard Gerstl had created portraits which were then among those which demonstrated the least concern with versimilitude. Like Schiele, he made many self-portraits, destroying many before his early suicide. At least one of his self-images shows him naked. When painting others he created poses which were simpler than Schiele's, with neither faces nor limbs emitting any real emotion, the emotional tone of the painting being achieved through his application of paint, and through extraordinarily intense colour. He was deeply interested in the expressive qualities of this technique and the

FIGURE **71** SELF-PORTRAIT LAUGHING, Richard Gerstl, c.1905
Oil on canvas laid on board, 40x30 cm, 15¾x11¾ in, Österreichische Galerie, Vienna

extant portrait heads show him testing the effects of different drawing implements and different media (Figure 71).

The outcome of this was the creation of some of the earliest portraits which might be legitimately called expressionist. His *Portrait of the Schönberg Family*, about 1907 (Plate 29), shows the lengths to which he took the expressive process. The sitters can be recognized only with considerable force of will but the artist's intense feelings for the family, his excitement in being with them, are chronicled in the free brushwork and livid dashes of red. That the artist's reactions to his sitters have become the real subject of his art is partially explained by the fact that the mother in the painting, Mathilde Schönberg, was to be Gerstl's mistress, leaving her family for a time to be with him.

Some years previously, in about 1905, Gerstl had been engaged in teaching Arnold Schönberg to paint. Schönberg is, of course, famous for his innovatory approach to music and less attention is given to his painting. He exhibited however at the *Blaue Reiter* exhibition of 1911 in the company of artists of the status of Kandinsky. From the point of view of the portrait his production (which is of limited technical quality) is of interest since the major part of it comprises faces and heads, whether described as *Self-portraits*, *Visions* or *Stares* (*Blicke*) (Figure 72).

In the latter we witness the use of the head for expressive purposes alone, any real likeness being irrelevant. The influence of Gerstl would seem to be obvious save that Schönberg maintained that it was he who exerted the influence. This

FIGURE 72 ROTER BLICK (THE RED STARE), Arnold Schönberg, 1910
Oil on board, 32x25 cm, 12½x9¾ in, Städtische Galerie im Lenbachhaus, Munich

statement has been interpreted as being not entirely accurate, because of the painful memories aroused by Gerstl. Whatever the facts, Schönberg's heads are experiments into the expressive possibilities of the head, experiments which were either influenced by or known to Gerstl.

All four of the above artists created works in which the place of the artist in the creation of a portrait was pre-eminent, and seen to be so. Their work, had it been followed at all, might well have signalled the death of the portrait as a medium designed to produce a likeness. Its real influence was, however, to diversify the possibilities of portraiture and to increase the variety of items which are acceptable as 'portraits'.

The final word in Viennese portraiture of the era belonged to Oskar Kokoschka. In common with the others mentioned above, he had a desire to plumb the psyche, to reveal the unconscious. But he paid greater attention to his sitter. He seems to have been able to do this within the limits of the genre, producing decent likenesses that one can compare with photographs. He himself commented on the viewpoint he adopted while making a series of famous and influential 'psychological portraits' in the years 1909 to 1914: 'People were living in security, but they were all afraid. I saw through their refined, baroque manners, and portrayed these people in their anxiety and suffering.' Kokoschka's portraits of this period seem to achieve a balance between description of the sitter's physique, and expression of the artist's insights. More careful about physical likeness than Gerstl and Schönberg, more able to perceive the personality of others than

Klimt or Schiele, he made some of the most successful portraits of our century. Their quality is that they achieve a kind of psychological rather than physical realism. In his concentration on the inner life rather than on the social or professional achievements of the sitter, in his assumption that refined behaviour might be no more than a veneer and that every personality is in some way disturbed or repressed, Kokoschka is perhaps the true Freudian portraitist (Plate 30).

From the time of Kokoschka, the idea that a good artist can recognize and express the inner life of the sitter has achieved greater currency. The portrait-painter has been given greater freedom than in any previous century to express his own vision of his sitter. Discontent is aroused when the artist's interpretation does not match that of sitter, commissioning body or public. It is easy to understand Lord Beaverbrook's statement about his portrait by Sutherland, 'It's an outrage but it's a masterpiece', and to grasp the idea that the same artist's image of Churchill could be at one and the same time a revealing portrait and an unsuitable one.

LANDSCAPE AND STILL LIFE

Robert Cumming

Section Three

LANDSCAPE

At the time of the Constable exhibition held in 1976 to mark the bicentenary of his birth, *The Times* published a memorable cartoon which is worth recalling, for it makes a good introduction to landscape painting.

It shows two bearded art enthusiasts, whose natural sympathies obviously lie with the avant-garde and more arcane manifestations of modern art, peering, catalogue in hand, at one of the world's greatest and best-known and loved landscapes, Constable's *The Haywain* (Plate 31). After what we assume to be several minutes of silence, one enthusiast turns to the other and says, 'Yes, but what does it mean?'

It is a good joke. Debunking modern art and the apostles who insist on seeing a profound meaning in a pile of bricks is bound to have popular appeal. When reproductions of Constable's *The Haywain* hang in thousands of homes and public buildings, and Constable country in East Anglia attracts visitors from all over the world for the sheer enjoyment of seeing the countryside at its finest, how absurd and intellectually pretentious to want to see it in terms of meaning. Meaning is best left to less obvious and less natural forms of art. But the subtlety of the joke is in fact that it rightly challenges such an over-simplified view, and causes us to ask, without pretension, whether beneath its obvious charm and skill, *The Haywain* may not contain some deeper meaning.

Constable would not have devoted his whole life to landscape painting, often with little encouragement, if he had in any sense considered his work to be meaningless. Yet at the time other painters thought his work was worthless. Contemporary members of the Royal Academy could not understand what he was trying to achieve, and a generation later John Ruskin, one of the greatest and most perceptive of critics, who was certainly not insensitive to landscape or landscape painting—he was a champion of Turner—dismissed Constable's work as revealing 'about as much as, I suppose, might in general be apprehended between them by an intelligent fawn and a skylark', in other words meaningless in any philosophical or intellectual sense. Constable himself teased his colleagues when he was finally elected to membership of the Royal Academy, an honour which he had long coveted, and the story of how he did it is famous and instructive. (The account comes from W. P. Frith's *My Autobiography and Reminiscences*, 1887, 1, pp. 237–8.) The painting referred to is *Landscape, a Study* (*Water Meadows near Salisbury*), an exquisite small oil painting of willows by a stream (Figure 73). Constable, by virtue of being a Royal Academician, had the right to exhibit automatically without submitting to the verdict of the Council who decided whether work by non-members should be shown or not. Constable was on the Council, passing judgement, and he slipped in his painting anonymously to see what the reaction would be.

When Constable was a member of the selecting Council, a small

FIGURE **73** LANDSCAPE, A STUDY (WATERMEADOWS NEAR SALISBURY), John Constable, 1830
Oil on canvas, 46x55 cm, 18x21¾ in, Victoria and Albert Museum, London

landscape was brought to judgement; it was not received with favour. The first judge said 'That's a poor thing'; the next muttered 'It's very green'; in short the picture had to stand the fire of animadversion from everybody but Constable, the last remark being, 'It's devilish bad— cross it' [Reject it]. Constable rose, took a couple of steps in front, turned round and faced the Council.

'That picture,' said he, 'was painted by me. I had a notion that some of you didn't like my work, and this is pretty convincing proof. I am very much obliged to you', making a low bow.

'Dear, dear!' said the President to the head carpenter, 'how came that picture amongst the outsiders? Bring it back; it must be admitted, of course.'

'No! It must not!' said Constable; 'Out it goes!' and, in spite of apology and entreaty, out it went.

We know a great deal about Constable for he was a prolific letter writer and his letters tell us much about his attitudes. He was ambitious in an artistic sense. He was not content for his work to attract just popular approval. He wanted recognition in artistic circles that his landscapes, particularly large works like *The Haywain*, were Art in the highest sense of the word, on a par with History paintings and the levels of moral and intellectual meaning that these carried in the early nineteenth century. He thought that History paintings had become tired and unoriginal, but he did not deny that the aim of art was to inspire and uplift the mind, as well as pleasing the eye.

In the preface to *English Landscape* (published 1830–2) he wrote:

> In art there are two modes by which men aim at distinction. In the one, by a careful application to what others have accomplished, the artist imitates their works and selects and combines their various beauties; in the other he seeks excellence at its primitive source, nature. In the first, he forms a style upon the study of pictures, and produces either imitative or eclectic art; in the second, by a close observation of nature, he discovers qualities existing in her which have never been portrayed before, and this forms a style which is original. The results of the one mode, as they repeat that with which the eye is already familiar, are soon recognised and estimated, whilst the advances of the artist in a new path must necessarily be slow, for few are able to judge of that which deviates from the usual course, or are qualified to appreciate original studies.

Later in a letter of 1834 he wrote, 'I have not to accuse myself of ever having prostituted the moral feeling of Art.'

We could tell our two cartoon enthusiasts that, for Constable, *The Haywain* was, in fact, full of meaning.

Landscape and still life painting seem such obvious activities for an artist. Nothing seems more commonplace than to pack up a box of paints and take a portable easel and canvas to some beautiful corner of the countryside, or to arrange a jug or plate and some apples in the corner of the studio; and appreciation of 'natural' beauty seems to be an integral feature of our ways of seeing. Constable is a useful reminder that even as late as the 1830s this was not generally accepted as true, and although the natural beauty of untamed nature, Wordsworth's Lake District for example, had fired both popular and intellectual imagination, the domesticated and agricultural nature which appealed to Constable, inspired little interest in others. If we take our own century few highly ambitious artists have considered landscape a worthy subject for their talents.

In his introduction to *Landscape into Art*, Kenneth Clark writes,

> People who have given the matter no thought are apt to assume that the appreciation of natural beauty and the painting of landscape is a normal and enduring part of our spiritual activity. But the truth is that in times when the human spirit seems to have burned most brightly the painting of landscape for its own sake did not exist and was unthinkable. [and]
>
> In the West landscape painting has had a short and fitful history. In

181

the greatest ages of European art, the age of the Parthenon and the age of Chartres Cathedral, landscape did not exist; to Giotto and Michelangelo it was an impertinence. (Epilogue, p. 229, 1979, paperback edition.)

In the opening pages of *A Writer's Britain—Landscape in Literature*, Margaret Drabble observes with clarity.

The desire to turn landscape into art seems a natural one, though it is hard to say precisely why painters and writers should labour to reproduce in print or words what each of us can see with our own eyes. But we all see differently and every writer's work is a record both of himself and of the age in which he lives, as well as of the particular places he describes. The appreciation of landscape has evolved over the years, and fashions in viewing scenery have changed . . . the word 'landscape' itself is relatively new, dating from the end of the sixteenth century: the word 'scenery' is even more recent, dating from the late eighteenth century. Both are so familiar it is hard to imagine how writers managed without them. Perhaps, as some believe, the ability to enjoy scenery for its own sake is as recent as the language we use to describe it. If this is a new faculty, how did it arise, and why did the English develop it to such a marked degree? (Thames and Hudson, 1979, p. 7.)

182

Both these books are essential reading for anyone seeking a deeper understanding of the relationship between landscape and artistic creation and inspiration, and it is worth observing that literary and painterly attitudes to landscape run in close parallel. I would like you to come back later to these two statements by distinguished commentators, to ask yourself to what extent you agree with the stand taken by them. Also, consider Lord Clark's identification of the 'greatest ages' of European art. You might well feel that there was also a 'great age' of landscape painting. Would you agree with my view that there *was* a 'great age'—the nineteenth century?

Ask yourself first: How 'natural' *is* the desire to turn landscape into art? And second: How true is it, for painting, that a landscape is a record of the artist and/or the age in which he lives, as well as of a particular scene? These last two questions are much more difficult to answer, and I shall raise them again later.

The general aim of this section is to enable the reader to visit an art gallery and look at landscape and still life painting with heightened visual perception and greater understanding. Hard work is necessary, but there is great satisfaction in peeling away successive layers of observable fact and interpretation without knowing when, or if ever, a final layer can or will be reached. In particular we will consider:

i. the structure and techniques of landscape and still life painting;
ii. their historical context;
iii. the artistic traditions to which they belong.

Already we have seen that landscape painting is a less obvious, and for the artist, a more hazardous occupation than we might at first assume. However, much of our own observation and appreciation of landscape and everyday objects is shaped by artists' perceptions and their determination to convince us of the truth of their own vision. Thus if we instinctively call a scene 'worthy of Constable' or a sky 'Turneresque', we are acknowledging Constable's claim that the artist could discover 'qualities existing which have never been portrayed before' and through art capture them in a form which remains alive and meaningful to subsequent generations. A subsidiary aim is to send you back to landscape and nature and art itself with greater perception and awareness of why you react as and when you do.

183

THE SCOPE OF LANDSCAPE PAINTING

I have deliberately made the point that landscape painting has had a 'short and fitful history' (and I should add that so has still life painting) since a visitor to a gallery of Western art is likely to observe that there are a great many landscapes and still lifes on display, maybe more than any other category of painting. We cannot draw any conclusions from mere numbers, however. More to the point is what was painted and when. It is important to observe the sheer range of landscape painting—from large and highly polished masterpieces such as *The Haywain* (Plate 31) (Constable referred to them as 'six-footers' on account of their size, and 'machines' on account of their ambitious construction and finish) to tiny sketches a few inches in dimension painted with only a few strokes, such as Corot's *The Roman Campagna* (Figure 74).

In spite of their physical variety and differing layers of meaning, all landscapes and still life paintings have one feature in common: they (like other types of painting) are flat, man-made objects, intended to be looked at directly, not by looking at a reproduction, colour illustration or television film, however good these may be. Size, nuances of colour, delicate effects of light and shade, or the texture of paint itself, which are often at the heart of landscape and still life painting, can only properly be perceived in front of the painting itself.

Let us suppose for a moment that we have been asked to join a committee whose purpose it is to select for exhibition a range of paintings of landscape and still life. I think we would find a fair measure of consensus among the art historians there. Most lists would probably contain specific schools of painters: Dutch seventeenth century and French Impressionists for landscape; Dutch seventeenth century again for still life, plus French Cubism, for example. There will almost certainly be a list of major names: for landscape Turner, Constable, Ruisdael, Monet, Cézanne—for still life Chardin, Matisse, Picasso, Cézanne. In spite of the repetition of certain schools and names under the heading of landscape and still life, I think there would fairly soon be agreement that for practical purposes we would need to divide the exhibition in two, or hold two separate exhibitions, one for landscape and one for still life. This is, in fact, what I shall do here. I will now concentrate on landscape and return later to a consideration of still life.

Some members of the committee will have names and schools on their list which are less familiar: Claude Lorraine, Richard Wilson, Caspar David Friedrich, the Norwich School, the Hague School. But in general I think we would find a concentration on works which are finished oil paintings, executed between the seventeenth century and the end of the nineteenth, with the greatest emphasis on artists of the nineteenth century. Thus we might well find that the committee's final list has instinctively reflected the summary of Clark's *Landscape into Art* (page 229): 'It is only in the seventeenth century that great artists take up landscape painting for its own sake, and try to systematise the rules. Only in the

FIGURE **74** THE ROMAN CAMPAGNA WITH THE CLAUDIAN AQUEDUCT, Camille Corot, c.1826–8
Oil on paper on canvas, 22×33 cm, 8½×13 in, National Gallery, London

nineteenth does it become the dominant art, and create a new aesthetic of its own.'

Such general agreement would be highly satisfactory, but then the troubles begin. Besides major oil paintings should they also include watercolours? If so, what proportion of the exhibition should they give to each? If they include highly finished watercolours, what about detailed pencil drawings? If watercolour sketches, should they not also include pencil and chalk sketches? In fact, ask yourself to what extent you would limit the choice to fully resolved works which we know were intended for exhibition, and to what extent open the door to preliminary works which are fascinating for the extra information they give about an artist's thoughts and technique? How far do we work chronologically? Do we take Clark's statement at its face value, or do we look back beyond the seventeenth century? Did the Renaissance really produce no landscape painting? What about the landscapes that appear in the backgrounds of religious and mythological paintings? Should we include these to give a run up to later developments? What about medieval painting; should there be some reference to classical antiquity? Indeed did the Greeks or Romans develop any sort of landscape painting? How far should we go into the twentieth century? Are there any twentieth-century landscape painters who we could claim confidently are worthy to rub shoulders with the great landscape painters of the past? If not, why not?

I have thrown a barrage of questions at you to indicate the sort of issues our committee is likely to face, and to show how difficult the process of selection is.

At the end of the day we must have a finite number of paintings which will look good when hung together and have some common link between them. And some members of the committee will want to extend the exhibition into very closely related and equally interesting subjects such as townscape and seascape.

Before committing yourself to an opinion you should hear the arguments on either side, and you would no doubt ask your committee members to spell out some general principles around which a coherent decision can be reached. As a matter of interest, however, why not attempt some answers now to the questions I have asked, and then return to the questions after reading this section and see whether your opinion has in any way altered. Ponder also the issues which our committee may not have raised. Although certain members may have fought hard for the inclusion of a particular artist, or a favourite picture, did anyone fight hard for the inclusion of a particular view or place regardless of by whom or when it was painted? I think that such an issue is most unlikely to have been raised, and this seems to me to be most significant. If we formed a committee to consider an exhibition of History painting or portraiture, I am fairly certain there would be a strong and legitimate demand that certain stories ought to be represented—the Judgement of Paris, for example—or that certain famous faces should be included. If I am right, why should there be this difference? Are we saying that in landscape painting the style and personality of the artist weighs in the balance much more strongly than a place, or than nature herself? How many great landscape paintings are really of nowhere in particular, in the sense that they make no claim to be an accurate depiction of a specific place from a specific viewpoint, in the way that a portrait is an accurate depiction of a specific face, and a History painting an interpretation of a specific story? Perhaps the answer to this question is one reason for the 'short and fitful' history of landscape painting.

186

GENERAL PRINCIPLES

I propose to establish some general principles about landscape painting by examining in detail two works by Turner, and by relating these principles to works by other artists and of different periods. I have chosen Turner, the great English Romantic artist of the early nineteenth century, because he is, for me, the most versatile and simply the greatest landscape painter of all. Not everyone will agree with this judgement, but I think that any fair-minded person would have to agree that the case is very strongly arguable.

Turner, *Crossing the Brook*

(Plate 32) The first painting I have chosen is *Crossing the Brook*, painted in 1815 when Turner was forty, and half-way through his life.

Format and size

It is a large painting, over 6 feet high and 5 feet wide (193 × 165 cm). It is important to register size since it has a crucial bearing on technique and the artist's purpose. Here we need to realize that we are faced with a studio work, a set piece of deliberately impressive size. A small oil sketch is tackled quite differently and presents different problems. It is notoriously difficult to sustain an idea and composition over a large area so that it retains a coherent and integrated image without collapsing into a confusion of unrelated images, or ceasing to have a focus of attention. How successful is Turner in achieving this visual cohesion? There is one aspect of this painting's format which is unusual for a landscape painting. Can you say what it is?

I think there is no doubt that Turner has produced a brilliantly taut and coherent image and I shall elaborate later on the way he does this. The unusual feature of the format is that it is vertical. Most portraits employ a vertical format, whereas the great majority of landscape paintings are horizontal. This must in part be a reflection of the dominance of the horizon in landscape (as opposed to the vertical stature of the human figure), and the fact that when looking at a landscape the head and eye scan naturally from side to side rather than vertically from the ground to sky overhead. A painter is not bound to use a horizontal format for landscapes, but it is clearly more natural and comfortable to do so.

The large size indicates that Turner is making a public statement, not a private observation. Small domestic interiors require small paintings, and many of the Dutch landscapes of the seventeenth century are small-scale for precisely this reason. Thus, sheer size indicates that Turner had a different setting in mind. This painting would only look comfortable in the large rooms of a noble house, or, as we might suspect here, on the walls of a Royal Academy Exhibition. This is exactly where Turner aimed to make a mark with this painting. He was a devoted

FIGURE **75** ST FRANCIS IN ECSTASY, Bellini, c.1475
Panel, 124x137 cm, 48¾x54 in, the Frick Collection, New York

member of the Academy (elected at the unusually early age of twenty-seven).
When first exhibited in 1815, *Crossing the Brook* attracted favourable attention
in the press (which would have pleased him) although it failed to sell.

Subject-matter
It may seem unnecessarily obvious to state that the subject-matter is a landscape,
but it is extremely important, given the date. By this I mean that the landscape
is not subsidiary to another subject in the way that it is in Bellini's *St Francis*
(Figure 75), or Claude Lorraine's *Cephalus and Procris Reunited by Diana* (Figure 76). In both of these landscape dominates visually but is not the motif. The
subject of Bellini's painting is St Francis receiving the stigmata. The landscape
plays a supportive role and carries a symbolic meaning to supplement the subject,
as we shall investigate later. In Claude's painting the landscape is subsidiary to
a literary theme which carries with it references to classical antiquity and Ovid's

FIGURE **76** CEPHALUS AND PROCRIS REUNITED BY DIANA, Claude Lorraine, 1645
Oil on canvas, 102x132 cm, 40x52 in, National Gallery, London

Metamorphoses, and the title is an encouragement to look for this connection. Turner's title is entirely neutral, and there are no classical temples or play-acting figures. What is the significance of Turner producing a more or less straight landscape at this date? If you recollect Professor Lynton's comments on the importance and status of History paintings in the eighteenth century (pages 47–8), you should be able to provide the answer, but before discussing it I am going to pose another question. Which country is represented in this painting?

I have asked this question of many different audiences, and the most frequent answer has been Italy; the least frequent answer, England. Curiously, both answers are correct. In overall visual terms the landscape is more Italianate than English (the left-hand tree is certainly not typical of England), the dry, hot, dusty light is far removed from the archetypal silver-grey moist English light of Constable's *The Haywain* (Plate 31). Yet we know from contemporary accounts that Turner's direct source of inspiration was the Tamar Valley in Devon, and in the painting there are details in the hills beyond and to the right of the bridge which are clearly Devon tin mines (not so easily discernible in a reproduction). Turner had made pencil sketches in a visit to Devon in 1813, and

FIGURE **77** HAGAR AND ISHMAEL, Claude Lorraine, 1646
Oil on canvas, 53x44 cm, 20¾x17¾ in, National Gallery, London

these were the basis of the present picture. Turner has deliberately cultivated an Italianate air so that spectators of the painting should be put in mind of Italy.

In the early nineteenth century serious painting was still dominated by the league table of subject-matter which placed History painting at the top and Landscape and Still Life at the bottom. Turner sought to raise the status of landscape painting in Britain, much as Sir Joshua Reynolds had raised the status of portraiture a generation earlier. Turner did this, not by convincing people that the hierarchy was wrong (that was Constable's approach and he failed), but by allying landscape with History painting. Turner's approach succeeded. At this period, he frequently painted landscapes which contained an illustration of or reference to classical literature, in the manner of Claude or Poussin. Here there is no such reference but the visual appearance is so close to a landscape by Claude that the connection has served to elevate its standing. The model is, in fact, Claude's *Hagar and Ishmael* (Figure 77) which Turner knew. This conscious manoeuvre by Turner may seem highly artificial, and of course it is. But it is important to grasp it since much landscape painting can only be understood correctly in this sort of context. Turner knew exactly what the conventions were regarding History painting and landscape and he was prepared to play the game to the limit within the rules. His contemporaries knew this and admired the skill with which he did it. By the end of the nineteenth century the rules had changed. Landscape painting had become as important to artists as History painting was at the beginning of the century, and it is this revolution which makes nineteenth-century landscape painting so important and so prolific.

Space and light

A landscape painter turns to nature itself—trees, hills, clouds, foliage, flowers— and has to contend with two features on which all successful landscape painting depends: space and light. There are many artists who have been successful at recording the details of nature but have failed to achieve an overall unity because they have been unable to depict a convincing recession of space or to convey the sense that all parts share the same source of natural light. Incidentally, it is worth observing that although we use one word 'landscape', the majority of paintings are fifty per cent about the sky. Constable observed, 'the sky is the source of light in nature, and governs everything' (Letter, 23 October 1821).

I propose to consider them separately, and deal first with space. Let us take *Crossing the Brook* (Plate 32) as our starting point once again, and ask whether Turner has achieved a convincing illusion of natural space, and if so, how has he sought to achieve it.

The horizon is drawn just under half way up the canvas, and this provides the high viewpoint. We look down into the valley in the far distance, and we also look down on to the brook in the foreground as though we are standing on a bridge. So, whilst observing the scene, we are not a part of it: to join the figures and the dog we would have to leave our 'bridge' and find a way down to the brook. By contrast examine Constable's *The Haywain* (Plate 31). What view-point has he taken and what is the difference of effect? I hope you can see he has taken a relatively low viewpoint and that by sweeping the riverbank across the front edge of the painting it offers an invitation to step straight into landscape. The carefully placed dog helps to emphasize the effect. Have a look at a selection of landscapes to consider the use of viewpoint, and ask why in some landscapes you are deliberately excluded and in others consciously invited in. (Turner uses both approaches at different times.) In some cases it is clearly appropriate for the spectator to feel barred from entry (Bellini's *St Francis*, Figure 75, for example); elsewhere, when the artist is trying to convey a sensation of the heat, light, smells and feel of the actual countryside, it would be inappropriate. Since Turner wishes us to think more about Claude and Italy than Devon it is probably appropriate that he should use a high isolating viewpoint. What viewpoint is used in Claude's *Hagar and Ishmael* (Figure 77)?

Turner achieves a consistent unity between our viewpoint and the placing of the distant horizon. Does he also achieve an even transition from foreground to horizon? I think the answer is 'Yes'. But he is extremely cunning in the way he does it. See how he keeps the foreground entirely self-contained within the hori-zontal band of the trees. He then concentrates our attention on the left-hand side of the picture, so that we look over this dark band immediately to the far distance, and it is our imagination which supplies the middle ground behind the trees. He then switches our attention to the right so that we look into a dark

191

FIGURE **78** MARTYRDOM OF ST SEBASTIAN, Antonio and Piero del Pollaiuolo, 1475
Wood, 291×203 cm, 114¾×79¾ in, National Gallery, London

tunnel in the trees, but now it is the far distance which is hidden and has to be imagined beyond the edge of the wood. Thus he sets up visual tension as the eye switches from the left-hand vista, where the eye is pulled into depth, to the right where it is pulled up short. In both cases he asks the imagination to supply the missing feature. This is a brilliant manipulation of space, and a virtuoso performance to bring such disparate and missing parts into a tight overall unity.

Achieving a convincing illusion of space in landscape painting caused artists difficulty for a long time and I would like to digress here to consider some of the solutions. Mathematical perspective with its structure of converging lines meeting at the vanishing point worked well with interiors and streets, but was less fitted to landscape where the straight line is notably absent and a broad horizon has no single vanishing point. Sometimes a mathematical structure was appropriate, as in Hobbema's famous *The Avenue, Middelharnis* (Plate 33), though

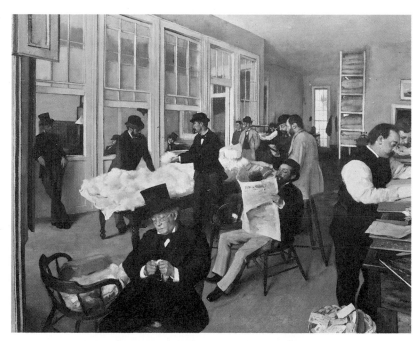

PLATE **23** PORTRAITS DANS UN BUREAU, NOUVELLE-ORLÉANS (Le Bureau de Coton)
(PORTRAITS IN AN OFFICE, NEW ORLEANS (The Cotton Office)), Edgar Degas, 1873
Oil on canvas, 74x92 cm, 29x36¼ in, Musée des Beaux-Arts, Pau. See page 160

PLATE **24** PORTRAIT OF PRINCESS DE METTERNICH, Edgar Degas, after 1870?
Oil on canvas, 41x29 cm, 16x11⅜ in, National Gallery, London. See page 162

COLOUR PLATES

PLATE **25** BERTÉLÉ ÉCREVISSE AU SINUS, Jean Dubuffet, 1947
Oil on canvas, 90x73 cm, 35½x28¾ in, Kunsthaus, Zurich. See page 163

PLATE **26** ADELE BLOCH-BAUER I, Gustav Klimt, 1907
Oil on canvas, 138x138 cm, $54\frac{1}{4}$x$54\frac{1}{4}$ in, Österreichische Galerie, Vienna. See page 170

PLATE **27** ADELE BLOCH-BAUER II, Gustav Klimt, 1912
Oil on canvas, 190x120 cm, 75x$47\frac{1}{4}$ in, Österreichische Galerie, Vienna. See page 170

COLOUR PLATES

PLATE **28** ARTHUR ROESSLER, Egon Schiele, 1910
Oil on canvas, 100x100 cm, 39x39 in, Historisches Museum der Stadt Wien, Vienna. See page 172

PLATE **29** THE SCHÖNBERG FAMILY, Richard Gerstl, c.1907
Oil on canvas, 89x119 cm, 35x47 in, Museum Moderner Kunst, Vienna. See page 173

PLATE **30** HANS TIETZE AND ERICA TIETZE-CONRAT, Oskar Kokoschka, 1909
Oil on canvas, 76.5x136.2 cm, $30\frac{1}{8}$x$53\frac{5}{8}$ in, The Museum of Modern Art, New York. Abby Aldrich Rockefeller Fund.
See page 175

COLOUR PLATES

PLATE **31** THE HAYWAIN, John Constable, 1821
Oil on canvas, 130x185 cm, 51¼x73 in, National Gallery, London. See page 179

PLATE **32** CROSSING THE BROOK, Joseph Mallord William Turner, 1815
Oil on canvas, 193x165 cm, 76x65 in, Tate Gallery, London. See page 187

PLATE **33** THE AVENUE, MIDDELHARNIS, Meindert Hobbema, 1689
Oil on canvas, 103x141 cm, 40¾x55½ in, National Gallery, London. See page 192

PLATE **34** HUNTERS IN THE SNOW, Pieter Brueghel the Elder, 1565
Oil on oak panel, 117x162 cm, 46x63¾ in, Kunsthistorisches Museum, Vienna. See page 209

PLATE **35** POPLARS ON THE EPTE, Claude Monet, 1891
Oil on canvas, 92x74 cm, 36¼x29 in, Philadelphia Museum of Art: given by Chester Dale. See page 210

PLATE **36** NORHAM CASTLE, SUNRISE, Joseph Mallord William Turner, 1840—5
Oil on canvas, 91x122 cm, 35¾x48 in, Tate Gallery, London. See page 212

202

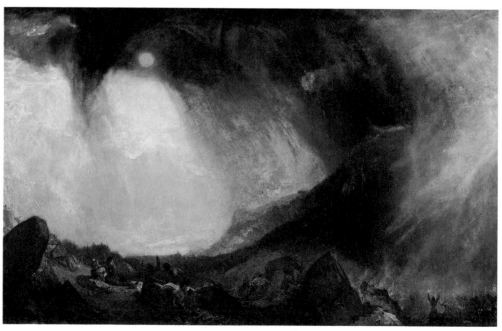

PLATE **37** SNOW STORM: HANNIBAL AND HIS ARMY CROSSING THE ALPS,
Joseph Mallord William Turner, 1812
Oil on canvas, 145x236 cm, 57x93 in, Tate Gallery, London. See page 214

PLATE **38** CHRIST IN THE HOUSE OF MARTHA AND MARY, Joachim Bueckelaer, 1565

Musée Royaux des Beaux-Arts de Belgique, Brussels. See page 252

203

PLATE **39** STILL LIFE, AN ALLEGORY OF THE VANITIES OF HUMAN LIFE,
Harmen Steenwyck, 1640–50?
Oil on oak, 39x51 cm, 15½x20 in, National Gallery, London. See page 254

204

PLATE **40** STILL LIFE, Gerrit Heda, c.1642
Oil on oak, 54x74 cm, 21¼x29 in, National Gallery, London. See page 254

PLATE **41** LE BOCAL D'ABRICOTS (THE JAR OF APRICOTS), Jean-Baptiste Chardin, 1758
Oil on canvas, 57x51 cm, 22½x20 in, Art Gallery of Ontario, Toronto. See page 258

206

PLATE **42** STILL LIFE WITH A PLASTER CUPID, Paul Cézanne, c.1895
Oil on paper, 71x57 cm, 28x22½ in, Courtauld Institute Galleries (Courtauld Collection), London. See page 260

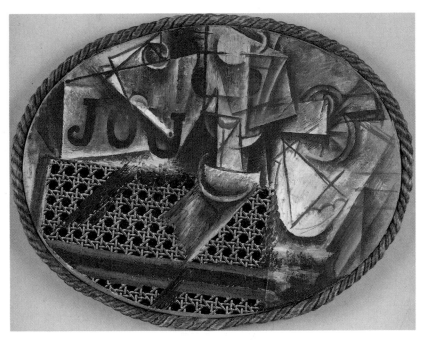

PLATE **43** STILL LIFE WITH CHAIR CANING, Pablo Picasso, 1912
Collage: oil, oilcloth, paper on canvas, with rope frame, 27x35 cm, 10½x13¾ in, Museum Picasso, Paris.
See page 263

PLATE **44** COMPOSITION WITH RED, YELLOW AND BLUE, Piet Mondrian, c.1937–42
Oil on canvas, 72x69 cm, 28½x27¼ in, Tate Gallery, London. See page 265

COLOUR PLATES

208

PLATE **45** LEMONS AGAINST A FLEUR-DE-LIS BACKGROUND, Henri Matisse, 1943
Oil on canvas, 66×50 cm, 26×19½ in, The Museum of Modern Art, New York. Loula D. Lasker Bequest. See page 265

FIGURE **79** THE BODY OF PHOCION CARRIED OUT OF ATHENS, Nicolas Poussin, c.1648
Oil on canvas, 114x175 cm, 45x69 in, National Museum of Wales, Cardiff, by permission of the Earl of
Plymouth Estates

this is obviously a special case. Many Renaissance artists who were extremely gifted in other ways, in the depiction of the human figure for example, failed to find a solution. Thus in *The Martyrdom of St Sebastian* (Figure 78) the background is rendered with wholly convincing accuracy, but the transition from foreground to horizon is fudged with a clumsy and artificial mound which divides rather than joins the foreground and far distance.

Within the framework of a solution designed to appeal to the formal intellectual mind, the most convincing solution was evolved by Poussin who used a road zigzagging backwards across the middle distance (*The Body of Phocion Carried out of Athens*, Figure 79).

A less intellectual though equally formal solution is employed by Brueghel in *Hunters in the Snow* (Plate 34) where he constructs his landscape on the basis of a series of carefully receding planes, each self-contained and slotting behind the other, in much the same way that a theatre designer uses a series of flats leading up to a back cloth to give an illusion of depth on a narrow stage. On each plane figures and objects diminish to the appropriate size, and by interlinking them with figures and trees Brueghel manages to lose some of the more obvious stagey effects.

Claude also uses a construction of successive planes but blends them further by two means. He uses a more elaborate pattern of animals, figures, tree stumps and bridges to connect the separate planes, and also uses light so that the planes are illuminated by sunlight or plunged into shadow. He also uses colour to define space. It is well known that warm colours appear to come forward and cool colours recede. Thus in *Cephalus and Procris Reunited by Diana* (Figure 76) the foreground planes are consciously warm in colour, the furthest distance cool blue and hazy in outline, the middle distance a careful balance between the two. Notice how Brueghel does not use colour in this spatial way; his far mountains are as clear in outline and of the same hue and tone as the foreground figures. Since nature herself knows nothing of separate planes, zigzag lines and perspective constructions, but does know colour, it is arguable that colour alone should be able to produce the illusion of space. This was indeed one of the stands taken by the Impressionists. Their acute sensitivity to tone and hue, and their ability to match them with the greatest accuracy with their pigments, did enable them to enhance the illusion of space, as in Monet's *Poplars on the Epte* (Plate 35).

In *Crossing the Brook* (Plate 32) Turner has also used the opposition of relative warm and cool tones to draw forward the foreground and push back the distance. Using another Claudian device, he frames his pale and silvery distance between two dark masses, and this too has the visual effect of pushing the pale area into a distant plane relative to the darker ones.

Space and light have, in a sense, to be created by a painter out of nothing. There is no real third dimension on a two-dimensional canvas; light has to be created out of coloured pigments and/or the juxtaposition of light and dark areas. We have discussed some of the difficulties in creating the illusion of space and the means by which this can be done. In some ways light creates even greater problems because it allows the painter greater flexibility and more choice.

Compare Constable's *The Haywain* (Plate 31) and Turner's *Crossing the Brook* (Plate 32) and ask: Which artist has tried to record observable effects of actual daylight and which has created a light effect which is essentially fiction and invented? The answer, surely, is Constable for the former, Turner for the latter. You may say you have seen light like Turner's, but I would seriously question whether you have seen such light in England: indeed, as I have already suggested, Turner did not want you to see or think of England.

The Haywain and *Crossing the Brook* represent two different approaches, therefore: the real and the invented, and each presents its own difficulties. For example, can you tell what time of day it is in Constable's painting, and what month? Such questions were of interest to Constable. We know that he made many oil sketches out of doors of the sky, on which he made a written note of both the weather conditions and the time of day. We know that he believed the sky was all important, for what happened in the sky dictated the pattern and quality of light on the land. He criticized the Dutch painters of the seventeenth century for not being truly accurate in this respect and for treating the sky more as a decorative backcloth than as a proper source of light. If you compare his Haywain with Hobbema's *The Avenue, Middelharnis* (Plate 33) you may feel he has a strong point (and note, incidentally, how Constable layers his clouds so that they recede in space whereas Hobbema's are simply piled vertically). Constable must also have known, as we all know, that light and the sky are constantly

210

shifting, both within the day and from day to day. To be truly accurate and realistic means somehow freezing a fugitive moment, not easy in a painting which may take months of work, and if a large studio painting is completed away from the scene itself. (*The Haywain* was painted in a studio in Charlotte Street in the centre of London.)

The proper title of *The Haywain* is *Landscape: Noon*. This is Constable's own title; he is very specific about the time of day but not about the season. If you examine a selection of his paintings you will find that time of day and season are more easily detected by what people are doing on the land than by light itself. Ultimately he has to make many generalizations about light although these are done with great brilliancy. Even if we cannot name the exact time of day he gives us a sensation of being in the open air, before nature herself, such as no one had done before, and not that many since. The Royal Academician, Henry Fuseli, a champion of literary paintings, once cracked a joke at Constable's expense saying that all he thought about in front of one of his paintings was 'his greatcoat and umbrella'. Fuseli simply could not appreciate that Constable considered that painting *ought* to be about such open air facts.

As Constable's point of view gained favour in the nineteenth century, the problem of accurately recording light, and not making do with generalizations, became of increasing concern to landscape painters, and elaborate schemes were invented to cope with the problem. Probably the most famous is Monet's houseboat which enabled him to paint in front of nature, and which was fitted out with racks to store a considerable number of canvases. He kept the same motif but as the light changed he would change his canvas for one which was closer to the new effect. Thus throughout the day and over a period of days he could hope to come near to producing a record of particular light effects (*Poplars on the Epte*, Plate 35 and Figure 80).

It is important to realize that something so apparently straightforward as recording an observed light effect is fraught with difficulty for the painter. Constable's method was in effect to stop the clock and make permanent what is necessarily a transient effect. Monet desired that his *Poplars* should be hung together so that the transience itself would be permanently recorded.

Why did Turner transform England's light in *Crossing the Brook* into Italianate light? We have already discussed one reason—the need to bring Claude to mind—and if you look again at Claude's *Hagar and Ishmael* you will see how close the two paintings are in the handling of light. The other reason lies in Turner's response to light which was quite different from Constable's since it interested him more as an emotional stimulus than as an observable fact. Most people have been affected emotionally by light, especially by brief and unusual phenomena— a brilliant sunset, a rainbow, the sudden clarity before a storm, a full moon. Light is also very evocative of a place, and places frequently have emotional associations, as I am sure Turner well knew while painting *Crossing the Brook*.

I would argue that any discussion of light in landscape painting necessarily leads to a discussion of emotional impact, and that the artist has three basic

FIGURE **80** POPLARS ON THE EPTE, Claude Monet, 1891
Oil on canvas, 92x74 cm, 36½x29 in, Tate Gallery, London

choices. First, he can record the light he perceives. Second, he can intensify light effects. This can be done in two ways. He can intensify all observed colours so that in the paintings they become richer and stronger; I think Monet does this to some degree in *Poplars on the Epte* (Plate 35). And he can intensify a light effect by enabling the spectator to look at length at something which is necessarily brief, for example a sunset or a rainbow. Third, the artist can create a light effect that can never be observed in nature. Turner's *Crossing the Brook* is such a case. The Italian light which he uses in the picture is not observable in England, and through it he manipulates our emotional reaction. Many twentieth-century artists have exploited this sort of effect.

Incidentally, when Turner painted *Crossing the Brook* in 1815 he had not been to Italy (he did not go until four years later in 1819). Italian light was something he only interpreted from other men's paintings. When he did reach the Mediterranean he found its impact far greater and more exciting than he could have imagined, and gradually his whole art changed. His celebrated late works like *Norham Castle* (Plate 36), are a flowing sea of brilliant colours and the visual expression of all that is implied by his dying words 'The Sun is God'.

Aesthetic context

All artists work in a climate of opinion that is generated by tradition, by academics and critics, patrons and collectors, and to some extent by their fellow artists. It is in this sense that I use the term 'aesthetic context'. Few artists can afford to work in total isolation, and even when supported by a private income, like Constable, there is an understandable desire to seek recognition from the most respected opinion of the day. Most artists need patrons and collectors to buy their work in order to live and keep on working, and so their work must usually make an appeal to the prevailing taste.

Which painting has more popular appeal today, Constable's *The Haywain* or Turner's *Crossing the Brook*? And which had more popular appeal in the early nineteenth century? You have probably guessed that I have posed the question because the two answers are the reverse of each other. *The Haywain* appeals today, but failed singularly to do so in 1821. *Crossing the Brook*, on the other hand, was well received in 1815, but now scarcely ranks as Turner's most admired painting. It succeeded on two levels. It appealed to the intellectual taste of the Royal Academy circle by virtue of its technical skills and cross-references to old master paintings; and it appealed to popular taste by virtue of its picturesque quality. *The Haywain* failed because there was no intellectual or popular aesthetic into which it easily fitted in 1821.

In the late eighteenth and early nineteenth centuries the 'picturesque' was a cult which was much discussed and written about. People made tours of England and Scotland and Wales to look at scenery that was deemed to be picturesque. Travel books with engravings were published both as guides and souvenirs, and between 1827 and 1838 Charles Heath published an ambitious series *Picturesque Views in England and Wales* in twenty-four parts with engravings based on watercolours which he had commissioned from Turner. There were no cameras but a conscientious traveller would take a 'Claude glass' to compose picturesque views. The Claude glass was a convex mirror of a dark colour which diminished the landscape reflected in it and gave it a brownish look like that of an old master painting. The traveller stood with his back to the landscape and moved the mirror about until what he saw reflected came as near as possible to looking like a painting by Claude Lorraine. A simple game, but a significant one, for it becomes clear that what Turner has effectively done in *Crossing the Brook* is elevate this activity to a high status without losing any of its popular appeal.

Not just any scenery was deemed to be picturesque, however. There had to be qualities of roughness and wildness, and the most popular areas were the Peak District of Derbyshire, the Lake District, and the appropriate regions of Scotland and Wales. I am sure the Tamar Valley in Devon also qualified in its own way. Constable's Stour Valley, with its flat lands, cultivated fields, agricultural activity, and general lack of wildness did not qualify. So although *The Haywain* may seem more picturesque today it did not fulfil the aesthetic criteria of the early nineteenth century. Indeed Constable had no instinct for the picturesque— he said of the Lake District that it oppressed his spirit—and this is another reason for the contemporary failure of his paintings. Turner at this date kept knowingly within the rules. Nonetheless it is a tribute to Constable's genius and the strength of his imagery that when we use the term 'picturesque' today it is probably his work that lies at the back of the mind rather than anyone else's.

The cult of the picturesque had already begun to decline by the 1830s, and Heath's publication failed to sell in sufficient numbers, causing him to go bankrupt. By then profound changes in attitudes towards the countryside were taking place as the growing population moved into urban and industrial centres. From being a part of everyday life and the main source of economic support the countryside became something outside daily experience for a great many people, a place of refuge, relaxation, and sometimes consolation, rather than a means of livelihood. In Britain the 1851 census showed that for the first time more people lived in urban areas than country areas. This gradual shift in social organization led to a gradual shift in aesthetic values as well, and beauty became associated not with wildness and roughness (of which town and industry provided plenty of examples though of a different sort) but with a harmonious and bountiful countryside. Constable died in 1837, and so did not live to see his paintings fulfil this popular need.

Turner, *Snow Storm: Hannibal and his Army Crossing the Alps*

(Plate 37) I do not propose to consider this painting by Turner, painted in 1812, in the same depth or with the same cross references as *Crossing the Brook*. But I shall use the same headings: Format and size, Subject-matter, Space, Light, Aesthetic context. I hope to confirm that they form five useful headings for analysing and discussing any landscape painting.

Format and size
This is another large painting and another public set piece in spite of the looser finish and handling of paint compared with *Crossing the Brook*. The conventional landscape format is used, though with exaggeration: it is unusually wide compared with the height, and this gives us a clue that exaggeration may be one of the key features in the painting.

Subject-matter
Although Turner hedges his bets in the title, do you think that the true subject-matter is the Snow Storm or Hannibal crossing the Alps? Consider the portions of the painting devoted to each: Hannibal's army clings to the bottom quarter of the composition and is not easy to see in detail even in the actual painting. Nor is it apparent that it is Hannibal's army but for an elephant silhouetted against the horizon at the bottom of the inclined shaft of light which connects the sun to the land. The storm predominates and occupies about three-quarters of the painting. Why, then, has Turner added Hannibal's armies when his real interest is the snow storm? The question will be considered again below under the heading 'Aesthetic context', but here I will give the account of Turner's first inspiration for the painting.

In 1810 Turner was staying with his patron Walter Fawkes at Farnley Hall on the edge of the Yorkshire Moors. The son of the family, Hawkesworth Fawkes, gives us this report (Thornbury, *Life of J. M. W. Turner*, vol. ii, p. 87 (1862)):

> One stormy day Turner called to me loudly from the doorway, 'Hawkey, Hawkey!—come here—come here! Look at this thunderstorm! Isn't it grand? Isn't it grand? Isn't it wonderful—isn't it sublime?' All this time he was making notes of its form and colour on the back of a letter. I proposed some better drawing block, but he said it did very well. He was absorbed—he was entranced. There was the storm rolling and sweeping and shafting out its lightning over the Yorkshire hills. Presently the storm passed, and he finished. 'There', said he, 'Hawkey; in two years you will see this again, and call it Hannibal Crossing the Alps'.

Space

Let me start with a rather oblique question: At what height should this be hung? I put the question since it is actually very important for this picture, and an important consideration for all landscape painting. We have discussed (pages 191–210) the importance of the viewpoint in a landscape and its integration with the horizon and intervening space. The fact is, however, that this carefully calculated effect can be ruined or even negated in a large work by hanging it at the wrong height so that your eye enters the painting at the wrong point. Please be conscious of this when you visit an exhibition or gallery and do not be shy about sitting on the floor and experimenting to find the right level. Many curators today hang paintings on a wall merely to make an attractive arrangement like postage stamps on a page and completely ignore this sort of consideration.

215

When it was shown at the Royal Academy Turner insisted that *Snow Storm: Hannibal and his Army Crossing the Alps* should be hung low so that the spectator's eye would be drawn to the centre of the storm, not held on a level with the soldiers at the bottom. In this way he intended, I think, that the spectator could be drawn into the picture visually and emotionally, and so share at least some of Turner's own experiences.

Light

Has Turner sought an accurate rendering of light, or has he distorted it for dramatic effect? The light is not totally artificial, but Turner has selected particular phenomena and then exaggerated and arranged them. The sun is veiled by cloud so that it takes on a sinister glow; the shaft of bright light and the dark clouds have been arranged within a swirling vortex which threatens to burst the confines of the painting. There are strong contrasts of light and shade, so that the clouds seem particularly threatening, and the light particularly forceful.

I think we can safely say that when Turner stood on the Yorkshire Moors what struck him was not the detailed appearance of the storm, but the general effect, and in particular the force of it and the drama of the light. Thus his immediate reaction (besides making notes of what he saw) was to respond emotionally, turning to thoughts of human destruction, the frailty of man in front of nature, the transience of great empires, the constancy of nature and so forth. I admit I am speculating about Turner's exact thoughts, but I regard this as a supreme example of light being intensified (but not transformed) for emotional effect.

Aesthetic context

Turner was aware that the Royal Academy would not be impressed by a snow storm *per se*, but might be by a painting that contained references to literature and antiquity. (He included in the catalogue some bad epic verse of his own to reinforce the point.) It is another exercise in elevating landscape painting to the category of History painting, and to judge from the newspaper criticisms, it succeeded.

Turner is consciously appealing to the aesthetic doctrine of the Sublime, just as he deliberately appealed to the picturesque in *Crossing the Brook*. In 1757 Edmund Burke had published an influential treatise entitled *Philosophical Enquiry Into The Origin Of Our Ideas Of The Sublime And Beautiful*, in which he distinguished between different types of aesthetic response and identified the supreme response as the Sublime. He also claimed that 'terror is in all cases whatsoever, either more openly or latently the ruling principle of the sublime.' This principle was widely known and respected, gaining great influence at the turn of the century, and a visitor to the Royal Academy would have recognised that Turner's painting was designed to trigger this specific aesthetic reaction. You may find it a somewhat odd definition of a reaction we might be more inclined to call breathtaking. The point I wish to re-emphasize, however, is that in looking at any painting there are two aesthetic contexts to consider: our own today, and that which is contemporary with the painting.

A visitor in 1812 might also have been aware that Burke had written in connection with painting of the Sublime: '. . . a judicious obscurity in some things contributes to the effect of the picture; because . . . dark, confused, uncertain images have a greater power on the fancy to form the grander passions than those have which are more clear and determinate.' Turner might be said to take this passage as a set of instructions, interpreting them with customary brilliance in the certain knowledge of giving people the type of beauty they expected and wanted.

As a footnote it is worth remembering that 1812 was the year of Napoleon's occupation of Russia and retreat from Moscow, so that the fate of empires was a topic of daily discussion. No visitor to the Royal Academy would have been oblivious of the topicality of the painting.

PRINCIPAL TYPES OF LANDSCAPE PAINTING

In the section which follows I am going to describe the major types of landscape painting, but before doing so there are a number of points I wish to make, to summarize what we have already discussed and to draw attention to other issues.

1. So far I have suggested five headings for investigating individual landscape paintings: Format and size, Subject-matter, Space, Light and Aesthetic context. However, there are two other considerations which I have not mentioned but which are important. The first is paint. I have already mentioned that a painting is a physical object as well as an image. Paint handling (or facture), that is, the way an artist applies paint, his brushstrokes, his choice of colour, his use of thin or thick paint, is extremely important both from a technical point of view and as an insight into an artist's intention. Artists whose approach is essentially objective or investigative tend to use a fairly dry, or hard edge, technique, with careful delineation of forms or carefully placed discrete (i.e. separate) brush strokes, each of which may be judged to correspond to something seen. An artist whose approach is essentially emotional tends to use a more intense palette, with thicker paint, greater generalization of form, so that one feels aware of colour and the gesture of the brush in the paint responding to an instinctive feeling, rather than a careful description. Please compare the difference in this respect between Constable's *The Haywain* and Turner's *Hannibal*. I hope the discussion of techniques which follows later will amplify this aspect, but I shall not go into it in detail since no reproduction, even in colour, either captures or conveys the actuality of paint handling. In an art gallery, however, please do not overlook it.

217

The second additional consideration is the use of the human figure in landscape, and the relationship between figures and landscape. Human figures and human activity tend to be a focus of attention, and because there is an instinctive identification with them they influence our reading of and interpretation of landscapes. As a worthwhile exercise we might take a number of landscapes and classify them into those in which nature may be said to dominate man, or man to dominate nature. Thus we might contrast Pollaiuolo's *St Sebastian* (Figure 78) and Bellini's *St Francis* (Figure 75); Turner's *Hannibal* (Plate 37) (where the focus of attention is the storm) and Constable's *The Haywain* (Plate 31) (where the focus of attention is the hay cart. It is in the stream at noon for two reasons: to rest the horses and to wet the wheels. In hot weather the wood shrinks causing the spokes to become loose and the wheel shrinks from its iron rims. The problem is solved by regularly soaking the wheels.)

Figures are also used to give a sense of scale: either actual, when the scale is true to life, or emotional where figures are made to appear much larger or smaller than a true to life rendering. Since nature often provides no artistically useful composition, figures are sometimes used to draw attention to a particular feature, and to draw the spectator visually into the painting. (The technical name for this use of the figure is 'staffage'.) Figures, perhaps unintentionally, can give a sense of period through their dress and poses. Left to herself nature is timeless; only man dresses up and imposes on nature a historical progression by the way he records it and by the way he shapes it. Observe at what point artists start to leave the human figure and activity out of landscape painting and allow nature to speak directly without the use of a human intermediary.

2. Analysing and classifying paintings can add enormously to our understanding of them and this is the justification for it. It can be a highly satisfying exercise, but do not fall into the trap of regarding it as an end in itself. It is all too easy to begin to want to treat paintings as documents in which everything has a factual explanation, so leaving nothing to the imagination and the emotions. However far you take your analysis a great painting should leave you with a sense of something beyond analysis and incapable of classification. One of the satisfactions for me of a painting like *The Haywain* is that it continually reveals some new previously unobserved factual detail, and surprises my imagination with its freshness and vigour. One of the reasons so many great twentieth-century artists owned (and own) works by Cézanne is that his paintings are like wells that give endless supplies of refreshing and stimulating water.

218   3. All classifications are to a degree artificial but there is plenty of evidence that landscape artists do think in terms of categories. Turner went further than any landscape painter before or since. Between 1807 and 1819 he published his *Liber Studiorum*. He described it as 'Illustrative of landscape compositions: Historical, Mountainous, Pastoral, Marine and Architectural' and it was both a theoretical treatise on landscape painting and a demonstration of how he, Turner, was master of all of them. Another example of classification is provided by the early nineteenth-century landscape painting of North America. Although the landscapes observed were entirely new they are recorded in terms of conventional categories—notably the sublime or the picturesque. The classifications I am using are not absolute or complete; merely useful and well recognized. Turner did not, of course, stick rigidly to his classifications and most great landscapes have elements of several categories. In this, however, I find much of the fascination. Do not think of the headings as pigeon holes; think of them rather as skeins of coloured wool. As the skeins are twisted and plaited together they form different patterns; thus the interest lies in detecting which skeins an artist takes and the manner in which he threads them together. The response of an artist of sensitivity and creativity to landscape and to art changes continually over his lifetime. Thus it is not possible to classify artists; it is only possible to classify individual works. If someone tells you that they like Turner, ask them which Turner.

4. I am conscious that my brief descriptions of categories try to compress a great deal of information into a short space. However, I think it is important to have an overall view of the major types of landscape painting, especially if you are hoping to confront a wide range of unknown works in an art gallery. If the brevity of the summary makes you want to know more, dispute some of the issues raised, or better still put the summary to the test in front of specific works, then I shall have fulfilled my main purpose.

5. There is no great landscape painter who has not responded with conviction to both nature and art. Many a gifted amateur has found that to be passionate about a landscape is not enough; there has to be an aesthetic and artistic framework which will provide sufficient common ground and general understanding between the artist and spectator, so that the artist can endow his personal passion with meaning. Similarly, there are many landscapes in which one admires the dexterity and ingenuity of the art, but in which one senses that there is no real or personal response to nature. Landscape painting of the highest quality should increase our understanding of art and send us back to nature with fresh eyes and increased awareness.

Symbolic Landscapes

Let us look again at the painting of *St Francis in Ecstasy* by Giovanni Bellini (Figure 75). As already indicated, this is more than a figure in a landscape. It shows St Francis of Assisi either at the moment he receives the stigmata—marks identical with the wounds of Christ's crucifixion—or offering a prayer of thanksgiving to God. Whichever interpretation is correct the relevant question here is why has the artist chosen to show this event in a landscape setting, and give such prominence to it? The setting does not accord with traditional accounts of the incident which say that St Francis was in retreat on Mount Laverna and that in his vision he saw a man like a seraph with six wings. Here there is no mountain, no seraph, and the background landscape is Venetian in character, rather than at the actual setting which is near Assisi. We could give a dismissive answer and reply that like Turner he was using the subject as an excuse to indulge in what he enjoyed most, but such an answer would be misleading and historically wrong. There can be no question of Bellini manipulating artistic genres, as Turner did, for the idea would have been quite unthinkable at that early period. Clearly he does have a very profound response to landscape and has closely observed its detail; and he may well have been a deeply religious man (although we can only guess at this). Observe the shadows and the direction of the fall of light. Is it not implied that St Francis is facing the sun, and that from this source comes his ecstatic and mystical experience? Further, is it not implied and shown that this source unites all things? From this we can fairly say that the landscape is in some sense symbolic: the light symbolizes the mystical experience, and God's presence is in this unifying light. Contemporary evidence does, I think, bear out this interpretation.

Behind St Francis (who is the protecting saint of animals and birds) is a structure with a flourishing vine. This is not placed there without reason. The structure implies the cross of the crucifixion, the grapes symbolize the wine of the eucharist; the vine is representative of Christ's words, 'I am the vine, ye are the branches.' Bellini is thus using the landscape in two ways to carry symbolic meaning: first through itself and the manner of its illumination (notice how everything is portrayed in a perfect or 'divine' condition); secondly, the objects within the landscape carry meaning according to a code which was well established and consciously used by painters: for example, the crane to the left of the ass is the standard symbol of vigilance.

Landscape and landscape-forms were frequently used in this manner in medieval and Renaissance paintings; they are surveyed (as are most of the categories) in Clark's *Landscape into Art*. Bellini's painting is a particularly spectacular example, a true miracle of a painting, and he has added to symbolism a deeply-felt mood and emotion, generated by his handling of light. Venetian painters were far more responsive to landscape light and mood than any other Italian Renaissance painters and they had a deep influence on subsequent generations of pioneering landscape artists, e.g. Rubens, Gainsborough, Turner and Monet.

220

Brueghel's *Hunters in the Snow* (Plate 34) does not use the symbolism of Bellini's *St Francis in Ecstasy*, but figures are used to portray winter as a scene full of incident which fulfils expectations of how a winter scene ought to look, and in particular what people ought to be doing. Although with hindsight Brueghel can be shown to be a key figure in making the first tentative steps towards establishing landscape as a genre in its own right, it should be noted that there is a long way to go before figures representative or symbolic of winter disappear from landscapes altogether to leave only snow, trees, hills and light as a satisfying and aesthetically fulfilling image of winter. Monet was the first to achieve such an image some four hundred years after Brueghel.

This sort of interpretation of landscape carries with it many satisfying pleasures and revelations although it is an exercise which must be done with care. Any such interpretation, to be valid, must be firmly based on historical context and fact. You may find you have your own imaginative interpretation derived from the imagery of the painting but be aware that this may have nothing to do with the artist's conscious use of symbolism. For example, I like to see God's presence in the rocks in Bellini's *St Francis in Ecstasy*, but I have to remember that this is *my* fantasy, not Bellini's symbolism.

There is a high degree of objectivity in Bellini's type of symbolism. It was the nineteenth century, with its rapid development of landscape painting, that added another, and highly subjective and personal type of symbolism. We have already seen one example in the late paintings of Turner where his luminous glowing light-filled landscapes symbolized a complex personal, and ultimately incom-

FIGURE **81** AUTUMN, Caspar David Friedrich, 1834?
Pencil and sepia, 19x27 cm, 7½x10¾ in, Kunsthalle, Hamburg

prehensible, mystical belief about the power and divinity of light (*Norham Castle*, Plate 36).

Van Gogh is another artist who uses landscape to express his own complex image of a worldly paradise in which the sun has a strongly symbolic role. The great German artist Caspar David Friedrich, a contemporary of Turner, also endowed his apparently factual landscapes with a deeply romantic and tragic symbolism in which dramatic light effects also contribute a strong sense of mystery. His *Autumn* (Figure 81) carries the following symbolism (I am quoting from Will Vaughan's exemplary Exhibition Catalogue of 1972):

> The path of life leads down the hill towards the town, which is probably a symbol of political ideal, is set in contrast with the high mountain, which symbolizes the Divine. The man, whose patriotic mission is identified by the coat of arms and the uniform, is making towards the town past the war monument beside the oak tree, while the woman, who is associated with the fir trees, chooses to climb a narrow path leading to the nearest peak, which has a cross on top of it. Friedrich characterises here the different relationship man has with politics and religion.

[Elsewhere Vaughan explains that the oak tree symbolizes a pagan and heroic concept of life, the fir tree the Christian ideal.]

LANDSCAPE

Factual Landscapes

The depiction of a town, or place, or a view which records nothing more or less than what is observed, is known technically as a topographical painting or drawing. I say nothing less since, in claiming to be an accurate record, it does not consciously select or alter details of the landscape; nothing more since it makes no attempt to add an aesthetic dimension by embellishing it with details or characteristics that would bring it within the ambit of any aesthetic theory, e.g. the sublime or the picturesque. Before the days of the camera, topographical drawings and paintings fulfilled an obvious commercial need, and many are things of great technical skill and beauty in their own right. Many of Canaletto's paintings are topography on a grand scale. There is an unbroken tradition of topographical painting which goes back at least to the fifteenth century.

Topography can be distinguished from landscape painting in that the latter is painted for aesthetic enjoyment and this is achieved by deliberately departing from observed fact. Many watercolours are more closely associated with topography than landscape.

Let us turn now to Hobbema's *The Avenue, Middelharnis* (Plate 33) and try to make a judgement as to whether this is an example of topographical or landscape painting. First-hand knowledge of the place itself would help, but nevertheless it is possible to observe the artist's treatment of the scene before venturing a conclusion. Remember, size is not a factor. In favour of this being topography is the very factuality of the scene in which avenue, distant town and even incidental details appear to be rendered with remarkable precision. Can such details be invented without accurate first-hand observation? On the other hand is it possible to believe that nothing of significance has been omitted, or that there is no conscious selection? It is on this last point that I feel uneasy. The quite exemplary good order of the landscape makes me wonder if Hobbema has not been very selective and has not undertaken some rearrangement of the landscape to make it fall neatly into three vertical sections, with the avenue in the middle, like an altarpiece with supporting side wings. If this were just topography why should the sky be painted with such obvious attention, and does the sky not lend a mood to the whole painting? Mood is not a concern of topography. Observe also the figures. Are these more than incidental, or are they included to give scale or act as staffage? The figure on the right is attending to some bushes. To the right of the avenue by the building a man and a woman are in conversation. A man walks down the avenue with his dog, presumably having come from the town, and behind him are other figures in the far distance. Hobbema's painting obviously treads a narrow line between topography and landscape, but my argument would be that on the evidence of the sky and the figures there is that further dimension which suggests this is more than a topographical painting; and if we turn to the painting's aesthetic context we shall find this supposition confirmed.

The Dutch were among the first to establish landscape painting as a genre in

222

its own right, and they gave topography an aesthetic dimension. That dimension was unique and very much a product of their age and politics. The United Provinces, the country we now call Holland, struggled for half a century to seize independence from the Spanish. When they succeeded, in the seventeenth century, and rapidly established themselves as a prosperous trading nation, they evolved particular types of painting: Dutch landscapes, still lives, and Genre painting. I will summarize the reasons for this. The Dutch did not want paintings that reminded them of Catholic Spain; thus, religion and mythological subjects were out of favour. New subjects had to evolve to fill the gap. Their Protestant religion encouraged a sober appreciation of simple observable fact, and the idea that this itself might have spiritual meaning. They appreciated landscapes which reminded them of their own country, for which they had fought and for which they had now won independence. In other words, political and aesthetic satisfaction walked hand in hand. In a prosperous country with little land as a store of wealth, painting was popular as an outward indication of prosperity. People bought paintings for investment.

The Dutch painters of the seventeenth century built on the example of Flemish artists of the sixteenth century like Brueghel. In his turn, Constable a hundred years later built on the example of the Dutch, their love of observable fact, but adding a different aesthetic dimension. *The Haywain* has no political or religious overtones (they were not necessary); Constable's opinion was that observable fact could form a valid aesthetic in its own right and that nature was rich in moral qualities. 'In such an age as this', he wrote, 'painting should be understood not looked on with blind wonder, nor considered only as a poetic aspiration, but as a pursuit legitimate, scientific and mechanical. . . . Imagination alone never did, and never can, produce works that are to stand by a comparison with realities.'

This is the first substantial claim to a purely factual and realist aesthetic which by the 1860s was the dominant fashion, especially in France. But this brings us to one of the major areas of development of nineteenth-century landscape painting which I shall consider again later under the heading '*Plein Air*' (page 244).

Ideal Landscape

Seventeenth-century Italy established a tradition which contrasts with the factual landscapes of northern Europe, and this tradition remained the dominant landscape formula until the flowering of *plein air* painting in the mid-nineteenth century. The two great originators of the style were Claude Lorraine and Nicolas Poussin, both French, but both working in Rome and the Roman Campagna.

Look again at Claude's *Cephalus and Procris* (Figure 76) and Poussin's *The Body of Phocion Carried out of Athens* (Figure 79). Obviously in neither case could I ask you to debate whether or not they are topographical. Although based on observed fact each are clearly composed according to an artificial plan

223

FIGURE **82** LA DANSE DES NYMPHES (DANCE OF THE NYMPHS), Camille Corot, 1850
Oil on canvas, 99x132 cm, 39x52 in, Musée du Louvre, Paris

224

or concept. In both, the artist has idealized or improved upon nature. Examine each carefully in detail and try to say how this idealization has been achieved.

Poussin's landscape contains a very firm framework of verticals, horizontals and connecting diagonals, and all the parts are arranged and selected to suit the format and composition of the painting. Light and dark are carefully contrasted to form artistic patterns, and the buildings in the background have the appearance of geometric blocks rather than actual structures. The landscape is also dominated by the presence of the figure and a deliberate piece of story telling. Much the same can be said about Claude's painting (with the exception of the buildings) although Claude's whole treatment is much softer and less rigid. His use of colour and light is more luminous and delicate. He does not use the sharp outline and bold contrasts of Poussin, but introduces sentimental details, such as the cows and the shepherd reclining on a tree stump. Both artists make reference to antiquity. Poussin's figures are in classical dress (and could almost be statues). Claude illustrates a story from Ovid's *Metamorphoses*.

The academic hierarchies of art and the dominant example of Italian High Renaissance postulated that idealism not naturalism was the end which artists should seek in all things, and the formal ideal landscape evolved to fit this order of precedence. We have already looked in detail at Turner's *Crossing the Brook*. There were many minor masters throughout Europe who used this sort of formula.

It was not easy to break loose from the formula and, as Constable found, academic acceptance of serious landscape which did not conform to this theory

FIGURE **83** SOUVENIR DE MORTEFONTAINE (MEMORY OF MORTEFONTAINE), Camille Corot, 1864
Oil on canvas, 66x90 cm, 26x35½ in, Musée du Louvre, Paris

of the ideal was impossible to come by. Corot, who produced exquisite and acutely observed sketches from nature, turned to the formula for serious landscape painting even in the mid-nineteenth century (Figure 82).

In his later work, he evolved a more realistic style, although one that has strong poetic and sentimental overtones. (*Souvenir de Mortefontaine*, Figure 83). He is quite typical of many nineteenth-century painters who clearly found it difficult to resolve the conflict in loyalties between the old idealism and the new realism. Even Cézanne, who pursued a relentless realism, looked back to artists like Poussin and stated specifically that he wished to preserve something of his ideal and heroic spirit in his landscape paintings. Seurat also blended modern ideas of factual perception with idealization *(Une Baignade à Asnières*, Figure 84) and it is perhaps only in the twentieth century that the tradition of the ideal landscape has disappeared altogether.

Pastoral Landscapes

The pastoral vision is based on the idea of an Utopia or the Golden Age in which man and nature coexist in perfect harmony, and nature delivers unending bounty for the satisfaction and pleasure of man. It has obvious attractions. It is not a vision to be believed in realistically, for it is wholly escapist. The tradition stems essentially from literature, rather than observed fact, and has for obvious

FIGURE **84** UNE BAIGNADE À ASNIÈRES (BATHERS AT ASNIÈRES),
Georges Seurat, 1883—4
Oil on canvas, 201x301 cm, 79x118 in, National Gallery, London

226

FIGURE **85** FÊTE CHAMPÊTRE (COUNTRY IDYLL), Giorgione and Titian, before 1510?
Oil on canvas, 110x138 cm, $43\frac{1}{4}$x$54\frac{1}{4}$ in, Musée du Louvre, Paris

FIGURE **86** THE MARKET CART, Thomas Gainsborough, 1786
Oil on canvas, 184x153 cm, $72\frac{1}{2}$x$60\frac{1}{4}$ in, Tate Gallery, London

FIGURE **87** A RUSTIC SCENE, Samuel Palmer, 1825
Sepia and gum, 17x24 cm, 6½x9¼ in, Ashmolean Museum, Oxford

228

reasons remained a popular theme for writers and painters. The key literary works, to which painters also referred, are Virgil's *Eclogues* and *Georgics*, poems written in the first century BC. In Book IV of the *Eclogues* Virgil describes a 'land where goats shall walk home their udders taut with milk, and nobody herding them; the ox will have no fear of the Lion. . . . Then grapes shall hang wild and reddening on thorn trees and honey sweat like dew from the hard bark of oakes. . . . The Soil shall need no harrowing, the vine no pruning knife, and the tough ploughman may at last unyoke his oxen.' In the *Georgics*, which is a poetic guide to practical farming, Virgil says (Book 2), 'How lucky, if they know their happiness/Are farmers, more than lucky, they for whom,/Far from the clash of arms, the earth herself/Most fair in dealing, freely lavishes/An easy livelihood.'

It is a tradition which is easily recognized and each century has produced its own version. The outstanding examples in the Renaissance are the paintings by the Venetian painter Giorgione and his followers (Figure 85). In the seventeenth century Claude and those he influenced combined the pastoral vision with the classical ideal. In eighteenth-century France, Watteau and Boucher produced a highly refined and elegant version, whereas in England Gainsborough produced a more rustic version (Figure 86). Corot's late landscapes which I have already mentioned under the heading of Ideal Landscapes are also touched, I think, by this idea of the pastoral Golden Age. It has persisted into the twentieth century in artists like Graham Sutherland.

One of the most famous and endearing of pastoral visions was created by Samuel Palmer in his brief Shoreham period (1826–37) (Figure 87). Significantly, this was a moment when the Industrial Revolution was beginning to drive labourers from the land into the city slums, and 'fair dealing nature' thus became more remote than ever. These works have a quite magical quality. Not only are they superb technically but their stylization and lack of dependence on accurate description is exactly suited to the pastoral vision, as is their unselfconscious naivety and simplicity.

Landscapes of Disaster

Film directors and newspaper proprietors are well aware of the popular appeal of disasters, and for about two hundred years there was a flourishing vein of landscapes which depicted catastrophe, sometimes on an apocalyptic scale. Like disaster films, the paintings seem to succeed with convincing brilliance or fail altogether and produce only laughable nonsense. We have already looked at one famous and successful example, Turner's *Snow Storm: Hannibal Crossing the Alps* (Plate 37), and the sophisticated argument that elevated terror and disaster to the highest level of aesthetic enjoyment, the doctrine of the Sublime. Turner was a master of this type of painting, risking his own life to obtain background material and experience, and producing a series of outstanding storms, avalanches and shipwrecks. Many other artists followed his lead, although what had been for Turner a matter of great seriousness, became in other hands overblown and sensational. John Martin, a generation later than Turner, is a good example of an artist who exploited the landscape of disaster to please popular taste for spectacular sensations (Figure 88).

The originator of this type of landscape was the seventeenth-century Italian artist Salvator Rosa whose work was highly thought of in England in the eighteenth century (Figure 89). Poussin, at times, married the idea with success to his ideal and classical style; indeed Sir Joshua Reynolds thought that only Poussin was successful with this type of painting. In his fourteenth Discourse he roundly criticized his contemporary Richard Wilson, advising him to stick either to proper History painting, or to landscape alone, and not attempt any more examples of landscapes of disaster.

Trompe-l'œil Painting

A *trompe-l'œil* painting is one that literally fools the eye into believing that what is painted is the real thing. Its success depends on technical skills and the right setting. This type of painting is in complete contrast to, for instance, Turner's *Snow Storm: Hannibal Crossing the Alps*. This painting was never intended to fool people into believing they were looking at the Yorkshire Moors

FIGURE **88** THE BARD, John Martin, c.1817
Oil on canvas, 127x102 cm, 50x40 in, Paul Mellon Collection, Yale Center for British Art

FIGURE **89** LANDSCAPE WITH TOBIAS AND THE ANGEL, Salvator Rosa, c.1660–73
Oil on canvas, 147x224 cm, 58x88 in, National Gallery, London

FIGURE **90** VIEW OF THE DECORATIONS OF THE VILLA MASER, near Vicenza, Italy, by Veronese, 1561

or Hannibal or a snow storm; nor was Constable's *The Haywain* intended to fool people into believing that they were looking at Willy Lot's cottage and the Stour Valley.

Examples of true *trompe-l'œil* painting are probably familiar to you: for example, a notice-board with letters, photographs and newspaper cuttings on it, which turns out to be a clever piece of illusionistic painting; a room with a painted interior giving the illusion of architecture, and windows or doors through which the landscape can be seen. The satisfaction of such painting lies in having being fooled, and then realizing the mistake and the skill of the illusion. Landscape and still life motifs are particularly suitable for this sort of game.

The history of *trompe-l'œil* painting goes back to antiquity, which provides us with the earliest examples of landscape and still life in Western European painting. Thus the Roman writer Pliny tells how the Greek artist Zeuxis (420–380 BC) revolutionized painting by introducing the technique of representing light and shade. There was a contest between Zeuxis and Parrhasios in which Zeuxis painted a bunch of grapes so realistically that birds flew towards it to eat them; but Parrhasios won the contest when he painted a curtain which Zeuxis himself tried to pull aside to see what was behind it.

The frescoes which decorated Roman villas frequently contained *trompe-l'œil* still lifes and landscapes and this particular tradition has continued uninterrupted and with scarcely any variation up to the present day. Spectacular examples are Veronese's decorations of the Villa Maser in Italy (Figure 90), and Bergl's decorations for the garden room at the Palace Schönbrunn in Vienna.

232

Artificial Landscapes

When we looked at Turner's *Crossing the Brook* we discovered that picture making according to a particular set of aesthetic rules was a conscious motive, but that this was allied to a very strong personal response to nature. Later I made the general proposition that landscape painting of the highest distinction achieves a balance between a response to a particular aesthetic framework, and a response to nature.

I now want to consider some examples where the artist has been concerned to produce landscape paintings which have the aim, *not* of producing a personal or serious statement about nature, but to be essentially decorative.

If you examine almost any phase of the history of landscape painting you will find many painters who have had decorative picture-making as their prime consideration. There is of course nothing reprehensible about painters who aim to decorate or charm, and a good and distinguished early example of a decorative landscape painting is Niccolò dell'Abbate's *Landscape with the Death of Eurydice* (Figure 91), painted in the mid-sixteenth century. A comparison with Claude's *Cephalus and Procris* (Figure 76), a painting which it foreshadows, makes the refined artificiality of Niccolò dell'Abbate's painting even more apparent.

FIGURE **91** THE STORY OF ARISTAEUS (Landscape with the Death of Eurydice)
Ascribed to Niccolò dell'Abbate, 1540–71
Oil on canvas, 189x237 cm, 74½x93½ in, National Gallery, London

Claude's painting was based on the observation of natural phenomena, especially light, whereas *Landscape with the Death of Eurydice* always was, and remains, more like a stage set.

In the eighteenth century Gainsborough and Boucher both produced landscape paintings which were based more on the imagination than on a close observation of nature herself. Gainsborough's *The Market Cart* (Figure 86) is a delectable image of how bounteous nature can be in the mind's eye, but never is in reality (see also page 228). But neither Gainsborough nor Boucher occupy one of the major places in the history of landscape painting, and perhaps it is worth mentioning in passing that Gainsborough's picture, painted in the mid-eighteenth century, the Age of Reason, does reveal an underlying observation and memory of nature which Niccolò dell'Abbate's does not have, and that it is this aspect of Gainsborough that was important for the next generation of painters such as Constable. The status of landscape grew in stature as the observation of natural phenomena grew in importance, and as a result landscapes which were consciously artificial and decorative never occupied a prominent place. The subtle shifts in balance between the respective importance of art and nature is something to be constantly looked out for and critically assessed.

Another type of 'artificial' landscape is that which investigates or comments on aesthetic issues. Such landscapes become important in twentieth-century modern art, when many artists have deliberately sought to break with the artistic traditions of the past and to emphasize new ideas about picture making rather than offer fresh observations and records of the natural world. It has been a major change and it is not surprising that as a result the traditional development of landscape painting has been checked. A good early example of the sort of paintings I have in mind is Braque's *Château de la Roche Guyon* (Figure 92) painted in 1908. He has used a landscape to experiment with viewpoints and to comment on the way that a painter records the three-dimensional world on a flat, two-dimensional canvas. If you feel that he might just as well have used a still life for the experiment, or that you are more conscious of a struggle to make the picture be something different from conventional landscape, and that any specific qualities in nature have taken a back seat, you have begun to grasp the point. The end result of these types of experimental paintings, which are an outstanding feature of early twentieth-century art, has been to establish an aesthetic in which artists are no longer bound to follow the general or specific appearance of the natural world, but can arrange shapes and colours purely to satisfy the demands of the painting. The delight has been to produce painting and sculpture which deliberately has an appearance quite different from anything produced by the natural world. Many twentieth-century paintings, landscapes included, must be looked at with these sorts of considerations in mind.

The great forerunner of this important change was one of the finest landscape and still life painters of all time: Cézanne. Many of his works have a tantalizing dual personality which displays: (i) his passionate response to nature and well-loved places, something which he wished his painting to convey and which depended on creating an illusion of the natural world; and (ii) his acute consciousness that a painting is an artificial object consisting of painted marks on a flat canvas, namely something independent of, and unknown to, the world of nature. Cézanne balanced these two aspects, but the next generation of painters began to create paintings which were overtly artificial in the sense described above, and which made no attempt to be convincing illusions. In the section on Still Life I shall look at one of Cézanne's paintings in detail and discuss this duality and you may find it helpful to have a look at that painting now (*Still Life With a Plaster Cupid*, Plate 42).

A very famous statement from the early twentieth century which has been enormously influential on other painters is Matisse's *Notes of a Painter* (1908). (Matisse's paintings consistently put the points made into practice.) He said, 'I cannot copy nature in a servile way; I must interpret nature and submit it to the spirit of the picture . . . to paint an autumn landscape I will not try to remember what colours suit this season, I will be inspired only by the sensation that the season gives me; the icy clearness of the sour blue sky will express the season

FIGURE **92** CHÂTEAU DE LA ROCHE GUYON, Georges Braque, 1909
Oil on canvas, 92×73 cm, $36\frac{1}{4}×28\frac{3}{4}$ in, Stedelijk van Abbemuseum, Eindhoven

LANDSCAPE

just as well as the tonalities of the leaves. My sensation itself may vary, the autumn may be soft and warm like a protracted summer, or quite cool with a cold sky and lemon yellow trees that give a chilly impression and announce winter . . . I want to reach that state of condensation of sensations which constitutes a picture.'

These matters are not easy to grasp at first reading, and of course many people find modern art difficult to comprehend. Sometimes the incomprehension arises because people fail to realize, or accept, that many modern artists have consciously changed the rules which define what a painting is, or the means by which it conveys its message. On the other hand, we accept that there can be many verbal languages, vocabularies and sets of grammatical rules (some having no connection with each other such as English and Japanese), so why should we not accept the same visually? I shall return to these points again in my remarks at the end of the section on Still Life.

236

WORKING METHODS

From time to time I have mentioned techniques and I would like to consider them further since they are of such great importance and consequence in landscape painting.

The most obvious and convenient place for producing an oil painting on canvas is the studio, and if it is of any significant size it is probably the only place. It can be left *in situ* to be worked on over a period of days, weeks or months. Materials are readily to hand, and the familiarity of the studio may well be advantageous in settling the artist's mind and concentration on the job in hand. In the studio a still life or portrait painter can arrange his composition and model as he wants them, with space and light finely adjusted. A History painter can bring together his working materials—preliminary sketches, figure studies and so forth in order to work on the final painting. In all these cases the direct source of inspiration, the motif, the materials, and the artist are conveniently self-contained in the studio.

This highlights the practical problem for the landscape painter. If he wants to paint on a large scale direct from the motif which is his source of inspiration there are immediate problems: transporting materials, leaving them over a period of time exposed to wind, rain, passing cattle, and a host of other uncontrollable conditions. It has been tried, and there are first-hand accounts of Monet isolated on a Normandy cliff-top or beach, his easel weighted down by stones to prevent it and the canvas blowing away, lashed by wind and rain, and Monet himself wearing a waterproof cape trying to hold his palette and mix his colours underneath it out of the way of the elements. In one of his earliest attempts at large-scale painting out of doors he was forced to dig a trench in the garden so that his canvas could be lowered into it to enable him to reach the top! Few artists have had Monet's fanatical desire to paint directly from the motif in such extreme conditions. On the other hand, he emphasizes the crucial point that if the landscape artist returns to the peace and quiet of the studio he loses direct visual and emotional contact with the source of inspiration: the artist must therefore evolve procedures which will enable him to maintain contact since, with a few exceptions, it is in the studio that major landscapes are painted. In many cases we have little knowledge of the step by step procedures used (some artists deliberately destroy the evidence) but there are four well-documented examples which are valuable to refer to.

Gainsborough

There is a famous account of Gainsborough's landscape technique by Sir Joshua Reynolds, told in his fourteenth Discourse. The Discourses were lectures which he delivered annually to the students of the Royal Academy. Reynolds upheld the conventional hierarchy of subject-matter, and exhorted his students to aspire to the highest achievements through the study of the Old Masters. Gainsborough cared little for this theoretical and academic approach. He painted landscapes because they pleased him, even though they ranked low in the hierarchy, and they remained stacked in his studio corridor neglected by his clients and the critics. Reynolds, however, was visually sensitive and not so dogmatic as to ignore the merit of these works. Hence in the fourteenth Discourse which he devoted to Gainsborough he said: 'I am well aware how much I lay myself open to censure and ridicule of the academical professors of other nations in preferring the humble attempts of Gainsborough to the works of those regular graduates of the great historical style. Yet we have the sanction of all mankind in preferring the genius in a lower rank of art, to the believers of insipidity in the highest.' His account of Gainsborough's technique is as follows: 'He even framed a kind of model of landskips on his table; composed of broken stones, dried herbs, and pieces of looking glass, which he magnified and improved into rocks, trees, and water.'

How do Gainsborough's pastoral and idealized vision of nature and his technique marry together? Do you feel surprised by Reynolds' account, or perhaps inclined to disbelieve it? Or given Gainsborough's response to nature, do you think it natural that he should in fact choose to turn his back on it as the direct source for landscape painting, and rely instead on his own imagination and literary sources? (*The Market Cart*, Figure 86.)

238

Constable

Although Gainsborough was an early source of inspiration to Constable (he said 'I fancy I see Gainsborough in every bank and hollow tree') Constable's technique was entirely different, and I hope you can see why. Constable's desire, not for poetic inspiration, but for the 'dewy freshness of nature', meant above all maintaining contact with nature even when working on his 'six footers'. Some of his early works are clearly painted from windows—convenient but limiting— and the fact that a work such as *The Haywain* (Plate 31) does maintain a sense of dewy freshness is a marvellous tribute both to his sensitivity and to his technical skill. The painting is inscribed 'John Constable . . . London 1821' itself significant: I think many people would presuppose a studio at least in Constable country, the Stour Valley, rather than somewhere so far removed as London. Behind the painting lie many small studies and paintings of the general region, sketches and cloud studies all of which point to a wealth of experience and memory to draw on in completing the final painting. But there are also many specific studies of the scene of *The Haywain* which have come direct from nature and been used to build up the final painting, culminating in a full-scale study executed in the studio in which the final design is worked out. Thus *Willy Lot's House* (Figure 93), a sketch from nature, has been used as the source for Willy Lot's cottage.

FIGURE **93** WILLY LOT'S HOUSE, John Constable, c.1810
Oil on paper, 24x18 cm, 9½x7 in, Victoria and Albert Museum, London

FIGURE **94** STUDY FOR A BOAT, John Constable, date unrecorded (early 19th century)
Chalk on blue paper, 9x12·6 cm, 3½x5 in, Courtauld Institute Galleries, London

LANDSCAPE

FIGURE **95** THE MILL STREAM, John Constable, 1813–14
Oil on board, 20×29 cm, 8×11¼ in, Tate Gallery, London

The boat on the right derives from a small black and white chalk drawing, again done from the motif, *Study for a Boat* (Figure 94). The first genesis of a complete composition was made in a tiny oil sketch of about 1813–14 (Figure 95), and by 1820–1 this had evolved into the full-scale study which is now in the Victoria and Albert Museum (Figure 96). As you can see, there is only one major difference between this study and the finished painting—the elimination of the figure on horseback in the foreground; and this was at one time included in the final painting before being painted out. This painstaking step by step evolution is typical of Constable and it can be traced in the case of all his great six-foot canvases. It is a reflection of his methodical temperament and provides a chain, which he never allowed to become broken, linking the finished work to those oil sketches which were done, or at least started and largely completed, in front of the motif itself.

Turner

You have already read an account of Turner's approach in the evolution of *Snow Storm: Hannibal and his Army Crossing the Alps* (Plate 37) from a few pencil notes made on the Yorkshire Moors. Would you expect there to be a series of sketches and studies between these notes and the final work, in the manner of Constable? If your answer is 'yes', you have misjudged Turner and

FIGURE **96** LANDSCAPE SKETCH (THE HAYWAIN), John Constable, 1820–1
Oil on canvas, 137x188 cm, 54x74 in, Victoria and Albert Museum, London

the nature of his inspiration. Turner's response was largely emotional and imaginative. A series of studies would have added no benefit.

As well as having an extraordinary imagination Turner was blessed with a remarkable visual memory. He was a prodigiously hard-working artist, and on his travels filled scores of tiny sketch books with meticulous and exquisite pencil sketches of scenes observed. There are also series of oil sketches and watercolours done from the motif, and drawings which map out an idea for a complete painting. Those for *Crossing the Brook* (Plate 32) are a case in point. But Turner's aim in his major oil paintings was to transform rather than transcribe what he saw, so that these sketches become a leaping-off point: he goes directly from the first sketch to the large painting, rather than developing the first sketch through a number of stages prior to the final painting. Many of the watercolour sketches which have the appearance of being done direct from nature were in fact produced in the evening, from memory, by the light of an oil lamp in a hotel bedroom. Towards the end of his life Turner undoubtedly exploited his ability to work directly on to the canvas without reference even to notes and preliminary studies. There is a celebrated account of his using 'varnishing days' (the day before an exhibition opened on which artists were allowed to add a few finishing touches to their paintings after they had been hung) to complete his paintings:

> . . . the picture when sent in was a mere dash of several colours. . . . The managers knew that a picture would be sent there, and would not have

hesitated, knowing to whom it belonged, to have received and hung up a bare canvas, than which this was but little better. . . . Etty was working at his side and every now and then a word or a quiet laugh emanated and passed between the two great painters. Little Etty stepped back every now and then to look at the effect of his picture, lolling his head on one side and half closing his eyes, and sometimes speaking to someone near him after the approved manner of painters: but not so Turner . . . he never ceased to work, or even once looked or turned from the wall on which his painting was hung. A small box of colours, a few very small brushes, and a vial or two were at his feet, very inconveniently placed; but his short figure, stooping, enabled him to reach what he wanted very readily. In one part of the mysterious proceedings Turner, who worked almost entirely with his palette knife, was observed to be rolling and spreading a lump of half transparent stuff over his picture, the size of a finger in length and thickness. As Callcot was looking on I ventured to say to him, 'What is that he is plastering his picture with?', to which enquiry he replied 'I should be sorry to be the man to ask him.' . . . Presently the work was finished: Turner gathered his tools together, put them into and shut up the box, and then, with his face still turned to the wall, and at the same distance from it, went sidling off without speaking a word to anybody, and when he came to the staircase, in the centre of the room, hurried down as fast as he could. All looked with a half-wondering smile, and Maclise who stood near, remarked, 'There, that's masterly, he does not stop to look at his work; he *knows* it is done, and he is off.'

Monet

One of Monet's solutions to overcome the distance between the motif and the studio was to take the studio to the motif by painting from a boat, as we have already mentioned. In fairness, he was not the first person to do so, but characteristically Monet pursued the idea with greater single-mindedness and concentration than anyone before or since. However, in so doing he presented himself with another problem. His floating studio enabled him to work long hours on a single work, but this merely pointed up the speed with which natural landscape changes. The artist working in the studio from sketches and memory can isolate and maintain a particular moment or effect of light. Not so Monet in his floating studio, and he could not ignore the appearance of nature which he was so dedicated to pursue. Hence his use of the series of canvases, which I mentioned earlier (page 211). Other stories, which if not wholly true are certainly indicative of what people expected of him, recall him purchasing the poplars to prevent them being cut down before he had finished painting them, or removing young

FIGURE **97** CLAUDE MONET ON THE PATH LEADING TO HIS HOUSE AT GIVERNY
Photograph Musée Marmottan, Paris

leaves from a tree because it had inconveniently started to sprout whereas when he started his painting it was leafless.

Given the importance of the fully resolved complete oil painting (which I will elaborate on further in a moment), Monet's ingenuity is a useful reminder of two things: first, the practical problems of making direct experience of nature the subject of landscape painting; and second, the interdependence of what an artist would like to do and the material available to him.

Monet's final solution was to construct a landscape which would be wholly under his control and place a studio at the centre of it. This he did with his garden at Giverny, some eighty kilometres north-west of Paris on a tributary of the Seine (Figure 97). The construction of the garden occupied exactly half his life and dominated the last twenty years of his painting, the series of water-lily paintings being the best known. The garden is quite small, totally self-enclosed, richly stocked with plants and visually dominated by colour and water. Monet at one time had eight gardeners working daily, and ultimately had three studios in the garden in which to work. The garden has now been restored to its appearance when Monet worked there, and is open to the public. For anyone interested in Monet's work and the problems of landscape painting I would strongly recommend a visit, since it is, I suppose, the ultimate solution to the sort of problem we have just discussed. I am not sure Constable would have approved, but he might have acknowledged the thoroughness and dedication. It is also the point at which landscape and still life meet, since in the end it is difficult to know whether the garden is best described as landscape or an infinitely variable bunch of flowers.

Plein Air Painting

Plein air painting means open-air painting, and it is used in two senses. The first relates to a painting which gives the *sensation* of being painted outside in the open air (even though it was painted in a studio), and the second describes a finished painting executed primarily in the open air (as against a painting executed in a studio).

Constable was the great pioneer of the idea that a landscape should communicate what he called 'dewy freshness'. After his death the leadership in *plein air* painting passed to France and was taken up by the artists of the Barbizon School, who in the 1840s formed a small artistic colony in the forest of Fontainebleau, south-east of Paris. The leading artist of the group was Théodore Rousseau. Although his main works were done in the studio, and have a highly romantic view of nature, he believed essentially in recording the facts of nature as he saw them, avoiding use of the human figure. He did not want to comment on the relationship of man and nature. He wanted nature to speak for herself.

Of the two paintings, Rousseau's *The Forest in Winter at Sunset* and Ford Madox Brown's *Carrying Corn* (Figures 98 and 99), which do you consider most fulfils the *plein air* spirit in the sense of giving the feeling of being outside. Rousseau's work was completed in the studio (note its large size); Brown's small panel was initially worked on in the open air, and then abandoned because he found it too difficult and there were too many distractions and interruptions. I shall leave the conclusions to your judgement, adding that it is important to distinguish between an artist's aims or claims, and the actual result.

Rousseau was known as the 'Grand Refusé' because of his constant rejections by the French Salon where ideal landscapes continued to reign supreme. Only towards the end of life did his paintings win acceptance in official artistic circles (though it should be mentioned that all the Barbizon painters had a following of discerning collectors, notably the Americans).

Plein air painting reached its fullest expression with the work of the Impressionists. They united both meanings of the term by producing finished works which vibrated with the sensations of natural light, and, using new materials, were begun and in many cases completed out of doors in front of the motif.

Watercolours and Oil Paintings

I am sure you are aware of the basic differences between oil paintings and watercolours, but in the following paragraphs I would like to concentrate your attention more closely on the techniques and on the role and status of watercolour paintings.

244

FIGURE **98** THE FOREST IN WINTER AT SUNSET, Pierre Étienne Théodore Rousseau, 1845−6
Oil on canvas, 162·5x260 cm, 64x102½ in, Metropolitan Museum, New York

FIGURE **99** CARRYING CORN, Ford Madox Brown, 1854−5
Oil on panel, 20x28 cm, 7¾x11 in, Tate Gallery, London

LANDSCAPE

Watercolour uses the same colour matter or pigment as oil paint, but the colour matter is bound together by gum arabic, which is soluble in water, whereas with oil paint it is bound together by oil, traditionally linseed oil. Watercolour is quick-drying, relatively thin in consistency, and requires an absorbent base, usually paper. For all these reasons it is really only suited to small-scale work. Oil paint is slow-drying, relatively thick and juicy in consistency, and requires a non-absorbent base, usually wood or canvas primed with a suitable substance. Oil paint can be used equally for small and large-scale work.

Watercolour can be opaque or transparent, although it is at its best when used in thin translucent washes which allows light from the white paper to shine through. Both paper and the watercolour medium are delicate and liable to fading and damage. Alterations to the image are difficult because the paint is water soluble even when dry, and translucent washes reveal underlying structures. Oil paints are at their best when used to give richness and brilliance of colour, either by building up rich impasto or in glossy glazes, but oil paint can be removed with a knife or rag, and can be moved and manipulated over a period of days by brushes, knives and fingers. Once dry it can be built over with subsequent layers of paint. The end result is extremely tough and durable provided sound paint and good technique have been used.

Nowadays oil paint is readily available in tubes, factory produced in a vast range of colours. The tube and ready-mixed colours only came into being from the mid-nineteenth century onwards, by-products of industrialization. Until then artists had to grind their own colours with pestle and mortar as and when they required them, and store them in animal bladders, an inconvenient and messy procedure. Watercolours, on the other hand, were available already mixed in the familiar small pans and could be bought over the counter from the late eighteenth century onwards.

Given this background how would you expect watercolours to be used by artists? And which medium would an artist use to make the most ambitious and competitive statement of his abilities and his art?

I think the answers are fairly predictable. Watercolour paints and technique, small, portable and quick are ideally suited to the outdoor sketch executed in a few hours at most, recording an artist's immediate impression. The translucency of watercolour matches admirably the variety and delicacy of natural light. Most landscape artists have used watercolour in this way. Turner was the supreme master, but even in the seventeenth century Claude made watercolour sketches in monochrome in the Roman Campagna as preparatory work for his landscapes; van Dyck made exquisite watercolours from nature, as did Dürer in the early sixteenth century.

Oil paint, however, remained the most suitable medium for the full-scale work, by virtue of its flexibility and by being able to deliver the maximum visual impact in size and colour. It was also regarded as more difficult to handle, and therefore a better test of an artist's skill.

However, the ability of watercolour to match natural light led to the estab-

246

lishment in Britain from the eighteenth century onwards, of a strong tradition of full colour, fully resolved landscape watercolour paintings. These were more than sketches and the one example I have chosen, Francis Towne's *Ravenscragg with Part of Thirlmere* (Figure 100), shows how exquisite, subtle and complex they can be. I have juxtaposed a sketch by Turner, *Landscape Sketch* (Figure 101), which was executed rapidly, probably on the spot, so that you can compare the differences. Once established, the watercolour tradition had many followers among artists who specialized in the medium and among collectors, but it has always been something of a Cinderella. The Royal Academy would not give recognition to watercolour painters, so they formed their own professional and exhibiting organizations, notably The Old Watercolour Society founded in 1804. And curiously, although there have been a few masters of watercolour paintings outside Britain—Cézanne is the prime example—no other country developed the tradition.

Sketches

I think I should say a brief word about sketches, since I am conscious of using the word in two different ways: one, to describe a rapidly executed, on the spot record of first impressions and significant details (Constable's *Willy Lot's House* (Figure 93) is a good example); and two, the working out of an imaginary idea or composition on which the finished work will be based (Constable's sketch for *The Haywain* (Figure 96), is an example). Both have a looseness in the paint handling and a spontaneity which the finished *The Haywain* lacks. Museums now happily exhibit all three, and collectors would not spurn any one of them. It is, I think, relevant to ask you which you would rather have. Certainly there is a substantial body of opinion which would rather have one of Constable's large sketches, considering his finished paintings to be overworked and without the virtue of spontaneity.

As an alternative to this view, let me quote from a letter written by Constable in 1824 after *The Haywain* was shown at the Paris Salon. He said he found the French critics 'very amusing and acute—but very shallow and feeble. Thus one—after saying "it is but justice to admire the truth—the colour—and general vivacity and richness"—yet they want the objects more formed and defined'. In other words, the criticism was that the painting was not sufficiently worked and finished!

Between these two opinions lies an enormous aesthetic change. It is important always to remember that the preconceptions we bring to a painting may be quite different to those of the date when the painting was first shown. Along with the demise of History painting in the nineteenth century went the fall from grace of elaborate, formal, highly finished works in which no brushmark could be seen. The rise in landscape painting and eventual favour of *plein air* artists and Impressionism meant that spontaneity not finish became the principal virtue.

FIGURE **100** RAVENSCRAGG WITH PART OF THIRLMERE, Francis Towne, 1786
Watercolour and pen and ink, 15·5x23·5 cm, 6x9¼ in, Fitzwilliam Museum, Cambridge

Modern taste tends to applaud work whose paint handling displays, not hides, the activity and state of mind of the artist. Neither Turner nor Constable would have considered exhibiting publicly their sketches. The Impressionists were the first to do so in the 1870s, and this provoked a howl of protest from the critics and the public.

Remember that on page 185 I asked if watercolours and sketches should be included in our exhibition. What is now your opinion?

Palette

Let us compare Constable's *The Haywain* (Plate 31) and Monet's *Poplars on the Epte* (Plate 35) with two questions in mind. What is the palette used by each artist? In other words, what is the range of colours used by each; and what colours has each used for their shadows and highlights? Perhaps I could add a third question, and that is, who gives the more faithful transcription of natural appearances? Your list should show Constable using essentially what we call earth colours: browns, blacks, greens, dull reds, also white. Your list for Monet should show the range of rainbow colours, red, orange, yellow, green, blue, violet, with no earth colours or black. Until the mid-nineteenth century, the range of pigments available to the artist was limited, with a few exceptions, to

FIGURE **101** LANDSCAPE SKETCH, EDINBURGH FROM ST MARGARET'S LOCH,
Joseph Mallord William Turner, 1801
Watercolour over pencil, 13x20 cm, 5x7¾ in, British Museum, London

those which could be obtained from natural substances, earth, rock, shells, insects, which were crushed and bound in oil for oil paint or gum for water-colours. In the mid-nineteenth century scientists began to synthesize new chemical dyes, initially from aniline, and this led to the manufacture of many new and much brighter colours.

Technically, therefore, the Impressionists like Monet had a very different background to Constable. They had convenient and easily portable paint in tubes; a new and lighter palette; and a knowledge of basic colour theory—the way we perceive colour and the physical effects of juxtaposing different colours—which had been developed in written treatises of the mid-nineteenth century.

Their adoption of a new palette was not arbitrary. Monet painted with a range of rainbow colours since this spectrum is the composition of light. Notice how he contrasts various yellows for highlights with blues and purples for shadows, whereas Constable contrasts white and black. Monet realized that optically his contrast produces a much greater vibration in the eye than black and white, and that this vibration is much more akin to the sensation experienced when we look at light and shade. Constable realized the limitations of black and white, and in one of his lectures said: 'When we speak of the perfection of art, we must recollect what the materials are with which a painter contends with nature. For the light of the sun he has put patent yellow and white lead—for the darkest shade, umber or soot.' In his later works you will find white pigment laid on increasingly thickly as he struggles with the problem. He had neither the pigments nor the theoretical knowledge to arrive at Monet's solution.

To my eyes it seems that Constable remains convincingly faithful to local colours: the greens of foliage, the browns of earth, the grey sky; but that Monet is more convincing in his overall envelope of light which gives to the whole painting a very precise sensation of light. Thus my answer to my third question would be that both are convincing in their own way, and within the limits of the conventions they adopt. No painter can reproduce nature. He can give us a convincing image of it only by laying down certain rules and conventions, and we will be convinced only to the extent that we are prepared to adopt them as well.

You should be aware of this when examining paintings in general, and in the case of landscape be alive to the changing palette from the mid-nineteenth century onwards; also to the fact that this changing palette requires you to accept new conventions of picture making.

When Lord Clark described the history of landscape painting as 'fitful' I wonder if he was not being somewhat unjust to what begins to emerge as a fascinatingly rich and complex genre. It may be young compared with History painting or portraiture, but it may yet have a long way to develop.

As a conclusion to this section may I refer you back to page 182 where I raised four questions, and restate the last two: How 'natural' *is* the desire to turn landscape into art? And, how true is it that a landscape is a record of the artist and or the age in which he lives, as well as of a particular place? You may not have come to a conclusion, but I hope you can now see that they are questions which lie at the heart of a discussion about landscape painting, and the fact that they may have no definitive answers is part of the fascination of the subject.

STILL LIFE

I am not proposing to discuss still life at the same length as landscape, for a number of reasons. In the first place, its historical development is more straight-forward, and I will argue that, apart from the twentieth century, it has remained a less influential genre. The fascinating rise of landscape painting in the nine-teenth century has no parallel in still life painting. It seems to me that still life subject-matter does not have the scope and potential of the other genres. As we shall see, still life can have something to say which is more than a descriptive list of its individual items, but still life does not have the ability to tell stories, as does History painting; to comment on human nature and individual personality as does portraiture; or to enlarge our relationship with the physical world we inhabit to the same extent as landscape.

In the second place, many of the basic ground rules that were established for looking at landscape painting can be applied with equal validity to still life painting, and I would like you to bear in mind again my five headings: Format and size, Subject-matter, Space, Light, and Aesthetic context. I shall use them again to discuss in detail a number of paintings which seem to me to occupy a key place in the development and definition of still life painting (although I shall not spell them out quite so obviously as I did with Landscape), and this will, I hope, give you a good point of departure for investigating the other still lifes you will come across in the galleries you visit. I shall not attempt to outline types, as I did for Landscape, nor discuss techniques, since, although relevant, I do not think they are issues which arise with such importance for a commentary such as this.

If you are unfamiliar with still life painting look through the illustrations I have selected and then let me pose two questions: The first is: how should we define a still life painting? The question probably brings to mind the familiar table-top arrangements of fruit and flowers, domestic utensils such as jugs, glasses and cups, books, candlesticks, loaves of bread, dead fish and game, with perhaps the addition of more bizarre objects such as a skull. But let me ask how you would classify a painting of a geranium growing in a pot, on its own? What about a painting from nature, for example a clump of primroses growing in a corner? Would game, a pheasant or a hare, be a still life if painted to appear alive rather than dead? I suspect most people would agree that the live hare and the clump of primroses fall outside the normally accepted definition of still life. In other words, and for whatever reason, we tend to accept still life as a very restricted genre, and the essential quality is that the objects are motionless and inanimate. The English term derives from the Dutch word *still-leven*, 'still' meaning motionless and 'leven' meaning nature. The French term is *nature morte*, and carries the same implications. Furthermore, this definition has not changed significantly, and this is a major difference from landscape where definitions and types have undergone enormous development. Perhaps it is also relevant to add that there are very few comparable parallels such as that between landscape and literature. The pastoral theme inspired operas, ballets and orchestral works such as Beethoven's 'Pastoral' Symphony, but I can think of no significant equivalent link between still life and literature, music or poetry.

This leads me on to my second question: Why should any professional artist of ambition or merit turn to still life rather than one of the other genres? There are three reasons that I shall put forward which, singly or together, may offer an explanation. Some artists have simply not been interested in excelling in the fashionable or historically important genres. Chardin is a classic example, revered now as one of the great painters of the eighteenth century. He never attempted History painting, yet how many people today are familiar with the work of van Loo, his contemporary, who then was revered as a major History painter?

The second reason is that few artists have concentrated exclusively on still life as they have with landscape. Chardin also excelled with exquisite domestic scenes; Cézanne was a master of landscape, still life, and portraiture, for example. The major exceptions are the Dutch who in the seventeenth century produced artists exclusively concentrating on still life, although as I shall explain there are special reasons for this.

The third reason is that still life painting has flourished in very special environments. It has flourished in those countries which have a strong tradition of accurate and detailed painting from life, such as the Netherlands (see page 254); and it has flourished when the prevailing concern in painting has been primarily with things seen and observed, rather than with flights of imagination or interpretations from literature. France in the late nineteenth century is a perfect example.

Bueckelaer, *Christ in the House of Martha and Mary*, 1565

(Plate 38)

Format and subject-matter
This remarkable painting is enormous, nearly 7 feet high and over 8 feet wide (171 × 250 cm). Spend some time examining the subject-matter and do so methodically. I suggest looking across the painting from left to right and in view of its richness, perhaps compiling an inventory on the way. On the left is a still life arrangement: kitchen utensils at the top hung on the wall; on the table another jug with cover, a two-handled vessel, a duck in a basket, clothes, a metal flagon with a handle, a haunch of meat on a dish, three glasses and two bread rolls. To the right of this is a distant scene through an archway in an elaborate architectural setting. There are six figures in an elegant interior wearing costumes contemporary with the date of the mid-sixteenth century. The architectural style can also be dated to around this period. The group appears to be conversing.

252

To the right of this, and in the foreground are three more figures, two female, one male, in front of a fireplace which has elaborate female caryatid supports. They are not conversing. The left-hand female holds a dead bird in a way that suggests that she is about to pluck it; the standing female holds a plucked bird and a side of meat on a spit; the male figure sits with his back to us. Thus there are three separate centres of attention and we need to ask how they relate together. There is an obvious realistic and rational link between the still life and the foreground figures, suggesting, albeit in a very mannered way, a kitchen and kitchen activity. But how does the background scene relate to this domestic interior? Let us consider this in relation to two of our headings:

Space and light

There seems to be a concentration on the foreground, mainly because of its expanse; it occupies about eighty-five per cent of the picture area; and the background scene is given a sense of distance by enclosing it behind an archway. Given its small size relative to its foreground it ought to appear distant, but there is no middle ground to make a coherent link, and what there is suggests that the overall distance between foreground and arch is not that great. The light effects are also curiously irrational. The direction of the shadows suggests light coming from the left and from a high point. It also suggests a hard and intense source of light which shows up detail, isolating objects rather than binding them together. The whole arrangement makes me think of a stage with spotlights, posed figures, and a backcloth.

253

I think it would be fair to say that the painting is a curious mixture of the rational and the irrational. There is no need to be disturbed by this since there is no rule which requires a painting to be realistic. Indeed the ability to suspend disbelief is essential in coming to terms with the visual arts.

Aesthetic context

Have I cheated by choosing as my first example a painting which is not truly a still life? In many respects yes, although I have reason for doing so. The left-hand third of the painting is undoubtedly a still life, but consider the following. The date of the painting is 1565, and still life was not recognized as an acceptable genre at this date. However, there was a demand for still life images and this painting is proof of that; it is not an isolated example. Furthermore, and this is important, the accepted artistic genres at this time were history, religion and portraiture. In view of this, how could a still life be made acceptable in terms of the artistic genres? I suggest by the artificial means of painting a dominant still life image and adding the pretext that the subject matter is religious: Christ in the House of Martha and Mary, the scene in the background. (Cast your mind back to the way Turner made landscape aesthetically acceptable in the early nineteenth century.)

For anyone with a taste for artificiality this gross contrivance is almost certainly an added source of pleasure. The mainstream of taste in the mid-sixteenth century was indeed for distortion, exaggeration and images of the impossible. This is also a consciously secular painting, painted for a commercial market, and for sale to a collector who appreciated contemplating material goods and the type of artistic virtuosity which depends on technique rather than imagination.

My main reason for including this painting is that it enables me to point from it in several directions, all of them relevant to the heading of still life painting.

It emphasizes the continuing tradition of detailed and meticulous realism in Northern painting, stemming from early Netherlandish painting, and passing through the Flemish School (of which this is an example) to the Dutch School of the seventeenth century.

It is a significant advance from earlier religious paintings in which still life images played a significant but subsidiary and symbolic role. For example the still life objects in Joos van Cleve's *Virgin and Child Enthroned with Angels* (Figure 102). (The grapes are symbolic of the Eucharistic wine and the blood of Christ. Cherries symbolize the fruit of paradise and reward for virtue; the pomegranate held by the infant Christ symbolizes chastity and the Resurrection.)

It points ahead to the establishment of still life as a genre *per se* in seventeenth-century Holland and also to the Spanish still life tradition which grew under the influence of Flemish painting (the Netherlands being ruled by Spain there were close artistic links).

254An interesting example of direct influence is Velasquez's *Kitchen Scene with Christ in the House of Martha and Mary*, 1618 (Figure 103) which, though small in size and much less elaborate, shows a direct influence in subject-matter and use of space and light.

Harmen Steenwyck, *Still Life*, Gerrit Heda, *Still Life*

(Plates 39 and 40). Before reading further please examine the two paintings in detail with my five headings in mind. In particular, consider what similarities there are between them; whether there is any significance in the objects chosen; for whom would they have been painted.

Similarities

They are similar in size and quite small. Both have a very shallow space which is articulated only in the immediate foreground where objects project out over the edge of the table. The space at the far edge of the tables (both of which are scarcely more than a plank wide) is very ambiguous. Both use a completely neutral background which is completely flat. Both use similar compositions with the taller objects at the back, or raised to make them more visible, and cloths hanging vertically at the front. Both use objects placed obliquely to lead the eye into the picture, and in both the still life arrangement is placed to fall below one of the diagonals. Both use a high light source and a cold hard light which emphasizes shadows and the surface detail of objects. Both choose objects with hard surfaces.

FIGURE **102** VIRGIN AND CHILD ENTHRONED WITH ANGELS, Joos van Cleve, 1515—25?
Oak panel, 85×65 cm, 33½×25¾ in, Walker Art Gallery, Liverpool

STILL LIFE

FIGURE **103** KITCHEN SCENE WITH CHRIST IN THE HOUSE OF MARTHA AND MARY, Diego Velasquez, 1618
Oil on canvas, 60x103 cm, 23¾x40¾ in, National Gallery, London

Dissimilarities

The chief dissimilarity is in the objects chosen. Heda chooses rare and luxurious objects; firmly wrought silver, elaborate glass, mother-of-pearl, a crab which is a luxury food, a Chinese porcelain plate (this was a very great rarity at this date, recently imported from China by the Dutch East India Company. Europeans were unable to manufacture porcelain until they discovered the process in 1710. Until then their ceramic production was confined to relatively coarse earthenware). Steenwyck chooses more humble objects, a shell, books, an earthenware pitcher, a lamp which has gone out leaving a trace of smoke, and a skull with the bottom jaw missing. He also causes a shaft of light to fall diagonally on to the skull.

The significance of the objects

I think it would be fair to say that the objects chosen are not neutral in their implications. Luxury items, whether seen in a still life or a shop window, carry social and economic implications: they reflect positively or negatively on wealth, status and desire, and possibly authority and power. Is it possible to remain indifferent to the image of a skull, or does it necessarily contain an implication of death? My own view is that it would require a mind of quite extraordinary insensitivity or discipline to contemplate a skull with the same dispassion as an apple. If the skull is intended to carry a meaning in this sense, it probably follows that the other objects, superficially neutral, are also intended to carry hidden meanings.

For whom would they have been painted?

The small scale and fine detail of the paintings imply that they are intended for prolonged study at close range, and the most natural place for this is a domestic interior. Seventeenth-century Holland was, as I mentioned in connection with landscape, a prosperous mercantile community, which wished to dissociate itself from Catholic, foreign and authoritarian influence and imagery. Before the days of modern banking and paper credit, silver was one of the primary stores of wealth. So was land, but in Holland where land was in short supply, painting by contemporary artists became an important means of investment, as we have seen. Indeed, modern art dealing was established in Holland at this time. What to present-day eyes might appear as a meticulously executed collection of expensive (and antique) objects and an Old Master painting, was to contemporary eyes a painting of modern luxury items, which carried a wide range of implications for the owner, his family and friends.

Still lifes like Heda's were very common, and if such blatant materialism seems distasteful, the Steenwyck type of still life, which was less common, provides something of a counterbalance. The key to the meaning here is the skull, and discussing and extracting the implied meaning in a painting was an activity enjoyed by Dutch collectors which their artists played up to: the subject is known technically as a 'Vanitas'. The immortal phrase, 'Vanity of vanities all is vanity' may spring to mind, and the full quotation from Ecclesiastes 1:2 would have been well known in Calvinist Holland:

> Vanity of vanities, saith the Preacher, vanity of vanities; all is vanity.
> What profit hath a man of all his labours which he taketh under the
> sun? One generation passeth away and another generation cometh.

Vanity is used here not to mean conceit and self-importance, but the emptiness of earthly possessions. The pitcher would have been understood as a symbol of emptiness, the sword a reminder that arms cannot be a protection against death, and the watch a reminder that time passes—*tempus fugit*. The books and musical instruments are a reminder of earthly pleasures and experience which must be left behind; the shell is, I think, a reference to sexual pleasure. The lamp which has just been extinguished also refers to death.

Am I being unfair if I describe this painting as the classic case of having one's cake and eating it? How satisfying to be reminded of vanity whilst contemplating an object one is sure has been a good investment!

I hope this discussion shows how still life became established as a separate genre. Being anti-authoritarian the Dutch cared little for hierarchies either in social life or the arts. Still life painting grew in response to commercial demand. But it is often so. In discussing the hierarchies of art it is important to remember that many works are produced without, and in disregard for, academic theory.

The high-water mark for still life painting in the Low Countries was the seventeenth century. Many still life paintings have been produced there since then, but they have been repetitions of standard types rather than works of great originality. Two exceptions are Van Gogh (who was Dutch), whose flower still lifes are supreme—for him the sunflower carried deep personal symbolism (Figure 104)—and René Magritte, the Belgian artist who exploited the genre in the context of Surrealism (Figure 105).

Chardin, *Le Bocal d'Abricots (The Jar of Apricots)*

(Plate 41) Compare this painting with the still life by Heda (Plate 40) with the following question in mind: What are the similarities and differences between them?

On close examination I can find few similarities other than the small size and the fact that Chardin has also arranged his objects on a narrow ledge. When considering dissimilarities, an obvious one is that Chardin has chosen an oval format. (If we were to examine other still lifes by Chardin, where he uses a conventional format we would find that he always places his objects centrally, not on a diagonal.) Furthermore, notice how he uses a low viewpoint, unlike Heda, giving me the sensation of sitting and looking, rather than standing, and he comes much closer to the objects. The way in which the edge of the painting cuts into the still life enhances this impression. The low viewpoint and central arrangement leave rather unsatisfactory blank areas in all four corners, so in this example he has shaped the canvas to eliminate them. This acute sensitivity to a visual and decorative problem, and the somewhat craftsmanlike solution should give you a hint both as to his approach and the aesthetic background, a point I shall develop a little later.

The light in Chardin's still life is much softer than in Heda's. Outlines blur and there is an envelope of light which bathes and unites objects rather than separates them. The light, whilst not spotlighting textures and structures, nevertheless makes me feel very conscious of them (I can sense the crisp crust of the bread and the paper on the parcel) and I think this is partly the result of the texture of Chardin's paint, evident even in a reproduction. He does not try to hide the existence of paint or his working: rather the opposite. Nor do I sense any flashy showing off or consciously brilliant painting such as are evident in the peeled lemon and crab in Heda's.

Indeed Chardin's subject-matter is extremely matter of fact. Some bread, a jar of fruit, a tambourine, an ordinary glass of wine, a steaming brew of some infusion in a porcelain cup which by this date would be of European origin, and if a pleasant luxury, certainly not a great rarity like the Ming dynasty dish. I feel no great temptation to look for covert or symbolic meaning, largely because the whole approach in subject-matter and style seems to be to play things down, and secret meanings do not naturally fit with such an approach. The only genuine mystery I can find is: what is in the parcel, and what is the green object above it? On a more esoteric level I would be interested to know which porcelain factory made the bowl and saucer, but none of these questions are of very great consequence.

FIGURE **104** SUNFLOWERS, Vincent Van Gogh, 1888
Oil on canvas, 92×73 cm, 36¼×28¾ in, National Gallery, London

FIGURE **105** LE MODÈLE ROUGE (THE RED MODEL), René Magritte, 1935
Oil on canvas, 72×48 cm, 28½×19 in, Musée Nationale, Paris

STILL LIFE

Like Dutch still lifes, Chardin's were intended for intimate domestic interiors, and this particular example was brought by Jacques Roettiers, the King's jeweller. Chardin achieved great success with them, and demand was such that he frequently produced several versions of the same picture. He was not exclusively a still life painter. He also excelled in small scenes of domestic interiors with ordinary people involved in day-to-day activity. He was a member of the French Academy, but only elected to the fourth and lowest category reserved for painters of still life and landscapes. He never aspired to the higher categories and was criticized for his lack of ambition. Nevertheless, his patrons included the King, other European royalty, and the aristocracy.

This was a period when royalty and aristocracy openly played at the domestic and simple life as a relief from pomp and ceremony. They also collected Dutch and Flemish paintings of the previous century. It was an age of great visual awareness, especially in the decorative arts and crafts. Marvellously designed and beautifully made furniture was produced, inlaid with the finest marquetry, and French factories produced wonderful porcelain. The French encyclopaedists championed a philosophy of rational analysis, observation and common sense (all of them low-key activities) and Diderot, a leading influence among them, praised Chardin's work. France had, in the early eighteenth century, no still life tradition of meticulous painting from nature. Here, therefore, is a supreme example of an epoch with a strong visual and common-sense interest finding satisfaction and fulfilment in still life painting. Considering that the French Academy was more influential and more wedded to the hierarchy of genres than any other, Chardin's success makes this point even more vivid.

Still life painting in France remained insignificant for a hundred years until a strong, but different, visual aesthetic emerged in the latter half of the nineteenth century. This aesthetic championed the notion that painting should be primarily about observable facts and at the same time it consciously ignored the academic hierarchies. Artists such as Courbet, Manet, the Impressionists, and Post-Impressionists treated still life as a subject-matter as interesting as and equal to any other, and their attitudes had influence well beyond French culture. A useful *bon mot*, coined at the time, was that 'a well-painted turnip is better than a badly-painted Madonna.' To illustrate the maxim I will mention two examples and allow them to speak for themselves: Manet's *Bundle of Asparagus* (Figure 106), and Sir William Nicholson's *Pears* (Figure 107).

Cézanne, *Still Life with a Plaster Cupid, c.1895*

(Plate 42) Study this carefully with my suggested categories in mind. If you find it easy to describe in terms of subject-matter, space and light, look again since you must have overlooked many significant aspects.

Although you will not be able to tell this from the reproduction, the work is painted in oil on paper (which has been laid on wood to make it more permanent, an unusual method of working). It is small. Does the technique lead you to think

FIGURE **106** BUNDLE OF ASPARAGUS, Edouard Manet, 1880
Oil on canvas, 46x55 cm, 18x21½ in, Wallraf-Richartz-Museum, Cologne

FIGURE **107** PEARS, William Nicholson, before 1944
Oil on wood, 31x44 cm, 12¼x17¼ in, City Art Gallery, Leeds

STILL LIFE

that Cézanne was aiming to produce a marketable painting for sale, like the Dutch painters or Chardin? Look at the actual paint handling. Well finished or sketchy? If you answer 'sketchy', why should a still life, done in the studio, be painted in such a manner? My own view is that some areas are sketchily painted (for example the apples at the foot of the plaster figure), whereas others are relatively well finished (for example, the head and torso of the figure). I also notice that there is no signature and no date. These facts together would lead me to believe (even if I were looking at a work by an artist wholly unknown to me) that the painting is unfinished. Further, I would expect an oil on paper to be either a preliminary work for a finished painting, or something done for the artist's own experimental purposes. At least, that would be my first conclusion, and I would want evidence to persuade me to come to any other conclusion.

At first glance the subject-matter seems straightforward: a plaster figure of Cupid on a table, surrounded by apples and onions with a table top and cloth and an area of studio floor showing and canvases stacked around the studio wall resting on the floor. It is on further investigation that the problems arise. Are there three apples on the plate or four? Is the red mark to the left of the green apple a fourth fruit or not? To the left of the plate is a blue cloth, but how does it then seem to rise in the air like a conjuring trick and support a further two apples (or are they oranges, or is one an onion?). Is the levitating blue cloth the same as the one on the table or different? Or is it in fact not 'real' in the sense of the other objects but a painted image on one of the canvases in the studio—a painting within a painting? What is the object just below a canvas of a kneeling figure at the far end of the studio?

Before coming to a conclusion, consider Cézanne's treatment of space and light. The table top suggests a high viewpoint, yet if you isolate the head and torso of the plaster Cupid, they presuppose that the eye-level is straight ahead. The studio floor suggest an even higher eye-level, but with the canvas propped at the back it has flattened out again. If we take distance and its diminishing effect into account the object at the foot of this canvas must be a football; yet it looks more like an apple the same size as those in the foreground.

Light is equally confusing. Occasionally there are shadows indicating a definite light source—the foot of Cupid for example—but there is no consistency: elsewhere shadows are omitted altogether. Why is the blue cloth on the table in shadow, when the plate is brightly lit? The more I examine this curious painting the more ambiguities and inconsistencies I find, assuming of course that I demand the rational visual logic and good order of a Chardin or a Heda.

If you set up a still life like Cézanne's and began to record what you saw on a two-dimensional piece of paper over a period of days, consider what you would see. As you moved round the table and round the studio your viewpoint would change constantly. The fall of light and shadow would not remain constant. Would a day, an hour, a minute, a second come when you could say, 'I have observed all there is to see; there is nothing left to record. I have finished?' Who, then, paints a more faithful record of what he sees, Cézanne or Chardin? The

262

answer I think, depends on what set of rules you start with and the manner in which you define the aims and purpose of a painting in the first place. Neither is exclusively right or wrong. Each is correct according to his own terms of reference.

Cézanne worked almost entirely in isolation. He had a private income and therefore did not need patrons and collectors to buy his work. Consequently he did not need to produce works which would satisfy their prejudices and preconceptions about what a painting ought to be. More than any other artist before him he wished a painting to be a faithful record of what he saw, but as I hope I have demonstrated, this alone presented enormous difficulties. Yet this was not his only problem. He also responded emotionally to what he saw: he clearly had a very strong response to landscape, to a single tree, the female body, even simple objects like apples or a plaster cast. He was also concerned to produce a painting that would be a visually beautiful object. Much of the fascination of Cézanne's work is the way he struggles to balance these often irreconcilable aims. Sometimes he lets the analytical side move ahead, as in his earlier work, sometimes the personal and emotional side as in his middle work, sometimes the need to produce a beautiful painting, as in his late period. But he never sacrifices one for the sake of the others. Although strongly influenced by Chardin I think he might have argued that Chardin sacrifices truth to what he sees for the sake of producing a beautiful painting. This is speculation on my part as Cézanne wrote and said very little and did not explain his work in words, but I think the evidence for my summary is there in the most important source of evidence about any painter: the pictures that he painted.

The still life provided Cézanne with an ideal vehicle for this prodigious achievement: the endless ambiguities are evidence of his determination to remain faithful to what he saw, yet the overall rhythm and colour harmonies, the placing of the plaster Cupid to provide a marvellous curving form down the centre of the picture are evidence of his wish to produce a satisfying and beautiful painting. The furthest apple/football is there as large as it is because the *painting* demands it. Take it away (cover it with your thumb) and see how the balance and tension in the composition is seriously weakened. It is a tentative admission that given a choice between loyalty to exact appearances, and loyalty to the requirements of a particular painting, then the second loyalty must ultimately triumph.

Still Life in the Twentieth Century

For this section I have chosen three very different paintings to provide a focus for a commentary on some of the issues raised by Modern Art. The first is a small work by Picasso painted in Paris in 1911–12 (*Still Life with Chair Caning*, Plate 43). It is a curious object, and not a still life in the traditional sense. It is not exactly an oil painting on canvas, since the pattern of chair caning is not painted but is a piece of real oil cloth with a printed pattern of chair caning on it, cut out

263

by Picasso and stuck on the surface of the canvas. The area above and to the right of it is oil painting and around the outside is fixed a piece of rope. It is not easy to 'read' the picture in the sense of identifying what is represented. In the fragmented forms at the top there are suggestions of a glass, a slice of lemon and the letters 'JOU', bringing to mind a newspaper. These are traditional items found in countless still life paintings, but usually presented as a convincing illusion of the real thing. Here their existence is suggested but any faithful illusion is firmly denied. The chair caning is equally a puzzle. Should one 'read' it as a piece of oil cloth covering a table (the real life purpose of oil cloth), or should one 'read' it as an illusion of chair caning, i.e. the seat of a chair? Indeed should one regard this as a picture in the traditional sense of the word or is it something else? If it is something else, what is it?

The point, as you may have guessed, is that Picasso is deliberately playing with these questions: What is illusion? What is reality? Does the artist need to produce a complete or convincing illusion for the spectator to be able to read or understand a picture? What is a picture—a window on the world, or an independent, previously unknown object, made by an artist?

Still Life with Chair Caning is one of the earliest works in which an artist played with materials in this way, and raised these sort of questions so specifically. In the history of modern art this small work is a milestone. Picasso boasted that he had been able to produce a work of art out of the contents of his wastepaper basket, and he later went on to produce works in which the only technique he used was to cut up and glue fragments of newspaper, old tickets, cigarette packets and shreds of papers on to a flat surface. These refined an idea which is emerging in *Still Life with Chair Caning*, namely: if a picture is created out of still life objects (pieces of paper etc.), then is not the picture also the still life that it claims to represent? Picasso is saying it is not possible to define his picture as an illusion of still life objects, since still life objects are actually a physical part of the picture.

For Picasso's first examples, he and subsequent artists developed similar ideas, just as the aviators made even more elaborate aeroplanes after the first experiments in flight. Once artists accepted the proposition that a picture need not be made with traditional materials, or be an illusion of things known to exist in the natural world, then all sorts of new possibilities were opened up, and in due course there followed totally abstract paintings which have no recognizable subject-matter from the natural world. These are bigger issues than we can go into here, but the point I want to emphasize is that still life subject-matter was vital in these early experiments, largely, I think, because still life objects are so familiar and because a still life is something that an artist can keep under close control in front of his active eye and in his mind's eye. In other words, it can be a very simple subject which does not divert the artist or spectator from the aesthetic and artistic questions which are raised. *Still Life with Chair Caning* is not unique, simply an early and important example in a period of art that is noted for its free-thinking inventiveness and humour.

My second example is Mondrian's *Composition With Red, Yellow and Blue* (Plate 44). Once Picasso and his colleagues had shown how the old principles of picture making could be discarded, artists such as Mondrian began to construct (it is a good word) new types of painting. The elements that Mondrian chooses are as simple as can be: horizontal and vertical lines and the three primary colours, red, yellow and blue. It is obviously not possible to describe such a work as a still life, or a landscape in any traditional sense, yet I confess that the more I get to know this painting, the more I find in its balance and controlled order a sense that approaches my reaction in front of the balanced still life of a Chardin (Plate 41) or the harmonious landscapes of Claude Lorraine (Figures 76 and 77). Without recognizable subject-matter the way into this painting is more difficult. It needs a greater intellectual and imaginative leap, and I think that this may be so with all abstract painting. A study of Mondrian's complete works reveals that like Plate 44 they evolved out of landscape. Mondrian's desire was to extract from the seeming disorder of the natural world those basic elements that all matter shares in common and to make paintings that celebrate and affirm this. Through the progression of his work and over many years, one can see this view evolving into his abstract paintings. Many abstract paintings are difficult to comprehend properly in isolation and need the full context of an artist's work to reveal their underlying purpose and the reason for their particular form.

My third example, Matisse's *Lemons against a Fleur-de-lis Background* (Plate 45) will serve to make the point that not all twentieth-century painting has been concerned with establishing new definitions, new ideas, or new types of art, and that the traditional definition of the genre of still life has flourished vigorously. Indeed I think it can be said that the new spirit of freedom which experimental modern art encouraged, allowed artists like Matisse to bring a new breadth of vision to traditional still life painting. This painting is easy enough to read— lemons, flowers in a vase, wallpaper, a shelf—but Matisse clearly does not feel obliged to recreate their appearance in the way that Chardin and Cézanne did. If you examine the picture carefully, I think it becomes clear that Matisse is more concerned with colour than with lemons and flowers. The painting glows with a vibrating warm red, the yellow and the green adding notes and accents which amplify the sensation. In *Notes of a Painter* which I mentioned earlier (page 234), Matisse said 'A work of art must carry in itself its complete signifi- cance and impose itself upon the beholder even before he can identify the subject matter.' For me this painting is an outstanding visual example of the principle in that statement. I would argue that one reason for his choosing a still life subject-matter is its familiarity, and because he thought that the simplicity of still life would offer the least distraction from his main purpose, namely a revelation of the power and magic of colour. Obviously one could argue that Matisse, like Mondrian, could have dispensed with recognizable subject-matter altogether, but Matisse wanted his work to be easily accessible and seductive to people who had no great knowledge of aesthetics. He also thought that the simple pleasures of life, like enjoying flowers, fruit and colour, were of great importance; and he knew that the 'pleasure of recognition' is one of the most basic rewards of looking at paintings, a reward that is not to be despised.

I am conscious that I have invited you to put your toe into the invigorating waters of modern art, and that I am not going to accompany you further. This is inevitable in a book which discusses the traditional genres of painting, since modern art has been concerned to break with the past and tradition. Perhaps in so doing it has merely created new genres and a new hierarchy, with abstract art succeeding landscape just as landscape succeeded History painting. It is difficult even now to tell with any certainty. Perhaps the old genres will find new life, following the example of still life. Nevertheless, I hope that my remarks and observations on landscape and still life will have given you the urge to go and examine paintings at first hand, and will have provided a framework of recognition which you will be able to develop with pleasure and personal reward.

266

PHILOSOPHY LOOKS AT PAINTINGS

Diané Collinson

Section Four

PHILOSOPHY LOOKS AT PAINTINGS

So far this course has guided you in the activity of looking at paintings. But this, its final section, is somewhat different. It makes a brief incursion into the philosophy of art, directing attention to some of the large general questions that underlie our interest in paintings. In particular it considers questions about our aesthetic experience of them.

Those underlying questions sometimes present themselves in a vivid and arresting way. How curious it is that many people are so deeply interested in, derive so much pleasure from, ascribe such importance to and study with such care, certain flat surfaces coloured with paint. How strange that we can endlessly dwell upon, investigate, discuss, and feel enriched by such objects. Why do people paint, study, enjoy, analyse, value and disvalue these things, and what is the meaning of it all?

Musings of that sort tend to generate further questions of the same kind; questions about the nature of art and our experience of it; about what makes something a great work of art; about the place of art in human life. Such questions indicate that a radical shift of stance has taken place. They move us away from a direct engagement with the paintings—from the looking, analysing, studying, and so on—to a stance in which we are talking *about* those direct activities. This is a move from a first-order to a second-order activity. We stand back from immediate engrossment in the works in an attempt to give an account of, to describe and characterize, what it is that we—both painters and spectators—are up to. Instead of attending to the paintings we ask questions about our attention to them, about the kind of objects they are and about their significance for us.

Such 'standing back' or underlying questions are philosophical ones. They beckon us to seemingly limitless areas of speculative enquiry. So the task now, in confronting such a vast terrain, is to choose a topic that will enlighten rather than confuse us. We need to find a vantage point from which we can relate our actual looking at paintings to the philosophical questions I have mentioned. To reach that vantage point I suggest we start off, once again, with the business of standing before a painting.

There are many different ways of regarding paintings. Imagine a person, whom I shall call 'the ordinary spectator', strolling through a museum or art gallery without much purpose beyond that of 'taking a look round'. This spectator's experience of the paintings would, I think, contain elements of a number of the different responses and attitudes I have in mind. Those responses and attitudes would occur, I surmise, in an extremely haphazard way. They would be made up of a mass of fluctuating feelings, comments, judgements, questions, and half-thought phrases and words: all that seething conglomeration of fast-moving, semi-articulate activity characteristic of a person's mental life. If we could capture some of the unspoken phrases or put into words a few of our imaginary spectator's fleeting impressions, the results might be something like this:

What a huge painting . . . I'll have to stand back here . . . Some kind of battle . . . how fierce and terrible . . . Red coats there . . . red in the flags and banners . . . Blood, carnage, trampled bodies, fallen horses . . . So much detail . . . What battle is it? . . . Is the painter famous? . . . So much wild movement, rage, terror, brutality . . . Are those French soldiers? . . . These are the ones who are being beaten, over to the left, and that central figure on the large grey horse is leading the charge into them . . . It looks a hot, dry country . . . Why was the picture painted? . . . Was it for a public building? . . . Perhaps commissioned by the victorious general . . . There is so much in it . . . I'm in the middle of the fighting . . . I can sense the force and fierceness of the battle.

Here's a smaller picture . . . a country scene . . . Greens and yellows and blues, peaceful . . . A beautiful light on the water . . . I'd like it on my wall . . . I wonder if it's valuable, what price it would fetch? . . . Would it be a good investment? . . . I love that far cornfield with the sun on it . . . How do they get that effect of shining light? . . . Who's the painter? . . . Is it an actual place? . . . I'm not in the middle of it as I am with the battle, I see it from a distance and it stretches into the distance . . . Would it fit on that end wall in my room? . . . Oh, that light on the cornfield . . . And the water . . . I wonder if it's a *good* painting?

This next one . . . a portrait . . . It's—fascinating, compelling . . . Perhaps all portraits are . . . I'm not sure if I like it or not . . . Is it seventeenth century? . . . It's rather harsh . . . a flat, expressionless face . . . carefully composed . . . She's a secret person . . . What was she like . . . her life? . . . What is the significance of the casket on the table? . . . That's beautiful lace, her dress is soft . . . That hand doesn't look very real . . . holding a Bible . . . Perhaps he wasn't any good at hands, had someone else paint them for him . . . I like the rosy colour and softness of her dress . . . He has painted the hand-stitching on it . . . There's an arch over there and a very small thin dog . . . Did they have special breeds in those days? . . . Was she an aristocrat? . . . She hasn't any jewellery . . . I must go back to that sunlit cornfield again . . . Oh, here's one I missed . . . A voluptuous woman, naked except for a wisp of something . . . Various figures grouped around in rather fraught postures . . . Draperies furling and flying . . . Large man almost naked . . . Leaning over the woman; *what* is he doing to her? . . . I wish I understood those types of paintings . . . Wonderfully sinuous lines and shapes but what is it all about? . . . Here's the country scene again at last . . . Ah, that sunlit field.

And so on. But now let me try picking out remarks which, I suggest, indicate or are expressive of particular kinds of experiences and attitudes. For instance, 'What price would it fetch? Would it be an investment?' might be said to reveal the *economic* attitude; 'Why was it painted? Was it for a public building?' the *historical* attitude; 'Would it fit on that end wall in my room?' the *practical* attitude; 'Is it a *good* painting?' the *evaluative* attitude; 'How do they get that effect of shining light?' the *technical* attitude. But what about 'How fierce and terrible . . . Ah, that sunlit field . . . I like the colour and softness of her dress . . . Wonderfully sinuous lines and shapes . . . It's rather harsh'? I shall class those remarks together and say they are manifestations of the *aesthetic* attitude and the aesthetic experience. And with that remark I have brought us, I hope to the vantage point we require.

What exactly is it that marks out aesthetic experience of a painting, distinguishing it from other kinds of experiences of it? A ready answer is to say that aesthetic experience is of the beauty of a painting. But the answer, although not one to be rejected, is incomplete, even though it is endorsed by the kind of definition given by a concise dictionary which tells us that 'aesthetic' means 'having to do with appreciation of the beautiful'. A fuller dictionary definition is more helpful, for it gives something of the roots and history of the word. 'Aesthetic' is to do with 'things perceptible by the senses'; by sight, sound, touch, smell, taste. Simply, then, aesthetic experience of a painting consists of response to its *look*; it is experience of visual appearance and meaning. Thus it is not only to do with beauty, for things which are ugly, dull, repulsive, indifferent, and so on are also perceived by the senses and therefore are elements in aesthetic experience. And this shows us in a moment how complex and rich the notion of aesthetic sensibility is, once we have moved away from the confines of a merely snappy (though useful) definition. For something may be ugly, in some sense of that word, and yet be aesthetically pleasing; or may be beautiful, in some sense of that word, and yet be aesthetically cloying. Another aspect of the complexity of 'aesthetic' has to do with what, in the present context, is to be understood by 'sense perception' or 'sensory experience'. For if we tried to give an account of the sensory perceiving of a picture we might well begin with a fairly straight-forward physiological report of the mechanisms of sight, describing the impact of light rays on the retina, the functions of lenses, processes of refraction, and similar occurrences. We might continue with talk of seeing colours, shapes, dark and light areas, roughness and smoothness; then of depth, space, distance; and eventually of perceiving objects, forms, movement, stillness, scenes, events, persons, and even moods, emotions and ideas. We move—somehow—from matter to meaning. It is obvious that sense experience is itself a complex subject, and although it need not be pursued here we should note that its complexity becomes incorporated into any detailed account of aesthetic experience.

So far I have maintained what is unexceptional: that sensory perception is the basis of aesthetic experience, and that an aesthetic response to a painting is to do with whether we like or dislike the way it looks. Several of the remarks I invented to characterize my 'ordinary spectator's' aesthetic experiences—'I like the colour . . . It's rather harsh . . . Her dress is soft . . . etc.'—certainly suggest a dwelling on sensations. But as the transition from sensory activity to mental concepts suggests, that is by no means the whole story. Perhaps aesthetic experience is even better typified by the gaps between 'the ordinary spectator's' phrases; by the wordless moments when the spectator is poised in the act simply of apprehending the painting rather than when remarking on it. Indeed, if we think back to the remark 'Ah, that sunlit field', it is the 'Ah' more than 'that sunlit field' that reveals the sensuous immediacy of the aesthetic moment. For it is not an experience in which we formulate an intellectual judgement to the effect *that* a vision of a sunlit field has been wondrously depicted. Rather, we experience the vision for ourselves; we are admitted to the painter's point of view. It is a distinguishing mark of aesthetic experience that it is one of participating in, or inhabiting, the world of the picture. Most of the comments or remarks indicative of the experience are retrospective in that they are *about* it rather than a part *of* it.

There are qualifications to be made and questions to be asked about what I have now said, but I shall come to them later. For the moment I shall develop the account of aesthetic experience, saying more about what it is like in its most vivid instances and considering variations of it. First it must be made clear that, in trying to isolate and describe certain pronounced characteristics of aesthetic experience, I am not claiming that this kind of experience, even though highly prized by many, is superior to other forms of experience or that it is narrowly homogeneous in its nature. Nor am I suggesting that it is in any way an exclusive experience, available only to the initiated or the ultra-sensitive. My view is that it is one particular aspect of conscious activity in general and that it is latent in all our investigations of the world. In what follows I shall try to isolate and describe aesthetic experience, but it is important to remember that in daily life it is usually inextricably mixed with many other experiences.

The most frequently noted mark of an aesthetic regard is its *disinterestedness*. Being disinterested does not mean that we are *un*interested in the sense that we lack curiosity about or alertness to what we are looking at, but that our attention is unbiased in that we have no axe to grind; we do not see the painting as a means to the fulfilment of some practical purpose. In experiencing it aesthetically, we do not learn lessons from it, grade it, or compare it with other works. Instead, the painting arrests and holds us within its own orbit, its own limits and evocations. It is present to us as a self-contained and self-validating entity.

Think back again for a moment to some of our 'ordinary spectator's' stream-of-consciousness thoughts. Those indicative of an aesthetic regard—phrases such as 'Beautifully sinuous lines . . . It's rather harsh . . . A secret person . . . How fierce and terrible . . . I can sense the force of the battle . . .'—do not relate to concerns as to the history or origins of the painting, the techniques deployed in its production, the uses to which it might be put, its saleroom value, or whether it is a better painting than the one next to it, but to its intrinsic properties. They relate to what the picture itself is: an object for the senses which embodies meaning. They are not reflections on the painting considered as a means to some further end, but the tentative beginnings of an imaginative move into the world of the picture, to investigate *it*. It is in this sense that an aesthetic regard is a disinterested one.

Aesthetic disinterestedness does not imply a severance from whatever knowledge of life and history and culture a spectator may possess. Indeed, to attend appropriately to a painting we need as much knowledge and experience as possible. But we need to use them in the service of what is essentially an imaginative enquiry. For in aesthetic exploration it is not that we seize upon a work to incorporate it as swiftly as possible within the confines of an already-existing intellectual framework, manipulating or taming it to conform to present presuppositions and capacities. Rather, we become receptive to a new—sometimes a strangely new—particularity. We have therefore to confront a painting as the whole of what we are; that is, as persons with histories and with some acquaintance with history, but with that body of knowledge and experience open to development and revision. What we already are, in that sense, enables us to establish points of contact with a painting, though not by subduing, or classifying what we do not fully grasp at first. When we explore a painting successfully we are able imaginatively to inhabit another segment of reality. That we are able to 'lose ourselves' or are 'taken out of ourselves' in contemplating works of art are profoundly apt sayings. Such losings are not escapist flights. The self is lost in that it becomes absorbed in what is explored; but subsequently it is found, bearing about it the authenticity of its new experience. And here we have a glimpse of how any analytical, historical, and technical study of a painting interacts with, may serve and be served by, aesthetic experience of it. For an immediate, intuitive, aesthetic apprehension may direct one's analysis, while analysis and scholarship can correct an intuition or point towards fresh insight into the work as a whole. As we develop visual skills, learning to look more carefully, closely, analytically, and for longer periods of time, at paintings, so our likings and dislikings may change and develop.

Aesthetic approval of a painting is frequently described as delight or enjoyment. This may seem a puzzling idea since many pictures are of tragic or sombre events, or are melancholy or harrowing in one way or another. It is the same with other art forms. Music may embody the whole gamut of moods and emotions; novels and plays be tragic and dark as well as funny, lyrical or exciting. How is it, then, that we can speak of enjoying, or delighting in a fine work of art, whatever mood or emotional quality the work itself may embody? The answer, I think, is as follows. In attending to a painting we certainly do perceive and are able to experience, among other things, its particular emotional content, recognizing sadness, joy, foreboding, or whatever is there that we are able to apprehend. Thus the term 'aesthetic delight' cannot refer to some delight-producing element that is a necessary ingredient in any painting worthy of attention, even though there may be some paintings which are, in every sense, delightful. What the term describes, I suggest, is a delight in the clarity with which what is perceived has been presented, a delight in vividly experiencing the world of the painting. It is this delight in the perspicuity of something that makes us return to look again, to experience more of the painting, and to seek out others similarly rewarding. And so it is with other art forms. We are as glad to have seen a tragedy such as *King Lear* and a painting such as Turner's *Snow Storm* (Plate 37) as we are to have heard Mendelssohn's *Midsummer Night's Dream* overture or looked at Constable's *The Haywain* (Plate 31), even though the first two acquaint us with despair and suffering and the second two with happiness and tranquillity.

I have said nothing so far of the variety or the difficulty of aesthetic experience, although on page 274 I mentioned that I do not think it is a homogeneous one. The experience is not simply a matter of confronting a work of art, confidently arranging one's physical and mental dispositions in appropriate ways and then, inevitably, being suitably affected. One can, of course, try to adopt mental and physical attitudes conducive to aesthetic experience, and that may sometimes be helpful, but I am inclined to think that the more intensely and deliberately it is sought the more elusive it becomes. Certainly, for most of us, the occasions when we are arrested and held entranced in a deeply memorable way are rare; for, however experienced a person may be in the matter of looking into paintings, most occasions of viewing them are ones in which, like the 'ordinary spectator's', one's regard alternates, shifting rapidly between aesthetic, practical, historical, and analytical explorations. But aesthetic experience can sometimes be cumulative, in that after quite prolonged investigation that perhaps has little aesthetic intention in it, one can come to a realization and appreciation of a profound significance in a painting; an awareness of inexhaustible meaning. This realization has built up gradually, in an unnoticed way. Aesthetic experience may also be, as it were, delayed. One may visit a gallery, perhaps to look at a collection of a particular genre such as landscapes, or Flemish religious paintings, and seem to derive very little from the visit. But subsequently, perhaps days or weeks later, the pictures come to mind, compelling the kind of imaginative participation which had not been possible in the gallery. It is not surprising that aesthetic experience can manifest such variety. Paintings themselves are so various and differing, some easy to engage with, others recondite and strange, some having immediate personal appeal, others being enigmatically abstract, that it would be simplistic to think that experience of them could not be correspondingly varied and yet be still essentially aesthetic.

On page 274 I pointed out that there were questions to be asked about what I had so far written. I am conscious now of having raised many more questions. Perhaps that does not matter greatly, since much of my purpose has been to generate thoughts and discussion rather than to offer a fully-argued point of view. But not everything can be left in its present profuse array. I want therefore to take up just one or two of the issues that seem especially to need some discussion or comment.

A question which stands out clearly is one about the nature of works of art. Aesthetic experience is not confined to works of art. It is latent, I have suggested, in most of our investigations of the world, and occurs for many people quite often in the presence of the grandeur or loveliness of nature. But works of art are especially apt to demand an aesthetic response—indeed, that is what they are for, one might say—and we want to know what it is, in general, that makes them thus apt. The question is a large and difficult one which cannot be treated in any comprehensive way here, but we can perhaps start from a remark I made on page 274. There I said that a painting is an object for the senses which embodies meaning; and we can connect that remark with others that relate to it.

First of all, a painting (I shall speak of paintings here but what I say can be extrapolated to refer to works of art in general) has a density of meaning which is not only complex but which possesses as well a remarkably integrated internal order and unity. It is as if it has taken some of the world into itself and composed it there in such a way that when we contemplate it we are not, as it were, sent out into the world where meaning would become attenuated or diffused, but find more and more of the world contained in the density of meaning within the painting itself. This is why, at best, we can be entranced by a picture, held by a shaft of attention that excludes everything else. The painting is so densely-packed, its meaning so closely-woven, that it can seem illimitable. If we think of the painting as having taken the world, or part of the world, into itself, we can understand why an exploration of it can seem to extend our actual experience of the forms and life of the world. This is as true of paintings predominantly concerned with shapes, lines, colour and light as it is of those which tell a specifically human story, since all those elements have been derived in some way from perception of the world and then have been embodied meaningfully by the painter in the work.

This reminds us afresh of the importance of historical and analytical studies not as an alternative to but as, in the end, a necessary part of a full 'reading' of a painting. They help us to see what of the world is in the painting, to trace the elements of its orderly unity and thereby to sharpen recognition of the work's significance.

I have spoken of meaning as embodied rather than as expressed. This is an important distinction which connects closely with the idea of a work of art as meaning itself rather than referring to something else for which it stands. For if something is expressive, then it is expressive *of* something else; that is, it derives its meaning, acquires its significance, by reference to something external to itself. But a work of art essentially means itself in that its meaning is embodied in its content and form, and is inseparable from them. This is not to suggest that there cannot or should not be works of art which *are* expressive—of feelings, passions, moods, and so on—but that expression of feeling is not the necessary defining or qualifying characteristic of anything held to be a work of art. In short, it is not the essential function or purpose of art to *express* feelings, although some works of art may do so. The meanings of expressive works are still embodied meanings, just as the meanings of works that use referring symbols such as a rose for love, a cross for suffering, a dove for spirit, are still embodied rather than referred meanings. It has been said that the only proper reply to the question 'What does this painting mean?' is to point again to the painting.

Does a painting ultimately have some fixed and unequivocal meaning which readily yields to the discerning spectator? Surely not. For one thing, this would

277

be to deny the inexhaustible density of meaning characteristic of works of art. It would be to ignore, too, the boundless complexity of causes and reasons that generate the production of a particular work; and not only to ignore them but to fail to recognize as well that such causes and reasons may be described in different ways and be given different emphases by different people. And of course, people simply do *see* paintings differently. Not only are there differences between people but differences between occasions of viewing by one person, and differences between viewing a painting at the time of its production and viewing it decades or centuries afterwards. Having said that, it is equally clear that we do often share many opinions, have similar experiences and are able to agree in matters concerning works of art. And of course, it is shared experience and mutual understanding, as well as differences and controversies, that all the talk, all the looking into paintings, is about. A picture may not have a fixed and unequivocal meaning, but on the other hand it cannot mean just anything at all.

The last question to which I'd like to draw attention is difficult to phrase; it has so many aspects. It might be broached by asking: What is the value of art? What is it for? What does it do for us? What place has it in human life? These are all aspects of the very large question: What is art? Once again, thorough treatment is not possible here, but I will offer a point of view consistent with what I have said so far.

In aesthetic experience we see perspicuously, inhabit another segment of reality, enter the world of the painting; I shall therefore say that engagement with paintings, and with works of art in general, is a form of knowledge. It is not knowledge of a kind gained by a process of learning or ingesting information or opinions, but knowledge through visual experience. Moreover, it is knowledge for the sake of knowing rather than knowledge acquired for the purpose of achieving some further end. And this relates to the difference between aesthetic experience *of* a painting and information *about* it. For aesthetic experience is for the sake of what is there to be experienced, while information about a work— its saleroom price, or the circumstances of its origin, for example—is information relating to a purpose the picture might serve. Aesthetic knowledge is attained through participation and is an insight or illumination. What is known is a particular perception of something: a place, a structure, a form, a mood, a pattern, a drama, an emotion, a texture. It is knowledge not of a generality but of a unique particular.

Think back to the first painting we studied with care: Yeames's *And When Did You Last See Your Father?* (Plate 1). We do not learn from it simply that a young boy was questioned by his father's enemies; it is more as if we are present at this particular interrogation and are subject to its particular conditions. Its emotional tensions are readily imparted to us with a precision, subtlety and coherence made arrestingly vivid by the organization and deployment of the elements of the painting: those forms, lines, colours, spaces, depths, densities and textures that present and charge the emotional meanings of the work, its emphases, exactitudes, and ambiguities. The elegant feet glimpsed in the portrait

278

behind the table may well be the feet of the boy's father. They are elegant because the shoes are fine and have pointed toes. Moreover, they *point*: nonchalantly and unknowingly towards a heavy black hat, onwards to the interrogator's head, to the boy, and downwards to the solid boots of a soldier. Their painted presence declares their owner's real absence, their stance his ignorance of the grim scene; their whole configuration denotes a life-style and values which appear trivial and incongruous beside the solid shapes of the Cromwellians. The marginal placing of the partly-seen portrait within the larger picture vividly reminds us that its subject is similarly almost ousted.

The relationships of the forms, lines and colours in Yeames's painting are part of a dramatic and emotional meaning which can certainly be understood, to some extent, simply from the facts of the painting's story, without any conscious dwelling on the formal relationships themselves. But of course, not all paintings are of the kind whose meanings are bound within stories or events. In many paintings the formal relationships themselves command our attention and bear the meaning of the work. Often those formal relations, once recognized, subdue the human-drama emotions which we may, in a search for significance, attempt to impose on a picture. If we attend carefully to, for instance, Cézanne's *Apples and Biscuits* (Figure 1) our interest in whether the apples came from Cézanne's own garden, or in the role of the wooden chest in his domestic life, or in the uses or origin of the dish, and so on, may gradually diminish, so that what we come to dwell on is the placing of objects or forms on the canvas, the sense of their weight and density and their juxtapositions to other forms and colours; the planes, angles and curves; light and shadows; brush-strokes and surface textures; and the whole complex presence of what is before us. We are admitted to a particular perception or vision that is itself the meaning of the work: a visual meaning that requires a visual understanding.

279

A consequence of this kind of illumination and our delight in it is that we wish to repeat and deepen the experience. We wish to look again and to extend and refine intuitions through more careful enquiry. Perhaps this attitude, this wanting to engage again, tells us something of the value of art and provides the germ of an argument that might be developed to oppose those who insist that art is merely play and as such is peripheral to more serious matters, to the practicalities of human life and conduct. For it seems to me that the knowledge acquired in a proper exploration of a work of art is of a kind that we acquire in relationships that are appropriate between persons. We give time to the work of art; we do not impose preconceptions on it; we take care accurately to establish its details; we allow that it has a density of meaning not immediately perceptible. In aesthetic regard we do not see a painting as a means to some further end, but as itself and as meaningful in itself; just as, if we like and love another person, we wish them to flourish, to continue being just as they are. If works of art, by their very nature, are apt to evoke this kind of sensibility, then art should not be seen as peripheral to, but as central in human life.

GLOSSARY

Aesthetics/Aesthetic
A narrow definition limits aesthetics to the study of beauty, leaving discussion of the nature of art and theories concerning it as part of the philosophy of art. When more broadly used it describes philosophical discussion about the nature of art, theories of art, and the characteristics of beauty.

In common use, the meaning of the term varies a great deal, but generally aesthetic, when used as an adjective, refers to experience through the senses (as opposed to through the intellect). Aesthetic used as a singular noun as in 'Constable's aesthetic' refers to an attitude or to a theory of art as a whole, held consciously or unconsciously.

Altarpiece
A work of art placed upon an altar, which serves as a piece of religious instruction when no service is going on and as background or accompaniment to the service when it is. Most often altarpieces are paintings: on wood during the thirteenth to sixteenth centuries, thereafter frequently on canvas. But there is also a tradition of altarpieces in carved relief, and at times relief sculpture and painting have been combined. The forms of altarpieces vary and depend partly on the importance of the altar for which they are done—for instance, the altar of a modest side-chapel, or in a home, in contrast to the high altar which is the focal point of a church. A single image may serve but frequently altarpieces have consisted of several images on a multi-part support: a main area and subject surrounded or flanked by ancillary images, often on a smaller scale. A *diptych* is a two-part work, a *triptych* three-part, a *polyptych* a work of several parts. These can be hinged together, door-fashion, so that different parts of a polyptych may be displayed according to the feastday or canonical season.

283

Attribute
An object associated with a particular person and shown in a work of art to identify him or her, e.g. the keys of St Peter, given him by Christ; the wheel of St Catherine, on which the Emperor Maxentius sought to torture this Christian martyr; the tower of St Barbara, built by her father to imprison her.

Avant-garde
A term introduced by art critics in the nineteenth century, from the military term for troops sent ahead of the main body of soldiers, to indicate artists and art leading art away from traditional concerns.

Caryatid
A sculpture of a human figure serving as a pier or column to support part of a building.

Colour

A broad term that needs to be used carefully in discussing art and is associated with other terms which have more specific meanings:

Local colour: the colour of an object unaffected by the action of other colours upon it under particular circumstances, as by coloured light falling on it.

Hue: the specific shade of a colour, e.g. which of many reds.

Intensity: the strength of a hue. For example, setting a red against a green is likely to intensify both by contrast; a large area of a hue is likely to appear more intense than a small area.

Tone: the lightness or darkness of a colour, i.e. its position on a scale going towards white at one end, towards black at the other.

Dimension

The size, usually given in a conventional sequence. For two-dimensional works: height then width; for three-dimensional works: height, width, depth (taking the largest measurement for each). The word can also refer, elliptically, to the ratio between these. Thus a picture of broad dimensions is one in which width greatly exceeds height.

Donor Painting

A painting that includes a representation of the person who commissioned and donated it, with or without his family, in the context of a scene or subject of which he or they would not naturally form a part, e.g. a painting of the three Magi bringing gifts to the Christ Child with members of the Florentine Medici family forming part of the courtly crowd, or a *Virgin and Child with Saints* with the man who paid for the painting shown kneeling in front of the saints.

Engraving

see *Prints*

Etching

see *Prints*

Facture

The appearance and character of the painted surface, in particular the artist's way of applying paint.

Format

A term referring to the size and overall shape of a work of art.

Genres

The genres are the traditional categories of (principally) painting discussed by the ancients and established by the academies of art and accorded greater and lesser importance: History, Portrait, Genre, Landscape, Animals, Still Life. The word Genre (with a capital letter) refers to scenes of ordinary people and their activities.

Hue
see *Colour*

Icon
A form of representation of Christ and/or angels and saints, developed by the Orthodox Church of Eastern Europe, especially from the ninth century on. Produced as single images or to hang with others, their manner and matter of representation followed prescriptions laid down by theological writers. Some icons are made of mosaic, others are carved or cast in relief, but most are painted on panels. They were objects of intense devotion and veneration at all levels of society, especially in Russia.

Iconography
The study of the subject-matter of works of art and the developing conventions by which specific meaning is conveyed; used sometimes also to refer to that meaning and to the deciphering of symbols, which is iconology.

Idol
An image used as an object of worship, usually in the context of pagan rituals.

285

Lithography
see *Prints*

Medium
Used broadly to indicate the major processes and materials used in a work of art, as in 'the medium of sculpture'; or, more narrowly, to indicate a particular medium and process within a category of art production, as in 'the medium of oil painting' as against watercolour or some other form of painting. Specifically, the substance into which the pigment is mixed or ground in the preparation of paint, often linseed oil for oil painting, gum arabic for watercolour painting.

Motif
The focal object of (usually) a landscape or a still life painting that appears to be the main concern of the painter.

Perspective
A conventional geometric system by which the three-dimensionality of things and their location in space can be plotted on a flat surface. There has been a variety of such systems since Graeco-Roman times, but the Florentine architect and sculptor Brunelleschi is credited with inventing the more exact system, 'Legitimate Perspective', much used in Renaissance art and thereafter.

Picturesque

A term used first in the eighteenth century to suggest characteristics by which a landscape or landscape garden resembles a painting, especially a painting by Claude Lorraine and his imitators. Later it described landscape paintings which appealed to the imagination through their informality and variety.

Pigment

Specifically, the colouring substance which, together with the medium, constitutes paint; used also more generally, as an alternative word for the mixture, for the paint itself.

Plane

The word 'plane' has many uses, some of which are particular to art. *Picture plane* is normally identified with the physical surface of a painting (as opposed to any illusion or effect of depth or projection the painting may offer). At various times artists have preferred not to suggest spatial recession and to compose forms and adjust colours so as to emphasize the planar character of painting, especially in large paintings such as murals. The word is also used in a special sense in relation to some landscape paintings or large and complex figure compositions where spatial recession is organized in terms of discernible 'planes' (not unlike the wings or 'flats' used on the traditional stage), giving the appearance of each being some distance behind the other.

Prints

Two-dimensional images produced by a method that permits multiple production. The word is used to refer to the works themselves, as in 'exhibition of prints', and to a range of printing methods. The following are those most frequently encountered.

An *Engraving* is produced by cutting lines into a metal plate (usually copper). Ink rubbed into these lines (but wiped away from the smooth metal) can be transferred to paper under pressure.

An *Etching* is produced by letting acid bite into the metal after lines have been scratched through a coating of wax. This permits finer detail than engraving and greater control of light and dark.

Both etching and engraving came into use in the fifteenth century.

A *Woodcut/Wood engraving* is produced by cutting into a plane of wood (along the grain for a woodcut, across the grain for a wood engraving) to leave portions standing proud, as in type so that these can be inked and an image printed on paper. Woodcuts were made in Western Europe at least as early as the fourteenth century, but were made in China several centuries earlier.

A *Lithograph* is produced by drawing the image on a smooth stone with greasy ink or crayon. Water is then applied to the whole surface, repelled by the greasy image, but accepted by the porous stone. The whole stone is then rolled with coloured greasy ink, which adheres only to the greasy image, the damp areas being impervious, and the image printed onto paper under pressure (i.e. the whole process is based on the opposition of grease and water). Like the woodcut, two or more printings are possible in different colours and overprinting results in an even greater range of colours. Being an exceptionally direct medium it allows the artist to draw freely in a personal manner.

All these processes result in an image, which is the reverse of what was 'drawn' on the plate, block or stone. Wooden blocks (for woodcuts) wear out quite quickly; metal plates are able to produce more prints, but these too become less clear as the plates are worn down. The number of prints is often limited deliberately, partly because of the deterioration in the clarity of the image, and partly to allow each print a scarcity value. The plate or block is then destroyed. The total number of prints made is indicated on each print, and each print is individually identified by number. Thus $^4/_{75}$ means that the particular print is number 4 out of a total pulled of 75.

Realism
Often used more or less interchangeably with 'naturalism' to refer to an artist's accurate or convincing portrayal of the visible world. More particularly, realism can mean an emphasis on what can normally be seen in the world, as opposed to what may be imagined or held to be of supernatural origin. As Realism, it refers to a movement initiated by Courbet in the middle of the nineteenth century, in which subjects and scenes revealing the harshness of life of ordinary people are presented as subject-matter worthy of the highest artistic endeavours.

Renaissance
Usually refers (with a capital letter) to the artistic and intellectual developments originating in Italy and spreading across Western Europe during, roughly, the fifteenth and sixteenth centuries. The word 'renaissance' means rebirth, and is thus sometimes given to other periods when new life seems to surge through cultural activity. Thus twelfth-century Europe is credited with a renaissance in classical learning and art forms.

Royal Academy
(Properly, the Royal Academy of Arts, London.) Academies of art were founded in Italy and then in France and other European countries to be artists' professional associations (to some extent replacing the guilds), where principles and methods could be debated and taught to students (gradually replacing the apprenticeship system as a way of learning art), and, from the eighteenth century, to be places where works of art could be displayed for sale and the awarding of prizes. The Royal Academy, founded in 1768, included architects from the start; its first president was the painter Joshua Reynolds. During the nineteenth century academies came to be associated with conservative and even reactionary attitudes to change. There was justice in the charge insofar as the academies had been created to uphold standards of art associated with the ancients and

with Renaissance and post-Renaissance masters such as Raphael and Poussin. Thus academic became a derogatory term indicating not so much the tradition upheld by the academies as the wearing down and cheapening of that tradition by repetition and misapplication. In recent years the Royal Academy has abandoned its once outspoken opposition to avant-garde artists, and has enrolled them as members and exhibited their work.

Stigmata
The marks made upon the body of Christ by his Passion and Crucifixion, particularly the piercing of his hands, feet and side; also the marks corresponding to these wounds supernaturally imprinted on devout persons such as St Francis and St Catherine of Siena.

Sublime
In the eighteenth century, the word was used, notably by Edmund Burke, in relation to feelings aroused by certain natural scenes or works of art or literature, which were said to move observers in a pleasurable or exciting way, by inducing awe or even terror though no real threat was involved. Burke identified great size (mountains, oceans, night sky) and great power (storms, waterfalls) as characteristics of these scenes. The sublime is thus distinct from the beautiful, which is calm and stable and does not involve this theoretical threat, but also does not excite the observer in the same way as the sublime. Romantic art greatly depended on the dramatic effects associated with the Sublime, e.g. on darkness and mysteriousness as against clarity, on great contrasts of scale (especially of nature as against man), and on violence directly portrayed as against more restrained representations.

Symbol
A representation or sign that stands for something else, as in the instance of the white dove, symbolizing the Holy Spirit in a religious painting and love in a secular work.

Tone
see *Colour*

Woodcut/Wood Engraving
see *Prints*

288

FURTHER READING

General

Alfred H. Barr, *Picasso: Fifty Years of his Art* Secker and Warburg, 1975

J. Ferguson, *Signs and Symbols in Christian Art* Oxford University Press, 1959

M. J. Friedländer, *Landscape, Portrait, Still Life: their Origin and Development*
trans. R. F. C. Hull, Bruno Cassirer, 1949

Ernst H. Gombrich, *The Story of Art* Phaidon, 1984 (new ed.)

Ernst H. Gombrich, *Art and Illusion* Phaidon, 1960

Ernst H. Gombrich, J. Hochberg, M. Black, *Art, Perception and Reality*
Johns Hopkins University Press, 1970

J. Hall, *Hall's Dictionary of Subjects and Symbols in Art* John Murray, 1975

George Heard Hamilton,* *Painting and Sculpture in Europe 1880–1940* Penguin, 1978

Norbert Lynton, *Looking at Art, A History of Painting and Sculpture* Kingfisher, 1982

Norbert Lynton, *The Story of Modern Art* Phaidon, 1980

Peter and Linda Murray, *Dictionary of Art and Artists* Penguin, 1983 (new ed.) (1959)

Robert Rosenblum, *Modern Painting and the Northern Romantic Tradition, Friedrich
to Rothko* Thames and Hudson, 1975

Robert Rosenblum, *Art of the Nineteenth Century* Thames and Hudson, 1984

John Steer, *A Concise History of Venetian Painting* Thames and Hudson, 1970

R. Wark (ed.), *Reynolds' Discourses on Art* Yale, 1981

Narrative Paintings

Michael Baxandall, *Giotto and the Orators* (esp. Chapter 3 'Alberti and the Humanists')
Clarendon Press, 1971

L. Berti, *Masaccio* Pennsylvania University Press, 1967

Anita Brookner, *Jacques-Louis David* Chatto and Windus, 1980

Anthea Callen, *Courbet* Jupiter Books, 1980

L. H. Heydenreich, *Leonardo: The Last Supper* Allen Lane, 1974

Gilbert Highet, *The Classical Tradition: Greek and Roman Influences on Western
Literature* Clarendon Press, 1949

Roger Jones and Nicholas Penny, *Raphael* Yale University Press, 1983

John Rupert Martin, *Rubens: The Antwerp Altarpieces* Thames and Hudson, 1969

R. Weiss, *The Renaissance Discovery of Classical Antiquity* Blackwell, 1969

Portraits

Portraiture. A series of articles in the *Encyclopedia of World Art*, vol. XI, cols.
469–515 McGraw-Hill, 1966

Roger Berthoud, *Graham Sutherland* Faber and Faber, 1982

Robin Gibson, *Twentieth Century Portraits* (exhibition catalogue at National Portrait
Gallery, London) National Portrait Gallery, 1978

John Hayes, *Portraits by Graham Sutherland* (published for exhibition, June–
October 1977) National Portrait Gallery, 1977

D. Piper, *The English Face* Thames and Hudson, 1957
J. Pope-Hennessey, *The Portrait in the Renaissance* Bollinger Foundation, 1966
Alistair Smith, *Renaissance Portraits* National Gallery, 1973
Sara Stevenson, *A Face for any Occasion*, 1976 (exhibition catalogue at the Scottish
  National Portrait Gallery, Edinburgh) Scottish National Portrait Gallery, 1976

Landscape and Still Life

Kenneth Clark, *Landscape into Art* John Murray, 1976
Margaret Drabble, *A Writer's Britain* Thames and Hudson, 1979
Lawrence Gowing, *Matisse* Thames and Hudson, 1979
Luke Herrmann, *Turner* Phaidon, 1975
John House, *Claude Monet* Phaidon, 1978
C. R. Leslie, *Memoirs of the Life of John Constable* Phaidon, 1980
Phoebe Pool, *Impressionism* Thames and Hudson, 1974
Graham Reynolds, *A Concise History of Watercolours* Thames and Hudson, 1978
Jacob Rosenberg, *Chardin Exhibition Catalogue* Cleveland Museum of Art, 1980
Michael Rosenthal, *British Landscape Painting* Phaidon, 1982
Meyer Schapiro, *Cézanne* Abrams (undated)
Basil Taylor, *Constable* Phaidon, 1975
A. Richard Turner, *The Vision of Landscape in Renaissance Italy*
  Princeton University Press, 1974

Philosophy Looks at Art

Edward Bullough, *Aesthetics* Stanford University Press 1957
R. E. Collingwood, *The Principles of Art* Clarendon Press, 1938
Diané Collinson, 'Aesthetic Education', *New Essays in the Philosophy of Education*,
  eds. O'Connor and Langford Routledge and Kegan Paul, 1972
John Dewey, *Art as Experience* Putnam, 1934
R. K. Elliot, 'Imagination in the Experience of Art', *Royal Institute of Philosophy
  Lectures*, vol. 6, 1971/72 Macmillan, 1973
Roger Fry, *Vision and Design* Chatto and Windus, 1920
John Hospers (ed.) *Introductory Readings in Aesthetics*
  Free Press, Collier Macmillan, 1969
F. E. Sparshott, *The Structure of Aesthetics* Routledge, 1963
Leo Tolstoy, *What is Art?*, trans. Aylmer Maude Oxford University Press, 1930
Richard Wollheim, *Art and its Objects* Harper and Row, 1968

* This is one of a series A Pelican History of Art. These are volumes on the major periods and schools of art, all of which are useful and contain bibliographies. Many of them are available in paperback.

292

ACKNOWLEDGEMENTS

For permission to reprint material, the authors and publishers gratefully thank the *Burlington Magazine*, Harper and Row Publishers, Harvard University Press, the *Illustrated London News*, John Murray (Publishers) Ltd, the *Sunday Telegraph*, and Thames and Hudson Ltd.

Illustration acknowledgements:
Scala/Vision International: plates 2, 3, 4, 5, 8; Lauros-Giraudon: plates 6, 11, 12, 22, 23, 43, figures 1, 50, 51, 82, 83, 85, 105; Larry Burrows/Life Magazine © Time Inc/Colorific: plate 15; Mansell Collection: figures 3, 4, 5, 6, 11, 34, 40, 44, 47, 53, 54, 59; Camerapress/ Woodfin Camp and Associates: figure 20; DACS 1985: plates 43, 44, 45, figures 16, 17, 18; ADAGP 1985: plates 15, 25, 30, figures 21, 22, 24, 25, 26, 27, 28, 49, 92, 105; reproduced by courtesy of the Trustees, the National Gallery, London: plates 10, 14, 17, 18, 19, 20, 24, 31, 33, 39, 40, figures 32, 43, 74, 76, 77, 78, 89, 91, 103, 104; reproduced by courtesy of the Board of Trustees of the Victoria and Albert Museum, London: figures 36, 73, 93, 96.

295

INDEX

Page numbers in *italic* refer to black and white illustrations; those in **bold** refer to Colour Plates.

Where the <u>subject</u> of a painting has been indexed, the name of the artist is given in brackets immediately after the reference.

297

299

300

302